The Called
and
The Chosen

**The Called
and
The Chosen**
by
David J. Ayres

First published by
The LICHFIELD PRESS
2004
Copyright David J. Ayres

Printed by Penprint (Midlands) Ltd.,
Lichfield, Staffordshire, WS13 6RJ

David J. Ayres
has asserted the moral right to be recognised
as the author of this work

ISBN 0 905985 36 2

The LICHFIELD PRESS

For many are called, but few are chosen.
Matthew, Chapter 22, Verse 14

Prologue

Farewell and God help you, Old Antrim!

Those who left the countryside either went to the growing urban centres of Ulster or emigrated.

Ulster - an illustrated history   M. O'Dowd and B. Walker.   Batsford

I always tried never to cry in front of Peadar, but, well, sometimes you can't help yourself, can you? I was born O'Neill, Sinead O'Neill, and my Da told us the O'Neills never weep except in private.

Peadar and I were married in Armoy, County Antrim, five years ago and I've been Mrs Grogan ever since. God knows we tried to make a go of it in Armoy but everything seemed to be stacked up against Peadar and me. Though he's a bloody good man, sure he is, but he never had a chance in the Old Country.

I got with child so quick, and poor Dominic was born in the bitter cold of 1906 on our rickety kitchen table and I could hear Peadar stamping up and down and crying and swearing outside. Our firstborn was taken back to the Lord just two months after. Influenza - that saw little Dominic off. Oh, I wanted to die then, truly I did, but my man told me ours was not to reason why the Lord did to us the things he did. I so wanted another little one in these arms and so I'd pray and freeze and pray again and freeze again in our cottage.

It was just a labourer's cottage about a mile up the track from Armoy. It had a door, two windows at the front and one at the back, a thatched roof and a smokey chimney. In summer it smelled of hay but in winter - Mother of God! - sometimes I

5

thought we'd freeze in our bed.

Peadar was a tenant farmer like his father and grandfather before him. Antrim people. Proud and bloody pig-headed. We'd suffered poor harvests for years in the County and many of our neighbours were leaving for America and Australia because there seemed to be no luck to be had for sure. Women who'd made the linen for generations were being put out to grass by the new-fangled machinery. And then there was the troubles with the Orange people.

Still, in 1908, Colm came into the world soon after my twenty-third birthday, just as old Mrs Connolly had foretold from my teacup after Mass one Sunday. How I did love that little scrap!

Then he was taken from us after six months. Passed away in his cot. Suffocation, they said. I swore I'd bring no more into the world in that cottage. There was a curse upon the place, I promise you.

Then Mr O'Gorman started getting long-faced about the rent, which was a good few weeks behind, and said what a curse the Land Act was, that gave the tenant too many rights he did not deserve.

'Fair rent and fixed tenure, my arse!' he used to grumble to my man. 'Less than thirty years ago I could have pitched you and your lady wife out into the fockin' road.'

Well, Peadar had just about had his fill and started talking to me about England. I wasn't even sure where it was, except I knew it was nearer than New York or Australia. I asked if we had to go on a boat to get to England.

He said, 'Sure, woman, we have to go on a bloody boat to get to anywhere from here. This is a bloody island! It's got sea all round it!'

I'd never thought about that - sea all around us - so I wasn't so keen as he seemed to be. I said all we needed was to get away from Armoy and the cold and the damp and Mr O'Gorman.

He said he was going anyway and I could please myself. So that was that. All he would miss in Armoy was his precious fife and drum band. And even I could tell he had no sense of rhythm at all. Well, when you live with a a man, you know if he has no sense of rhythm, now don't you? All right, I realise you're an unmarried lady, but in your line of business you must soon come to know folk pretty well, helping them to come into this evil world and then helping them depart out of it. I suppose it's what goes on in the meanwhile that you know less about, being a spinster, like.

Mind you, you don't have to listen to Nationalist speechifying every night about a Dublin parliament and Ulster Catholics joining forces with all their Irish kinfolk. Mother of God! Sometimes I think I'll end up throwing myself in Stanley Dock!

At that time two of my sisters had gone to live in Belfast to work at Ewart's linen mill in the Crumil Road, and the older one, Siobhan, had written to me to say there could be work for me there, as it was expanding, so to speak, just like I so wanted to myself, if you catch my meaning, but Peadar, oh, he was having nothing of it. So there was to be no Ewart's for me. And then he turned down the chance of another farming job in Carnmoney, telling all and sundry that it would be the same old story as Armoy only in new surroundings. Maybe he was right at that, the daft old bugger!

So we came here in February last year and here we've stayed and I can't say I'm overwhelmed with gratitude to Our Lady for it. And now here's 1910 and me spreading me legs on the kitchen table for the third time in my twenty-five years, only this time in Liverpool. Help me this time, Nurse McEwan. You say it's twins. Well, let them live, please God, let them live this time! If they can just make the first year, I swear I'll come over to you at Eldon Street laden with groceries, so I will!

1910 - 1914

Chalk and Cheese

And so it was that at ten-thirty on the cold and wet and foggy morning of 14th October 1910, Seamus and Padraig Grogan tumbled into the stuffy dimness of Number 8 Oswald Street, Liverpool, their bawling vying with the sobs of their exhausted mother and the cooing of Nurse McEwan.

'Are they all right? Are they all right?' quavered Sinead, breathlessly.

'Two arms and two legs apiece, Mrs Grogan, and you took your time about it, Lord love us all! And you telling me your life history instead of concentrating on the job in hand! Two lovely boys, Mrs Grogan, two lovely twins!'

The jaundiced smoke-laden fog pressed in on the tall, grimy sash window, so that you could barely see beyond the narrow gutter that ran along the middle of the street. The gutter trickled into Dryden Street, which was cosidered something of a main road because it connected directly with the Scotland Road, which gave the whole ward - Scotland Ward - just north of the city centre, its name. 8 Oswald Street was a 'court' in a back street of courts, with four big stone steps leading up to the street door. On either side of the steps was a rusty iron hand-rail, all pock-marked and skinny to the touch. The house was a large terrace with three floors and a large population. The Morrisons alone had eight children in the top floor room, so that the toilet on the upstairs landing was almost permanently blocked or overflowing, with an overpowering stench all through the house.

'Bring us a cob of paper, you fockin' scally, and you can come next!' would be heard ringing in the dingy stairwell most mornings.

A single rented room and eight shillings and sixpence a week was home to the Grogans. It was on the ground floor, for which Sinead was eternally thankful, having been heavy with the twins for so many months, and the window looked on to the street.

The half of the room which contained the iron bedstead could be curtained off with a faded green curtain on a slack wire, and this arrangement was drawn back during the day, the curtain bunched up against the wall. Every time Sinead drew that curtain back, she would catch a whiff of Peadar's pipe tobacco and it would conjure up a strong impression of him when he was off queuing for work at the docks. She would stop, press her brown hair back from her forehead and fondle the dowdy curtain material, while gazing into space, across the angry Irish Sea to Antrim.

Though unlikely to own to it, Peadar Grogan had a grudging liking for working in the docks. He worked mostly at Stanley Dock, about a mile from Oswald Street, and was attached to a gang of eight men, who would meet up on the walk down to the dockside, go to the 'pen' together and queue, sometime for hours to sign on for work each morning. Peadar liked the work because it was matey, unlike the solitariness of his work as a farmer.

The charge-hand would stand on a box and call so many men out for a particular job, often using their well-known nick-names. He would try and keep the gangs together, because they were usually close comrades who worked well together, having an agreed leader, joker, tea-brewer and so forth. Having signed on, a man might get half a day's work or a full week, if he were lucky. Peadar and his gang did quite well as they were all hard workers and did not turn up only when the sugar boat was in dock and the best money was to be had. There was practically no trades union activity because men were simply too scared to join, though for the first few months in the job, Peadar had been appalled by some of the accidents he had seen: One man had been crushed in front of his eyes, when a huge crate of tobacco leaf swung into him, squashing him against the side of the ship's hold. Another was beheaded when a length of steel hawser snapped and whipped with a cannon crack through the air.

Peadar also noticed that he and his comrades stank. Now, it is true that he used to sweat and stink like a steam engine in the fields and bogs of Armoy, but that was in the fresh, open air. Here, men were cramped together on the dockside, doing demanding physical work, buried in the stifling hold of a ship with rats and 'roaches, and where some of the cargo itself - such as bone-meal, molasses and the like - was overpowering, especially in the heat of the summer, so that, as the day wore on they all reeked worse than a piece of over-ripe Stilton. Public baths there were, though few and far between. Peadar's nearest was the 'penny cold and tuppence hot' in Burroughs Garden, though he seldom saw the inside of it. How much nicer to be scrubbed down at the end of the day by Sinead with hot water and a big cake of Bibby's, and to watch her jiggling breasts as she stooped to wet the cloth. She knew he looked forward to it and bath-time was often the prelude to their love-making, though normally on the hard floor, the old bedstead having collapsed once too often in the midst of one of Peadar's orgasmic cries of 'Christ, woman, I do fockin' adore you!'

Still, they had had a cottage and now they had only a room. During those blissful moments when the twins were both asleep, Sinead would wedge a hand on her hip, push her hair back and look around her, exhaling slowly. Outside her window, which went up nearly to the high ceiling, she would often see sights which caused her to wrinkle her nose and turn away in disgust: a man stooping over the gutter, pinching his nostrils and blowing his nose into it, or an obvious drunk vomiting.

She would look towards the fireplace on her left. The mantle shelf above the fireplace was draped with a piece of green baize, which she ran her hand over absent-mindedly and picked up the photograph with the photograph of Peadar and herself with baby Dominic and the cottage behind them, proudly but kindly taken by Mr O'Gorman with his own camera, and then the other photograph of baby Colm lying asleep in her arms. So even Mr O'Gorman wasn't that bad.

The walls of room were two-tone, the lower half dark green up to waist level with a dull creamy colour above that and on the ceiling. Though she had washed and scrubbed the whole place time and again, still the general impression was of constant semi-darkness and damp. Running across the width of the room, from the left-hand side of the big sash window, right up high past the fire-place to the opposite wall was a line of steaming baby clothes and nappies. On the left of the fire-place hung her framed embroidery BE STRONG IN THE LORD, which she re-adjusted like a ritual every single morning as part of her routine. She felt uneasy until she had done that every day. There were two gas-pipes with jets but Peadar had no experience of gas and would have none of it, so they used oil-lamps just as they had in Ireland, one on the table to the right of the fire-place, called the kitchen-table, where the food was prepared and eaten, and the other on a little table beside the bed, which was against the far wall. Just beyond the foot of the bed was a good-sized sink which, though badly chipped, did not leak on to the utensils, cutlery and crockery curtained off underneath it. In various parts of the room were little tin lids containing rat poison for what Peadar called his 'little Orange boys'. Although there was no shortage of them in all the courts along Oswald Street, Sinead remained haunted by the story, a few years before, of a child who had been gnawed to death by rats.

In fact, one Saturday afternoon in early November, Peadar threw two dead rats into the gutter, swift-flowing that rainy day, as he stepped out towards St Domingo Street tat-yard to look for a pram for the twins or the bits and pieces to enable him to build one of sorts. His outing took a turn for the worse when, as he was picking his way over the tram-lines on the Scotland Road, his head down and his mind on rats, a blaring klaxon frightened him near out of his wits and he had to jump back to avoid being run down by a motor cab. It was not that he had failed to see several such automobiles going up and down the road, but he had simply misjudged the speed and forgotten that they could cross tram-lines very quickly indeed unlike the majority of horse-drawn cabs. And whereas the automobiles in summer threw up clouds of dust from the relatively soft road surface, in winter, as now, their wheels could splash a shower of mud and horse-droppings over the unfortunate bystander or pedestrian.

'Bleedin' scorcher!' yelled Peadar, looking down at his boots and trousers and raising a fist, as the cabbie slithered to a halt beside him, his two lady passengers lurching forward and then being thrown back in their seats.

'And who are you calling a scorcher, Paddy?' came the defiant response.

As Peadar was thinking of a suitable insulting rejoinder, bearing in mind the presence of the ladies, one of those very ladies piped up, 'Driver, driver! Drive on this instant, will you? We have no wish to be embroiled in a street brawl!'

'Who asked you, lady? You pay your fare, I drive you there. That's the company motto, but I just need to sort Paddy out first.'

'Drive on, I say! I won't spend any longer than is necessary in this dreadful neighbourhood.'

'Scouser, I could kill you in your cab,' said Peadar quietly and in complete control, leaning against the cabbie's door.

'Drive on or I shall fetch a police officer!' gobbled the panic-stricken lady, gripping her companion's arm.

The cabbie had had enough now and knew that he could possibly come off worse on this occasion, so he graunched his vehicle into gear, revved the engine and showered more mud over Peadar, shouting, 'Get off back to Ireland, spud-picking Paddy man!'

Suddenly, Peadar felt like a stranger all over again.

The tat-yard in the wet was an undulating mountain range of darkly shining debris. It was cold and it was slippery under foot. There were carts, wagons and coaches, some on their side, some upside-down, there were wheels, pots and pans and even parts of one or two automobiles, much to Peadar's disgust. There were also perambulators of all shapes and sizes, in all states of repair. Through the spattering of cold rain came the shrill cries of tattered boys, malnourished scarecrows, clomping over the tat in their clogs, some barefoot, their feet so filthy they looked at first glance as if they had black boots on. They were all trying to get a bicycle together. Peadar was struck by the number of young boys who smoked a pipe and spat like old men.

Using the tools in his brown canvas kit-bag and getting a good soaking in the process, he managed to turn a battered but basically sound perambulator into a tolerable baby carriage for the twins to travel in, top-to-tail, the same way they all slept in the bed at home. He kept the old newspapers he found in the bottom of the carriage, because it was all surprisingly dry and Sinead was always crying out for newspaper to put on the table when she was scrubbing the fire irons on a Sunday evening like a creature possessed. Peadar was a reasonable reader, if a very poor writer, and he read out the Bovril advertisement aloud, standing where he was, amidst a jumble of upturned railway goods trucks without wheels or axles, the perishing rain running off the peak of his flat cap: 'Bovril's Part in the South African War - Baden-Powell and Rudyard Kipling unite in bearing testimony to the great popularity of BOVRIL at the Front . . . .'

Realising that the newspaper must be nearly ten years old, he set to wondering what might become of himself and his family in the next ten years. As he did so, he put his kit-bag in the perambulator, raised the folding canopy and struggled over to the tumble-down wooden hut to pay the few coppers for it.

The boys grew fast and Sinead prayed that they would live and stay fit. Soon a light brown down dusted their domed heads, prompting their father to chuck them both under the chin and remark, 'Jesus, mother' they look almost human, so they do!' and Sinead to glow inside and stroke the new fine hair, willing them both to be strong, to be 'Strong in the Lord'.

Peadar said he hoped they would both grow up to drive flying machines like Monsieur Bleriot and fly over the Channel but Sinead just hoped they would grow up. She had kept silent about the tuberculosis round the back in Wilbraham Street, and about the Morrison boy upstairs with scarlet fever. But the weeks became months and by the spring of 1911 two distinct individuals were emerging in the Grogan household. Padraig had an eager, sometimes you might say almost desperate, look about him, his rich, brown eyes alert, always scanning around. His little mouth would compress sometimes into a determined line and he would make soft grunting sounds, as if struggling to grow and get to grips with the world. His brother, Seamus, on the other hand, had eyes of a softer brown, vaguer eyes, often half closed , and a beatific smile, giving him the air of a miniature Buddha, lolling back on the bed clothes, blessing the ceiling. The harder Padraig struggled, the more broadly Seamus would smile.

'Sure those boys have different fathers, mother! I think that young knocker-upper comes back round here after I've gone to the docks!'

'Listen, husband, by the time you get your body out of here and down the street, the knocker-upper is half way up Great Homer Street!'

'And how might you know his whereabouts, then?'

'Aren't I on my way to the market by then, Mr Suspicious Grogan?'

Peadar would by now have taken Sinead in his arms, both of them laughing.

'What has the market to do with it, wife?'

'I pass the knocker-upper on my way down to the market. "Good morning, Mrs Grogan," says he. "And what a fine one it will be today, unless I'm much mistaken." And I say, "And good morning to you, Mr Adamson."'

'Oh, do you, indeed?'

'That I do!' Sinead would chuckle, by now horizontal in front of the fire.

Their local market was the wholesale fruit, vegetable and hay market in Juvenal Street, run by Mr and Mrs Holz and their family, part of the large German community in Liverpool before the War stirred things up. The Holz family kept the market area scrupulously clean and litter-free, so that it had become quite a meeting-place for social chat as well as the best place in the city for spice balls, roast ribs, pig's cheek, beef and every kind of vegetable. Vast displays of fruit overflowed on to the pavement, the wet fish shop ran with water all day, there were clothes shops and clog shops, and Gales the Photographers had a shop there too. On the corner of the market where Juvenal Street ran into Cazneau Street, there was always an old man in a moth-eaten black suit, who stood from dawn to dusk singing Irish songs at the top of his cracked voice. The people packed inside the trams rumbling down Cazneau Street to the city centre would point at him and laugh, partly because they knew their laughter would set him off swearing and shaking his fist. Sinead avoided him because he spat green on the pavement and mumbled things about her being more beautiful than the spring morning, though his eyes never smiled the way Irish eyes are supposed to, the way Peadar's eyes smiled.

It was while the twins were still quite young that Sinead learned a very useful lesson about the complexities of human nature in the big city, thanks to Mrs Holz. They were standing talking by a mountain of carrots, watching 'Auntie Dora' collecting cabbage leaves off the concrete floor. She moved quickly, because Mr Holz would soon be round with his five-foot broom, sweeping between the stalls.

'What does Auntie Dora want with those?' Sinead asked, pointing to the old lady whose real name seemed to be unknown.

'To make cabbage water,' grinned Mrs Holz.

'Cabbage water? You mean she's . . .?'

'Constipated? Ja, mein Schätzchen!'

The two of them laughed as the cold fishy water from the fish shop swilled around their boots. Then Sinead remarked, 'But we shouldn't laugh at such a wonderful lady.'

'Wonderful lady? Are you serious, my dear? She's a dreadful person, a bloody thief!' She pronounced the last word 'teef'.

'How can you say such a terrible thing, Mrs Holz?' gasped Sinead, appalled.

'I cannot lie to you, Mrs Grogan, the woman is a thief. Ask my husband. He's caught her at it many times.'

'I won't hear bad things said about a godly lady, Mrs Holz. My husband says she's a saint.' Sinead was getting quite huffy now.

'Then more fool your husband, meine Liebe!'

Mrs Holz watched Sinead turn on her heel and splash her way between the stalls and displays to the Juvenal Street entrance, and she shook her head sadly as if to say, 'That woman has a lot to learn!'

But Sinead's lesson had only just begun.

One mild, grey Monday morning, as spring was creeping tentatively up Oswald Street and all the big sash windows rose a coy inch or two, and the soiled old net curtains stirred expectantly and the Echo forecast a summer as hot as last summer when some places recorded over 100 degrees, the big front door of No. 8 was bummed open and Sinead emerged, carrying baby Padraig in her arms. Two Morrison urchins playing with a hoop along the gutter called, 'All right, Missis?'

She smiled and nodded, thinking of the death of their brother of scarlet fever that winter and of the dignity of the mother through it all and how the old man had even stopped drinking since that terrible night. No. 12 was at the blind end of the street, where the high brick wall separated it from the Abercromby oil cake factory, whence all manner of noises and smells emanated. Nobody noticed the noise after a few weeks in the street, but the smells, it was said, led to consumption. The door to No. 12 was open for her, so she went up the steps and straight inside Mrs Kennedy's two-room place on the ground floor. While the old lady was settling Padraig in a cradle that had once been an orange box at the docks, Sinead went back to fetch Seamus. Once the boys were installed top-to-tail in the cradle, Sinead would always offer Mrs Grogan a few coppers.

'Lord bless you, no, Mrs Grogan!' she always answered. 'Just wash these few odds and ends for me while you're there and I'll be more than happy. If Padraig should cry, I'll give him his goo-goo!' She beamed at Padraig, dangling a small piece of chewed grey cloth before his eyes. Minutes later, Sinead was pushing the pram down Scotland Road towards Burroughs Garden Public Bath and Wash-house, the pram well down on its springs with its burden of dirty washing, some in a potato basket, some in a pillow slip.

With one hand steadying her swaying cargo, she squeaked into Dryden Street, past the biscuit factory to her right, then across the busy tramlines and down towards the junction at Bevington Hill. She looked down at the tips of her black boots moving in and out of the encompassing circle of her long skirt. Fascinated, she tried to mesmerize herself, as she used to do when she was a child, into believing that her boots remained on the spot while the flagstones were sliding backwards. She felt quite elated to find she could still do it.

'The new King's going to India next year, Mrs Grogan!'

'Oh, good morning, Auntie Dora.'

Sinead had almost knocked the old woman down. She kicked the brake on and gaped, at a loss, at the rotund figure before her, buttoned up to her stubbly chin in black, her tiny rimless spectacles perched on the end of her nose, a few white curls peeping from beneath an improbably large black hat. She appeared quite unaware that she had just walked into the path of Sinead and her juggernaut. Sinead, in turn, had forgotten that she was passing right in front of the old lady's door. Auntie Dora's little terraced house was well known to all the folk in the Scotland Road and surrounding area, because she catered for the poor and needy in the old Victorian tradition, though she did not run an official 'dinner-house', nor was she in the League of Well-doers, which she left to what she called 'that bunch of old dears in Portland Street'. Auntie Dora kept an open house, with a pan of scouse permanently on the simmer, day and evening, or a pancake with syrup and a beaker of hot, sweet tea all for a few coppers or for nothing at all if the diner looked sufficiently haggard and ragged.

Her one disconcerting habit was her sudden change of subject when she was talking. 'Doing your washing an' all, are you, Mrs Grogan?'

'That I am. Would you like to walk along with me?'

'Can't say I like your German friend at the market. What's her name: Holt? Hart? Hurt?'

'Mrs Holz?'

'Whatever she calls herself. Laughs at me, she does, I tell you.'

'Sure she does not, Auntie. It's just her way.'

The rest of her explanation was a drowned by yet another tram full of rowdies on the way to the Drill Hall opposite the Shakespeare Theatre in Fraser Street to disrupt a Suffragist rally. Needless to say, they were nearly all men, though, surprisingly perhaps, there were a few very vociferous women too, chanting, 'Fooligans! Fooligans! Fooligans!' - one of the many disrespectful names for the disciples of Mrs Pankhurst.

'How would you like to be able to vote, Auntie?'

'Aye, all right, I'll walk with you then, Mrs Grogan. Speak German, do you?'

'No. Auntie, I do not,' she smiled, shaking her head.

Auntie hitched a bulging pillow slip under her arm and prodded her spectacles higher up the bridge of her nose, accelerating to a brisk waddle to keep up with Sinead. They passed the Medical Mission Hall as they went down Bevington Street and then turned right into Burroughs Gardens, where the Public Wash House was to be found at the far end on the right.

The two ladies got a dolly tub next to each other, then shared a sink and scrubbing board, because the place was getting so crowded. Auntie then picked an argument with the attendant who doled out the soap, calling him a skinflint and swatting him with her empty pillow slip. Eventually, however, both finished boiling their whites and moved over to the big wringers. It was there that Sinead noticed that her big white towel was missing. There was so much noise and steam and there were so many women pushing and shoving that her first reaction was one of panic. She had a couple of other towels but that one was the biggest, the softest and the newest and she had sewn a G for Grogan in black cotton on one corner. Everyone assured her that they had not seen the towel, some insisting on handing over their washing for inspection, others shaking their head and lamenting the fact that theft was such a common occurrence in that place. Auntie volunteered to go back and check the dolly and the boiler but her glasses were all steamed up and she looked exhausted, so Sinead said she would do that as long as Auntie saved her a space on the maidens in the big heater for the rest of her stuff.

The towel was not found. The ladies finished their washing and for a while that was the end of the matter. It would probably have remained one of life's unsolved mysteries had a horse not fallen in Great Homer Street not long afterwards.

In those days, Great Homer street was cobble-stoned. It ran north and south, parallel to Scotland Road and in fact Dryden Street joined the two at right angles. A large volume of horse-drawn goods traffic coming to market at Juvenal Street clattered along that route, the noise of wheels and hooves echoing round the terraces, urchins scattering to to the uneven kerbside. In addition to the incessant traffic noise on market days, in wet weather the cobblestones became very slippery and both horses and heavy carts would slip and skid, sending terrified passers-by into doorways, often dodging a cascade of falling vegetables. Now and then it was something more serious.

Sinead had been delayed in Laugharne's, the tobacconist in

Dryden Street because of a torrential thundery downpour, for which she was not properly clad, the May morning having started close and humid. At Laugharne's she had purchased Peadar's usual tobacco, Ogden's Juggler, and a box of matches, and when the rain had abated she ventured forth into Great Homer Street towards the market to shop and gossip with Mrs Holz. Trundling precariously over the glistening cobbles came a weary looking grey horse, hauling an overloaded cart, bearing cabbages, carrots, swedes and potatoes. Just as it was passing her, leaving precious little space to walk, as it seemed to overhang the pavement, such as it was, the horse seemed to lose its footing. Its back legs went first with a loud scouring sound of iron on stone. Sinead cowered against the shop front of Louis Vogel, the pork butcher, as the grey fell heavily against the shafts, causing the cart to capsize and to shed its load and its driver all over the puddled street. Shouts and screams went up as the animal struggled desperately to regain its footing, its head thrashing about among the piles of vegetables, sending potatoes and swedes shooting across the street, some into Chalmers, the greengrocer, some against the wall of George Davison, the bread and flour dealer, and carrots and cabbages into Vogel's tiny shop, where they skidded to a halt in the pungent sawdust. Then the horse became still, its eyes big with panic, as if it understood young Mr Vogel's suggestion that someone send for the knacker man. Children approached the prostrate grey, leaning forward to look at its face and talk to it, but they were soon told to clear off. Then the assembled crowd turned its attention to the shocked driver, who had been given a stool to sit on outside Vogel's. He leaned his shiny bald head against the wall and looked up to heaven, mopping his brow and gesturing feebly with a shaky hand that he was all right. The commotion brought Mrs Clara Orrett downstairs from the rooms she rented above Vogel's. Despite her grubby and unwashed appearance and her strong body odour, she was ever practical in an emergency, bringing down with her on this occasion a washing bowl of water and a soiled-looking off-white towel over her arm.

Brushing aside the onlookers, who were now locked in earnest discussion over whether to send for a crane to right the wagon and raise the beast or to send for the knacker man to despatch the unfortunate creature, she dipped the towel in the bowl and applied it fiercely to the face of the trembling driver. When the bowl was more or less empty, Clara decided to go back upstairs to refill it. She thrust the towel at Sinead, obliging her suddenly to jerk into life, and gestured at the driver while she herself vanished in a waft of sweat with the bowl, dripping water behind her. Sinead, self-consciously at first, then with more application, dabbed the glistening, ruby face of the driver. Then she began to wring the towel out. She paused. She looked at the corner of the towel. She opened the towel out and looked down at it, holding it full length with outstretched arms. She felt her face going hot and a sick sensation in her stomach. Clara reappeared with another bowlful of water. Sinead stepped into her path and held out the towel, her brown eyes wild.

'And what do you call this, Clara Orrett?' She shook the towel accusingly in her face.

'I call that a towel, Sinead Grogan. And what, pray, do you call it?'

'Don't be getting funny with me, you hussy, and tell me what you're doing with my towel!'

The driver turned his head from one woman to the other as he lolled against the wall, his mouth opening and closing like a large beached fish.

'Your towel? And how do you come to claim my property as your own?'

Sinead turned the towel in her hands until she found the G in black stitching, and shoved that part of the towel into Clara's grimy face.

'There! What is that, Clara Orrett? It's a G! It's a G for Grogan, and that, Clara Orrett, is me!'

'Huh! That could stand for lots of names! Don't try that on me. You've got a husband to support you, I have none. So leave my things alone or I'll fetch a bobby!'

The horse and driver were temporarily forgotten, eclipsed by this new spectacle and the prospect of a street affray on market morning. Bystanders clustered round the two shouting women, kicking the spilled vegetables away from their feet and calling out encouragement like: 'You tell the dirty cow!' 'You tell the lying thief!' or, if they sided with Clara, 'Teach that Irish murphy bitch a lesson, Clara!'

'Where did you come by it, that towel?' Sinead yelled into her opponent's face.

'I was gave it, wasn't I? I was gave it. It was part of a parcel for the necessitous and this towel was gave to me, so leave off!' She spat on the pavement.

'Who gave it you? Who gave you my towel? It was stolen from me, so it was! That was my best towel!'

'Auntie Dora gave it me out of charity. It can't be yours. Auntie Dora gave it me, so it must come from gentlefolk.'

'Does it bugger! It comes from me, that's where it bloody comes from!' And Sinead, brown eyes blazing like hot peat, began folding the towel as if to take it off with her.

Clara, who had been puffed up with indignation, hands on hips, now snatched the towel from her adversary, spat at her feet again and shrieked, 'How do you like that, murphy thief? Now sod off where you bloody came from!'

With that, Clara turned on her heel, and, now oblivious of the wagon driver, stormed off to her rooms, leaving the water basin and a strong hint of body odour behind her. The crowd, for that is what it was by then, clapped or cheered and booed as the mood took them.

Sinead could see there was no point in arguing further with Clara and stood for a while, amid the scattered vegetables, as the people calmed down and began to withdraw, leaving the bemused driver, still leaning against the wall, looking at her with detached curiosity. She glanced at the old grey, still now, its eyes rolling in its head, waiting, so it seemed, for the knacker man. It had given up the struggle and indeed this was one of those occasions when Sinead herself felt the same way. One or two bitter tears rolled down her cheeks for Antrim and she felt an almost uncontrollable urge to run down to Stanley Dock, take Peadar by the arm, collect the twins and get on the boat back to Ireland. But the O'Neill in her blood prevailed and a few minutes later she was pouring out her troubles to Mrs Holz, who was pouring out tea for them both.

The two ladies sat on stools in Mr and Mrs Holz's office, elbows on a hardwood shelf which served as a work table and desk, and looked through the large barred window down on to the tumult of the market, several concrete steps below. The noise was of voices, shouting and singing, barefoot barrow boys, whistling or with clay pipes clamped between their teeth, the throng of shoppers, ladies in long black or dark blue dresses and complicated hats, men in brown cow gowns or dark suits with bowler hats or straw boaters and white shirts with shallow rounded collars. There were flat caps, moustaches, bicycles, children with hoops - it looked and sounded like bedlam. Sinead felt quite privileged to be up in the office, somewhat insulated from the hubbub.

Mrs Holz turned to her and smiled: 'Yes, Liebchen, that down there is the big city, the big bad city.'

Sinead shuddered.

'You must not fear it, Mrs Grogan. You must simply learn its ways. Clara Orrett is not a thief . . . .'

'No, but Auntie Dora is. You were so right. I should have listened to you.'

'Auntie Dora just spreads things round. She certainly would not consider herself a thief. She takes what she thinks might not be needed by someone and gives it to someone who needs it. Like that English outlaw in history . . . .'

'Robin Hood?'

'Ja, ja, genau so.'

'How is it you are so wise about the city, Mrs Holz?'

'I come from Berlin, Liebchen. The rules are just the same there. A city is a city.'

'Aye, but stealing is stealing, whether it be in Berlin or Liverpool, leastways that is what my folks taught me.'

'But, unlike in the country, you must never, never take your eyes off your own goods and chattels in the big city. Imagine everyone you meet is a thief . . . or a murderer!'

To emphasize the word 'murderer', Mrs Holz pulled a horrific face and made her eyes bulge, sending Sinead into a fit of giggling, at which Mrs Holz slapped her thighs and began to guffaw loudly too, sounding just like a man.

'Mrs Holz, you're an encyclopaedia!'

Mrs Holz dabbed her piggy eyes on her sleeve and winked at Sinead.

'And, if your pocket is ever picked or your bag stolen, go straight down to the drinking fountain in Scotland place and talk to the shoeblacks, because it's always one of those scallies that does it.'

Sinead gazed at her in admiration, this fount of urban knowledge.

'But,' Mrs Holz went on, raising a warning index, which she wagged from side to side, 'if they stuff the stolen goods down their shirt, you are in bad trouble.'

Sinead obliged by asking why that should be.

'Because most of those ragamuffins are sewn into their clothes, yes, sewn!'

Sinead was amazed.

Mrs Holz said, 'Not just for warmth in winter, but in case their clothes are stolen, stolen off their verminous bodies!'

Sinead thought about the Morrison boys, who always wore the same clothes and never seemed to take any of them off, and wondered whether they too were sewn into their clothes.

Mrs Holz made it quite clear that there was little point in expending energy having a confrontation with Auntie Dora. She should consider the whole incident a lesson learned. The towel had been not so much stolen as re-absorbed into the giant digestive system of the city. On another occasion, said Mrs Holz, Auntie Dora would be just as likely to give something to Sinead, something she really needed at the time, which had come into her possession in the very same way. So things moved round the city, redistributed, re-shuffled, but not getting less and always in the hands of someone in real need.

The end of October 1911, saw the death of one of the birthday goldfish. Purchased by their father for the twins on their first birthday, one had been called Padraig and the other Seamus, but, after five days, the one called Padraig had been found floating on the surface of the water in the glass bowl, sending Sinead into hysterics, crying that it was an omen. She was distressed for days, constantly walking up to her framed embroidery BE STRONG IN THE LORD and adjusting it, though it needed no adjustment, and ignoring Peadar, who shook his head and pulled sadly on his pipe of Ogden's Juggler, commenting, by way of diversion, on the noise from the new presses at 'the Abercromby', and the new smells.

He would say, 'They're going into soap production, so folk say.' But Sinead would press her brown hair back over her temples and pat it down and ignore him. She did not even notice the new infestation of cockroaches which used to happen every time the locust bean boat was in port and would normally be Sinead's signal for a manic round of spring cleaning, whatever the season.

Eventually, however, on Nurse McEwan's insistence, Peadar sat her down on the creaky bed and tried to make her see reason. The boys were over a year old, he told her. They were strong, they could crawl about and they could say 'ma'. She had stopped breast-feeding them a few weeks before and they now ate mashed up solid food. What more did she want? This was all she had prayed for and this she had been granted.

'You ask the Lord for something, wife, and he gives it you, then, without a word of gratitude, you start worrying about the future.'

Sinead thought hard and long about these words and, slowly, slowly, the strong faith of her childhood and adolescence came trickling back. Yes, she had asked for the survival and strength of her children and, yes, she had been given both. While other folk's children took sick and passed over, hers thrived. The O'Neills were a devout clan and Sinead came to realise that she was not living her life as she should.

Within a few days, she had wheeled the twins up the Scotland Road to St Anthony's and had met Father Castlereagh. The three of them began to attend Mass two or three times a week after Peadar had left for the docks. The twins' reaction to the cool, dark, fragrant interior of St Anthony's was quite different: Seamus would appear to relax completely, smiling soundlessly, whilst his brother would fidget and writhe and scream the place down, his tiny feet going like paddles.

'Peadar, go over to Nurse McEwan,' said Sinead one grey and blustery Saturday afternoon in November.

'Nurse McEwan was here only last week, woman!'

'I don't care if she was only here yesterday. I want to send her some potatoes and some cabbage.'

'You've given her plenty already.'

'Then I'll give her more.'

'But the wind's from the Vauxhall chimney. You can smell the sulphur in the street,' Peadar whinged experimentally.

'Then complain to Murphy's Chemical Works, for there's precious little I can do about the chimney or the smoke. Here's the spuds and here's the cabbage, and don't dally, you scally!'

Peadar smiled and tried to pat her bottom but she side-stepped and laughed at him as she handed over the vegetables.

'If Nurse isn't at home . . . .'

'Then I'll leave them by her door.'

'You'll do no such thing!' She could hear Mrs Holz, like an unseen counsellor whispering in her ear. 'You'll wait till Nurse comes back. You know she's very busy at present, because of some of the doctors.'

'You should work down at the dock, wife. You'd make a good charge-hand,' he said, lifting his cap off the iron hook on the back of the door and settling it over his springy brown hair, throwing

Sinead the look that always reminded her why she had married him.

To Peadar's eyes, Eldon Street was a cut above. Just a few minutes from Oswald Street, the three-storey tenements were barely six years old, a new sort of working-man's dwelling - prefabricated moulded panels of crushed clinker from the Liverpool refuse destructors and Portland cement, steel reinforced.

Nurse McEwan had two small rooms opposite a church and a school, and she would occasionally be heard shouting at the children coming home, because they liked to nosy-parker at her, wallowing in her chair quaffing a glass of milk stout.

'Eh, missis, give us a swig, why don't you?'

'You bugger off and leave me in peace!'

'I'll tell my ma you swore at us!'

'I'll tell her a thing or two about you, young Donovan! And remember it was me brought you into this world. Now be gone!'

And they always went.

Peadar tapped respectfully on the door, cap and vegetables in hand, squinting against the cold dusty wind. The street was deserted. Only a few tatters of flying litter stirred. The sky was heavy. There came the sound of movement behind the door. It opened an inch and an eye peered through the gap.

'Well, well! Mr Grogan himself come to pay me a visit! Come in, come in!' She flung the door back on its hinges and practically dragged her visitor inside.

The fire in her little shadowy parlour was small but intense. She pulled up a straight-backed chair for her guest and collapsed with a wheezy sigh into her own rocking chair. Peadar sat awkwardly erect, staring into the glowing coals, the bag of vegetables in his lap, his cap turning in his fingers. Then he turned shyly to Nurse McEwan, almost intimidated by her large, strong frame and big ruddy face. Even in repose she looked like a volcano, resting between eruptions.. Her short, wiry hair was almost completely grey and Peadar put her at about fifty. He began to explain tentatively, 'See here, Nurse, the wife has put a few bits and pieces together for you, and we would like . . . .'

She raised her large, capable hands and smiled, her hazel eyes crinkling at the corners. 'The Lord bless you both! And I trust those two lovely boys are still in the very best of health?'

Peadar passed the bag over and noticed how she took it from him with just one hand and lowered it easily to the mud-coloured rug at her feet.

'Both very well, thank you.' He watched as she took up her glass and drained half of it in one swallow.

'But, how rude of me, Mr Grogan! Here am I, sitting drinking like a bottomless pit, while you sit there parched, I shouldn't wonder.'

Peadar shook his head and began to deny any sensation of thirst, when the large, solid lady rose with surprising agility from her chair, rummaged around behind him for a few seconds, then returned to thrust a glass into his hand. 'Here!' she cried, as if giving an instruction, and gestured with a bottle of stout that he should hold out his glass. She stood and poured until he protested that that was quite sufficient, but she cut in with 'Stuff and nonsense! You shall be filled to the top!'

She remained standing to watch him drink, her black, buttoned bulk looming above him, one side of her face lit red by the coals, lending her a Mephistophelean quality, the other side in shadow. Peadar gulped eagerly to please her and, this apparently accomplished, saw her resume her seat.

There followed a pause, during which both parties gazed into the fire and drank, the visitor with decorum, the nurse as if struggling to extinguish a major blaze inside her stomach. At length, she set down her glass with a sigh: 'You know, Mr Grogan, you don't have to come here laden with gifts. I'm happy to see you or your wife come over empty-handed.'

Peadar tussled with his cap in his lap. 'The wife, you see, Nurse, is so thankful to you for the boys.'

'She must thank the Lord and Our Lady for that, as I've told her, not me. All I did was what I always do - deliver. That's my job. The rest is not up to us mortals, Mr Grogan.' Somewhere in a dark corner, a large clock was clanking away the seconds.

'Are you a religious man, Mr Grogan?' The question came with unexpected directness. She had even turned in her chair to observe his face, perhaps to see whether he intended to lie to her. 'Er . . ., I was brought up Catholic, sure, like Sinead, but I . . .'

'Tut, tut, Mr Grogan!' she admonished, frowning and pointing a large index in his face. 'And you have so much to be thankful for!' The coals began to spit and crack, as if joining in her spirit of condemnation of the unworthy sitting there. She moved her face closer to his and he saw how her thick, arched eyebrows looked heavy and dark in the firelight and the glow of the embers reflected itself in her eyes: she reminded him for all the world of a gargoyle - she was godly yet diabolical.

'So many of us are brought up Catholic, Mr Grogan, but so many fall by the wayside, as the parable goes.' She fixed him with a gimlet gaze and he shifted in his chair, suddenly aware that one of his legs was much too hot. He lifted the trouser leg delicately away from the skin of his shin and turned an attentive face to the formidable lady.

'The sower, Mr Grogan, the sower!'

He nodded, smiling weakly, while she warmed to her subject, speaking into the fire now. 'We are given the gift of our religion but we do not live up to it. It doesn't grow into faith, d'you see?' She rounded on him, knocking back her stout with fierce intensity.

Peadar hesitated, then ventured, 'And are you a religious person, Nurse McEwan?'

She threw her grey head back against the chair and laughed, then stared into her glass, coated with froth but almost empty: 'Lord bless you, no, not really! I just preach to others. It's different for me, you see, because I'm just an old maid. I've less to lose or protect than most folk. Not like you with a wife and family. Religion's a bit like this new Insurance Act that's giving me so much work.'

Peadar was lost now, so he sipped and waited.

Nurse McEwan heaved a sigh which lifted her great bosom, then let it subside slowly with a wheezy hiss: 'If you're insured under the new state scheme you're called a 'panel patient' and doctor is obliged - yes, obliged' - here she underlined her words with a wag of her finger - 'to come out and attend you.'

Peadar showed that he was suitably impressed.

She added, 'Only some don't.'

He wrestled inside his head to relate all these seemingly unconnected ideas. He had not considered religion as being like an insurance, or anything else for that matter.

'I do talk to the Holy Virgin in my prayers, Nurse McEwan, though I don't go along to Mass or to Confession these days.' He paused to await her absolution, while she ran her finger round the inside of her glass to pick up the froth, then popped the finger in her mouth and sucked on it, her giant figure flickering on the wall beside her.

'You keep talking to her, Mr Grogan. The long-suffering mother is a good image. I should know. I've attended to enough of them,' she added in an undertone, more to herself than to him, 'I see them at their weakest and worst and it's a good way for ordinary folk to talk to the gaffer.'

'The wife does take the boys up to St Anthony's,' offered Peadar, aware that his glass was well nigh drained and that the moment was approaching for him to engineer a tactful getaway.

'Well, that's good, that's good. So she's taken out the insurance, as you might say,' and she cast him a conspiratorial glance, followed by a wink. He knocked back the last drop of stout and made loud noises of appreciation, setting his glass down on the floor and grasping his cap with determination.

'You'll be getting back then, I've no doubt,' she sounded almost disgruntled.

'That I will, Nurse McEwan, and thank you kindly for the drink.'

After the door had closed behind him, he pottered off down Eldon Street towards Limekiln Lane, pondering the religious upbringing of his sons and burping milk stout.

By the spring of 1912 the youngest Grogans were tottering about on chubby, newly discovered legs. Padraig was by far the more active and exploratory, having distinguished himself by spilling and then crushing beneath his little boots his father's homeopathic tablets, which were for his lingering cold, or 'catarrh and rhinitis' as the little brown bottle announced.

'Talk about Mulligan's picnic, at fourpence a bottle! All over the floor!'

'Don't go on at poor Padraig, now. He couldn't help it, could you, darling? And see his hands as black as the hobs of hell.'

'And didn't I traipse all the road to Roscommon Street to the homeopathic?'

'We don't need the homeopathic now we're on the panel.'

'Old habits die hard.'

'Aren't you the antwacky one?'

'And proud of it, woman.

It was a Monday and no work to be had at the dock. Sinead was off to the wash-house, leaving the twins and the rent-money in Peadar's hands, and she would pop in to Mrs Kennedy's to see if she could take any of her stuff down the wash too, knowing she would say, 'Lord bless you Mrs Grogan! Just wash these few odds and ends for me and I'll be more than happy!'

She always said the same thing. Sinead rather liked that. You always knew where you were with Mrs Kennedy. But the old perambulator was going to be well down on its tired springs again, with or without Mrs Kennedy's two pennyworth. But the woman was a mine of information about the goings-on in the Old Country, better than the *Echo* and cost about the same with her washing. She had told of rumours of civil war in Ulster, of Sir Edward Elgar and Rudyard Kipling speaking in favour of the Orangemen, aided and abetted by Andrew Bonar Law, himself of Ulster descent.

'I'm away now, Peadar. Watch the boys now, won't you?' She

leaned over the sink to squint into the tiny oval mirror hanging on a nail above it, patting her hair fussily, waiting for him to say, 'Christ, woman, you're only going to the wash-house! You're not some Mary Ellen on the Scotland Road!' Then he would pause and add, 'Though we'd surely be a little better placed if you were!' But his cold was bad and he kept his peace, though his eyes still laughed at her and said what his mouth did not.

As Sinead and the laden pram rumbled through the chimney smoke and potato peelings, dodging young buckos who should have been in school, Peadar was rubbing his hands together looking forward to another game of 'fall and drop' with the boys. This stunt, Sinead protested, was brainless and dangerous and was, so she thought, banned. The game required that the blameless and trusting child be stood on the extreme edge of the kitchen table, facing the abyss before him. The mischievous and foolhardy parent then stood facing him, one pace back from the table edge. Then the latter would beckon the child, patting himself eagerly on the chest, as if calling a dog, the object being to persuade the child to fall forward voluntarily, relaxed and confident, into the waiting arms of the beaming and undeserving father. This was to plant the seed of trust, albeit blind, in the father-figure. Peadar shrugged off his wife's strong objections but never played the game when she was near. To her, it was not merely tempting fate, it was toying with God's mercy. Then, with a broad grin of pleasure, Seamus would close his soft brown eyes and allow himself to fall like a dead weight into his father's outstretched arms, whereupon his shrieks near drowned Peadar's laughter, as he swept him up, high above his head like a trophy. Padraig, in contrast, yelled and resisted, and, when propped up on the edge of infinity, showed wild, anxious eyes and no readiness to leap into the unknown. His father, therefore, was obliged to pull him gently forward in order to initiate the fall. Poor Padraig was always bawling uncontrollably by the time his little body crumpled into his father's distant arms.

'Have you no faith, young Padraig?' he would chide, his voice muffled by the child, now clasped close to his face.

The commotion that cut the game short seemed to come from halfway up the stairs where Mrs Morrison was making what Mr Vogel called a 'shemozzle' when it came about that someone began shouting in his shop. Peadar suddenly paid much closer attention when he heard her calling not just upon the Virgin Mary but also upon Sinead for mercy. Placing the twins delicately on the cold, worn floor tiles, he opened the door and a wave of chaotic humanity broke inside the room. Mrs Morrison, her two youngest tugging at her skirt, rushed straight past Peadar and over to the window, carefully pulling no more than an inch of net curtain aside and panting in distraction, 'Is he there? Is he there?' staring up and down the street, the little ones trying to bury their tear-stained faces in the folds of her clothing. Mrs Morrison must have been in her late thirties, though she looked over fifty. Monotonous childbirth had made her whole body sag, like a sad candle slowly melting and sinking into a waxy pool in its dish. True, she was not a fat woman, though her face was a collection of pockets and pouches, saggy disappointed-looking cheeks, a flappy turkey throat, two grey teeth in her lower jaw, and sunken, damp eyes. Her hard, round mobile chin moved up and down like a pink button, lending extra emphasis to her speech. Her lack of teeth made the sounds 's' and 'sh' a sort of lispy expulsion of air, accompanied by volumes of spittle, which accumulated round her puckered and shrunken lips. Her bony, veiny hands flailed in the air as she stumbled along groping for hand-holds along the way. Not even a spectre of the once attractive young woman was detectable inside the dishevelled black skirt, the worn grey blouse and the heavy woollen shawl. About three years older than Peadar, she could have passed for his mother. Even her grey hair was thinner than his, barely enough to scrape back into an untidy bun. Her youngest, six months older than the twins, had a permanent run of green snot down his upper lip and the other one, about four years old , looked shifty even when he was crying.

'Is who there, Mrs Morrison?' Peadar was recovering from his astonishment.

'Fletcher!' she spat, placing her hands protectively over the heads of the two unwholesome boys, who were gaping mistrustfully at Peadar as if anticipating some kind of assault.

'Fletcher, the landlord's agent?' asked Peadar, relieved.

'Aye, the same, and his bully boys!' More spit hit the window pane.

'Bully boys, Mrs Morrison?' He looked round at the twins but they were playing by the bed, as far from the Morrison boys as possible. Padraig always finished up sitting triumphant on the calmly quiescent Seamus, the former flushed with infant victory, the latter happy to lie beneath his brother's seat for as long as it appeared to make him happy.

Peadar sat Mrs Morrison at the kitchen table and raised the big black kettle from the hob. She shook her head, so he made tea just for himself. She turned her chair to the window, so that her back was towards him when she spoke.

'My Larry's been out of work for years, as you know. Well, he's not well any more, what with his back and his knees. He was a drayman when I wed him. These days he sells horse muck, begging your pardon, Mr Grogan, at a penny a bucket, and he takes our oldest lad down to Juvenal Street to the market to break up the old flower boxes and hawk them round as firewood, twopence a bag - you know, Mr Grogan, because Mrs Grogan's bought some off us. So we're not lazy folks, Mr Grogan, not layabouts.'

Peadar listened and sipped. Mrs Morrison gave a sob and gathered her children to her scant bosom.

'Well, Larry gave up the drink when our Michael was took away with the scarlet fever but now he's at it again, God help us! He's drunk the bloody rent!'

'But Mr Fletcher's a reasonable man, Mrs Morrison. I'm often on short time and we fall behind a week or two . . .'

'Oh, Mr Grogan, this is much more serious! We've missed over six weeks and we're in debt for many more weeks that we've borrowed off the sheeny man.'

'Sheeny man? What sheeny man?'

'A money-lender down the Scotland Road, next door to the Two-guinea Tailor's.'

'Oh, my God! Horowitz?'

She nodded and snuffled and so did her boys.

'A couple of Horowitz's fellows put one of my work gang in the infirmary.'

'But today is rent day and I haven't got it and Mr Fletcher warned me last week he'd sell our stuff and pitch us out in the street!'

She sobbed and the spittle flew. The next moment she and her children appeared to hold their breath, as the steps outside clattered with hobnails and the street door flew back against the wall. Gruff male voices sounded at the foot of the stairs.

'Right at the top you say, Mr Fletcher?'

'Aye, right at the top.'

'Shall we lead the way then, Mr Fletcher?'

'Aye, lad, you lead the way. I always start at the top and work downwards.'

'And the same when you're collecting rent, eh, Mr Fletcher?' The ruffian's leer was audible.

'You keep your filthy mind on the task you're paid for, young McGrath!'

Mrs Morrison had slid, terrified, from her chair and was squatting beside it, her shawl in her mouth, trying not to scream. The two boys also took up a squatting position hesitantly at her side. Peadar was at a loss. If only Sinead were there! She would know what to say and how to behave.

Padraig and Seamus were spellbound too. Their play was forgotten. They sat on the floor and remained silent. Only the fire made a sound. Only the fire moved.

Peadar inched the door ajar and listened to the sounds upstairs. Ringing down the stairwell came Mr Fletcher's rich dark voice: 'Mrs Morrison, it's me, Mr Fletcher, come to collect the rent. Will you open the door to me, if you please, missis?'

Silence apart from the mice on the stairs.

'Come on now, Mrs Morrison! Landlord has been a patient man but he has to make a living same as you and yours. I have two . . . colleagues, with me, Mr McGrath and Mr Riley . . . .'

Cavernous knocking on the door echoed round the dingy walls and ceilings, like nails being driven into a coffin lid. Had Peadar turned in his doorway, he would have seen his visitor flinching at every blow, sinking deeper with each one.

'If you don't open up, missis, my instructions are to effect entry by force with the assistance of my colleagues here.'

Mrs Morrison gave a little cry. Peadar turned and put a finger to his lips.

'Have it your own way, missis. I've got a job to do. Stand away from the door, if you please, and keep your little ones clear. Right, Mr McGrath, let's get on with it.'

Peadar stepped out into the hallway and cupped his hands to his mouth: 'Stop! Stop!'

Silence fell at once and, for a second or two, it was easy to imagine that the three men were not up there at all and it was all a nightmare. But reality can out-perform any bedtime chimera and the performance duly resumed.

'Who's that down there? That sounds like Mrs Grogan's old feller. Is that you, Mr Grogan?'

'That it is, Mr Fletcher,' shouted Peadar up the blind stairwell.

'We have business with the Morrisons. We'll be with you directly.

'The lady is down here with me, gentlemen. I'll thank you to come down here and join us.'

Further silence was followed by murmured deliberation. The footsteps crunched down the gritty bare boards of the stairs, hesitating only when the Morrisons' door flew open behind them and an adolescent male voice bleated with something akin to defiance, 'And you leave our mam alone an' all!' whereupon the door slammed shut again.

It was a strange trio that Peadar found himself facing at the foot of the stairs moments later. Fletcher he was acquainted with, a bear of a man, yet with an agreeable enough disposition and a voice which Sinead likened to warm, brown sugar, worthy of preservation 'on one of those how's-your-father phono . . .phono . . . phono . . . things.'

McGrath looked on the world through the eyes of a rat, dangled a long truncheon from his right hand and appeared flushed and constricted by a jacket and waistcoat which were far too tight and which obviously used to cover a far slimmer, and in all probability a far pleasanter, person. Riley seemed to be a man of few words with a bowler hat and a beard like the King's.

'May we have a few words with Mrs Morrison?' began Mr Fletcher.

'With the little lady?' sneered McGrath, exposing a row of worn, black teeth.

'We have not come to threaten the lady, merely to explain the situation.' Fletcher tried to stand in front of McGrath but the latter squeezed back into view.

'The very serious situation,' said the sneer.

'There may be certain options open even at this late juncture,' offered Fletcher, coughing respectfully.

'This very late juncture indeed,' grinned McGrath blackly, twirling his truncheon.

Peadar opened his door and stood aside. McGrath took a step forward but was eased firmly aside by Fletcher and, before he could regain his footing, Riley, too, entered before him, leaving him in their wake, his truncheon knocking clumsily against the door.

The three men stood in a line between the door and the sink, looking for all the world as if they were about to audition for some bizarre vaudeville routine in the music hall. The pathetic object of their visit upstairs still cowered on the floor, her two offspring cowering with her. The twins sat quietly by the bed, looking from one person to another, Seamus slowly tracing a pattern in the drying mud left by the wheels of the parked perambulator. Peadar raised Mrs Morrison back in her chair and said: 'Gentlemen, you can see the lady is afraid. She has a family problem, which leaves her short for the moment.'

'Leaves her short,' leered McGrath. 'Leaves the little lady short.'

He smacked the truncheon into the palm of his left hand, scowling as Fletcher motioned him to put it away.

'Yes,' said Peadar, 'so she asks you gentlemen to kindly allow her more time and offers her respects to landlord, him knowing her situation and all.'

'The little lady's situation,' muttered McGrath, struggling to loosen his collar with two dirty fingers, his face like a Sunday roast.

'Regretfully, Mr Grogan, I must insist on some kind of payment from this lady, if only as a gesture of good faith. The landlord, you see . . .,' Mr Fletcher gave a little bow towards Mrs Morrison as if by way of apology and glanced at Riley, who had removed his bowler and stood stroking his beard.

'Oh, Mr Fletcher, Mr Grogan, gentlemen, what am I to do?' sobbed Mrs Morrison, rising to face the fire, searching the coals for inspiration.

Peadar looked across at the Golden Syrup tin on the mantlepiece and wrestled to organise his thoughts.

'Just a small token, perhaps,' Fletcher almost pleaded in his baritone, eager to be away from the place now.

Peadar cleared his throat and looked from the tin to Mr Fletcher, both men visibly moved by the distressing proceedings. 'Now see here, Mr Fletcher. I see you to be a good man and cannot stand idly here watching a lady and a mother suffer for lack of money.' He went over to the mantlepiece, took the tin, prised off the lid with his nails and tipped out some coins into the palm of his hand.

'I would like to offer you this . . .'.

'No, no, Mr Grogan. Your rent is not in question here.'

'Allow me to finish, Mr Fletcher. I'm offering this rent money for Mrs Morrison, so she won't be thrown out in the road.'

Mrs Morrison fell at Peadar's feet, crying, 'God bless you, Mr Grogan! God bless you!'

He pressed the money into her hand and she knelt, weeping over it.

'Well, Mr Grogan, if you're sure,' boomed Fletcher. 'This sum will please my employer and help him to view this lady and her family more favourably, I don't doubt.' He held out his huge hand and the coins were poured meekly into it.

'Much more favourably,' nodded McGrath, grinning with one side of his mouth and scowling with the other. Riley dusted off his bowler, sensing the nearness of departure and then stared into it, as if reading a newspaper article inside it.

'As regards my own rent, Mr Fletcher . . .'.

'Do not trouble yourself about it this week, Mr Grogan.'

'An act of Christian charity, Mr Grogan,' said Mrs Morrison. 'I don't know how I can ever repay you.'

Peadar was speechless at the enormity of what he had done. It was probably he who would be thrown out in the street - by Sinead!

'That's why I love you, Peadar Grogan, and that's why I wed you,' murmured Sinead, squirming for more warmth against his back.

'Why? Because I gave the rent money away to the first worthy cause?'

The dying fire glowed. They had been too weary to bank it up. Sinead's breath blew on the back of his neck.

'No. Because you did a Christian thing, although you knew we were short too.'

'And although I thought you'd lay into me when you got back from the wash-house!' He laughed and reached back for her flank.

'Oh, so you fear me, Peadar Grogan, do you? You a hulking docker and me a slip of an Antrim country girl!'

She made as if to pull back from him but he gripped her firmly without rolling to face her. Out of habit now, they kept their feet clear of the boys at the foot of the bed, Sinead being adamantly against having them up at their end for fear of 'overlaying'.

Peadar sniffed the faint odour of carbolic rising from the chamber pot under the bed and reflected what a good woman Sinead was, how she had followed him all the way from the old country and given him two sons, and now her warm belly was pressed into his backside and he was beginning to stir. Yet when he rolled over to face her, she said, 'I've never caught since the twins.'

He answered, 'Nurse McEwan did warn you that might happen.'

'There's me hoping for signs of catching each time of the month and Mrs Morrison, whose rent we've paid, knocking back her bottle of 'mother's ruin' or mixing herself a hickey pickey when Larry's off her back.'

'Now what in the world might a 'hickey pickey' be, when it's at home?'

'It's something to get rid of the baby. A sinful concoction, with white lead in it.'

She felt his hands rise under the bedclothes and softly cup her breasts, then heard the noise of his greatcoat sliding off the bed on to the floor, at which he cursed but made no move to retrieve it. He would do that later, when it got really cold.

Now he pushed himself against her and asked, 'Now what do you think of that, my little Irish maid?'

'Mrs Kennedy's landlord's going to fumigate her place next week. It's crawling, she says, crawling.'

She was smiling when he kissed her.

'Crawling, is it?' he teased, sliding a hand under her heavy nightdress over her warm legs. Oh it knew where it was going!

'Aye, crawling,' she said, half suffocated by his kisses and by her own desire for him.

Most women told her that they wanted it over quickly, no fuss, no preamble, just doing their duty by their man, but she became aroused by his advances as much as when he first took her in the grass by the laneside on a warm summer's night in 1903, she not yet twenty.

She smelt the pipe tobacco on his breath and felt secure, and now her nightdress was up round her waist and she was panting, 'What do you think you're doing, Peadar Grogan?' yet she clamped him fast, breathing, 'Careful of my nightie, clean on tonight it is!'

She felt him pull up his shirt, gasping hot in her ear, 'Why did you not create merry hell about the rent? I was sure it would start a big shouting match, and - mind the babes, my love . . .'.

'You mind the babes, Lord and Master!' she smiled against his lips and stubble, and he felt her legs opening slowly and softly until his waist lay in the gap between her thighs, and as he shuffled upwards on knees and elbows he found himself brushing against the hot wetness that never ceased to surprise and delight him.

'But the money?' he fought to keep his whisper steady. 'The money - we needed it too. I can't think what possessed me.'

'The good Lord, I shouldn't wonder. I know we needed it too. But the money goes round and round and changes hands and whose hand it's in is no real matter. The same money goes round and round and you put off a terrible day for the Morrisons. Their need was greater than ours this morning.'

'Sure, you're quite the little thinker, aren't you?'

'"Thinker"or "tinker" was that, Grogan?'

'Take it whichever way you want, my love.' He was suddenly serious as he began to enter her, slowly and deliberately at first, and then with an urgency that seemed to generate itself with every second he spent inside her body.

'You have to think of money and things like a sea,' she paused for some deep breaths, holding him to her, 'that washes over lots of little shells, and we are all the little shells . . .'

Peadar was listening to her after a fashion but he too was rocking on an ocean and Sinead's whisper came to him from far away.

' . . . and we have so little control over it all, the tide of money and things, as it washes in and out, in and out, over us and around us. You got a God-given chance to push a bit of it someone else's way and you did it, and I'm sorry for us, sure I am, but it doesn't really, I mean really, matter.' She went on as if in a dream, her brown doe's eyes big and gentle, her body moving beneath him without effort or technique, to the rhythm of her own muscles and the silent music of Nature herself, playing in the cold dark, undeterred by bugs or vermin, unconcerned what century it was or where on earth they chanced to be lying.

'You're too good for me,' he gasped into her nose, the clean smell of soap about her face and throat, and she knew he would soon be finished, his breathing ragged, his grip like a vice, the animal side which she had once feared, which her mother had taught her to fear as a young girl, but which she had grown to love, rejoicing in his strength and manhood as a part of the strength of their union. Perhaps it was he who was too good for her. Or perhaps they were one in the sight of God, so it didn't matter. Then he gave the noise she had once feared was the death-rattle and his whole body stiffened and shook and she was filled with a warm flood inside her and she clasped him to her, because she knew this was his important time, and only a few seconds of it in the long onslaught of life, and she could always do this for him and keep the world out for just a short while.

It was nearly Christmas 1912, bitterly cold and murky, and Peadar and his gang had just finished their stint with the sugar boat, leaving them all reasonably well placed for the festive season. Sean Finnegan, the only member of the gang who was not a family man, went straight off shift to the dog track on Breckfield Road, leaving his mates counting their wages with relief and discussing rent arrears and even the chance of a penny ferry trip across the water. Great Howard Street rang to the clatter of boots and clogs in the freezing mist and dimness, clouds of breath hanging in the the dark, groups of weary dockers passing between pools of light, crossing the tramlines into Lightbody Street, their chat drowned by the thunder of a seemingly endless goods train crawling over the viaduct, its smoke and smuts falling over them and staying in the air, not dispersing. Clogs slithered and slid and lucifers popped and flashed as pipes were lit, clusters of flat caps like trays of mushrooms bobbing in the dark.

Peadar felt sorry for Sean, because he was not going home to a warm fireside and steaming fish or hotpot after Benediction, but from the dogs into the arms of what Sinead called 'a painted Mary Ellen', thence, depending on his luck with the dogs, to the music hall on Roscommon Street. In fact Sean was to be less fortunate than Peadar imagined.

The Grogan twins were well over two years old and Seamus had coped heroically with measles, never squalling or complaining. Both could walk and run, Padraig with precocious skill, and they could talk. Though they could both use the chamber pot quite successfully, it was poor Seamus who occasionally still had 'accidents', and try as she might, Sinead could not find it within her to scold the smiling, sunny-faced little mite, even when he stank like a byre. Seamus also took twice as long as his brother to eat his food. Padraig ate fast and had a wary look in his eye, as if he half expected someone to try and steal his food from him before he had finished it. When Sinead held the spoon to his mouth, he would thrust it in, casting about the dim room, in the shadows, the dark flickering corners, for potential predators.

Only a bitter winter can bring about the cosiness that Peadar found that Friday evening when he arrived at Oswald Street, the peak of his cap and his eyebrows hung with icy droplets. He scuttled to the blazing fire and stooped low over it, sniffing the broth and the fish with satisfaction, reassuring himself with a glance that the sagging brown curtains were tightly drawn to shut out the freezing rawness of the night. The twins were dozing at the top of the bed, covered by their father's old greatcoat, now a sleeve short and very moth-eaten, and, on top of that, Sinead's sacking apron that she wore to hearthstone the outside steps. The hearthstone dust was visible all over the apron, though she never used the new powders, fearing the tales that inhalation of the powder caused 'galloping consumption'. Peadar's suggestion that perhaps the powder was only the old stone ground up was met with cynicism.

Peadar noticed there was also bread and jam to eat.

'Thanks to Mrs Morrison,' explained Sinead, holding up a jar of strawberry.

'But the woman has nothing.'

'She still gives for the rent, my love. And I give her a few bits of coal and all. They must be frozen up there sometimes.'

'But where in the world did the Morrisons get jam from, pray?' He filled his pipe, squatting by the fire and the big, almost red-hot, pan.

'It was in the Goodfellows' Christmas parcel. Two were dropped in yesterday, one for old Mr Casey above and one for the Morrisons at the top. They got some tea, some sugar in a little pot, a bit of beef, a jar of jam and a jar of pickles - oh, and a toy for each of the younger ones. Mrs Morrison came straight down here with the jam.'

'But no Goodfellows' parcel for the poor Grogans?' grinned Peadar, spreading his hands to the hot coals.

'Holy Mother of God! We aren't poor! We're the lucky ones, you being in work most of the time and . . . no more little ones here or on the way.'

'It will happen, my love.'

'When the good Lord wills it.' She looked at BE STRONG IN THE LORD.

'But for now, the Grogans shall have strawberry jam on their bread until the cows come home!' He leaned his elbow on the mantle shelf and pulled on his pipe, beaming his satisfaction into the flickering room, the cold dying in his clothes and in his bones.

'No, beloved husband mine! Only tonight, so make the most of it.' She smiled and crossed to the bed to check on the twins.

'Why only tonight? What are you going to do with our strawberry jam, you scheming young colleen?'

'I shall spoon a dollop off for us and give the rest to Mrs Kennedy for all the times she's minded the babes - like tonight while we go to Benediction.'

'Bring the boys tonight, Sinead, now they're baptised. They'll be good.'

'Oh? And who's going to hold them for an hour?'

'I'll do my bit.'

'I shall still need Mrs K. to mind the fire and the cooking.'

'Tell her she can sup with us when we get back.'

'The range is a disgrace. I'm ashamed of it. I haven't leaded it for days and you can see rust. Make me up some more blacklead, would you?'

'Calm down, woman! Mrs Kennedy won't go over the place with a spy glass!'

St Anthony's Church and Roman Catholic Elementary School lay close enough to be very convenient, yet far enough for the cold to flay the nostrils and to go straight through shoe-leather to turn the feet to stone.

Over her best dress, Sinead wore a thick woollen shawl and, over that, her warm cape with the collar turned up against the freezing fog, and her hat, dark and broad-brimmed with a cluster of black ribbons on one side, the brim a bit distorted where the twins had tried to push the hat under the door.

Peadar wore his 'Sunday best' suit, from Paddy's Market off the Scotland Road, his best cap and his 'walking out' overcoat, which had looked tired even before he left Ireland. The frost stung his close-shaven face so that it shone like a beacon and the gaslight and the lights of passing trams were reflected in his ruby cheeks.

The twins sat face to face, almost too big for their pram. They were not yet breeched and wore white dresses beneath a shabby old blanket. Sinead had cut their hair in a 'prison crop' so that she could wash their heads using soda, water and Bibby's. Their father insisted that they would surely catch their death.

In spite of the mist and winter chill, the closer they came to the church, the more at peace Sinead felt, the further from her workaday cares, the nearer to her God. Peadar was thinking about Sean and how different his life was: dogs, colleens and music halls! Peadar did not envy Sean, he was just curious. He wondered whether Sean envied him. Paid-for pleasure could not compare with the love and loyalty of Sinead. He pondered in his imagination how it might be for Sean and was still going over the details when they arrived at the church.

Parking the pram inside the porch with much fuss and bother, they each carried a baby into the church. Padraig at once grew restive and red in the face, struggling in his mother's arms. Seamus lay in Peadar's crooked arm, smiling and limp, the soft candlelight glowing in his eyes. Mother and father crossed themselves, having dipped their fingers in the holy water, icy in its little stone stoup by the door. They also made the sign of the cross in front of the twins' faces. Padraig flinched and whimpered. Seamus followed his father's finger with his eyes, then stared at him, spellbound.

Peadar remarked that the church was as cold as the tomb.

''Tis comfort for the spirit, not the body,' murmured Sinead as she steered towards the genuflecting form of Auntie Dora.

'Why doesn't she go to the church in Collingwood Street?' Peadar whispered. 'Seeing as how it's closer for her?'

'She had a bit of a to-do with the priest,' Sinead said, nodding and smiling to Auntie Dora, who was staggering to her feet.

'What sort of a to-do?' Peadar had not forgotten the towel and did not subscribe to the philosophy that worldly goods were like a sea or whatever, but just that they cost money, which he worked hard to earn.

'Oh, the priest just reckoned that she had helped herself off the collection basket.'

Peadar rolled his eyes but before he could express an opinion, she said, 'Don't say anything, because I don't want to know.'

'No,' he jeered under his breath, 'because you know what I think!'

It was quite a small church, a simple white-washed vaulted ceiling, poorly lit by two gas lights, leaving all but the nave in shadow. Its magic came from the many candles, which gave the altar a dreamlike splendour. Sinead found it easily believable that Christ Himself might appear there at any moment, like a sudden reward for all the daily toil, the worries, the constant battle against dirt and bugs. Peadar turned his nose up at the gas lights and wondered at the Church pandering to modern inventions, wasting its money. Sinead, dazzled by the altar cloth, could not comprehend how anything earthly could be so white. It had to be holy and without sin to be so white. The gold glinted on the pages of the Bible, sitting sternly on the eagle lectern, the tabernacle hunched beneath its green cloth behind the altar table, bearing the Eucharist, a heavy gold cross rising behind it in turn, two tall candles making the gold burn as if alive, the two vases of blood red roses. Sinead always felt overcome.

'Why, in Heaven's name,' came Peadar's whisper, ' do you have to sit us all next to that old baggage?'

She scowled at him before turning to smile at Auntie Dora, who winked over her tiny spectacles and adjusted her plateau of a hat.

'And who's keeping the scouse boiling tonight in this bitter weather, Auntie Dora?'

'Good evening to you, Mrs Grogan, and to you, Mr Grogan, and just see these two fine little boys. A friend, Mrs Grogan, a friend.'

'I'm surprised she's got any left,' chuntered Peadar, deftly moving his foot away from Sinead's.

'Oh, there's always plenty left, Mr Grogan. I keep a full pan on the boil.'

'Pity she doesn't boil herself!' came the whisper again, now to the tuneful accompaniment of muted organ music.

'Indeed I do boil it myself,' Auntie Dora nodded proudly, 'but while I'm here in the Lord's house, I have another lady to take over for my poor lost lambs.' She drew her bedraggled coat closer round her fat shoulders and beamed at the twins, sitting on their parent's laps as the pews filled.

Eventually, just as Peadar thought he was going to freeze to death, the bell tinkled and the congregation rose ponderously with the movement and sound of a large wave breaking on a shingle beach. Out came two altar boys in white surplices trimmed with a deep red, one of them Francis Morrison, one of the many Morrisons, looking like a convict who had died and gone to heaven. This was certainly the cleanest any of the tribe ever looked, though who could know the filth beneath?

The boys clustered more candles on either side of the altar, Francis occasionally turning to snigger to his colleague, who ignored him. Then Father Brendan Castlereagh appeared, wearing bright green edged with white and gold. Having now seen Father Castlereagh, Sinead already felt warmer in both feet and body and was filled with an almost child-like expectancy. Her little charge fidgeted half-heartedly but made no sound. The many candles, now alive with light, seemed to empty and focus her mind.

Seamus stood supported upon his father, gazing transfixed as Father Castlereagh opened up the tabernacle, placed the Blessed Sacrament into the little glass pyx and put the pyx in its place in the gleaming monstrance. The priest's every move was followed by the little brown eyes as the monstrance was set carefully upon the altar.

Peadar nodded to the square-set figure of Patrick Connelly of Great Howard Street, victualler and betting man, who turned to wink at him, and to James Cassidy, coalheaver of 'back of Wilbraham Place', who waved a tattered copy of the Echo from several pews away.

The congregation joined in the *Adoremus in Eternum*, to a tune which was one of Sinead's favourites. Peadar moved his lips a little and smiled at Auntie Dora's loud rendition of the words and melody, wondering whether her hat acted as a kind of amplifying diaphragm.

'Isn't she a bleeding phonograph on two fat legs?' he whispered, expecting the sharp nudge.

The rosary followed in English, soporific and and relaxing to Sinead. The Divine Praises were also said in English and the responses went up into the shadowy vault, lifted on cloudy breath

48

like a living prayer, and the sweet incense wafted into Sinead's nostrils and she floated above her seat, her child weightless upon her. The Sacrament was put away to the accompaniment of *Tantum ergo Sacramentum* by the congregation and a violent fit of coughing by Auntie Dora.

Sinead adjusted Padraig, in order to put a concerned hand on the old lady's broad back, while Peadar tutted and rolled his eyes again. 'Stupid bloody woman! A common thief, scouse or no scouse!'

Still the coughing shook its victim's heaving frame, causing her to detonate a wet sneeze which burst like a sudden fountain jet into the frosty air. Sinead stroked Padraig's prison crop abstractedly with one hand and tried to comfort Auntie Dora with the other.

'What a shame, Auntie Dora. Shall I take you outside?' she cooed.

The rotund old lady raised a veiny hand and shook her head, so that the plateau on it suffered a mild quake. She then fumbled in her sleeve and produced a fine white handkerchief, delicately feminine and beautifully embroidered, which she applied with dedication to her whiskery nose.

'Well now, that's nice, Auntie,' whispered Sinead, but the handkerchief was already being stuffed back into the sleeve. 'Who gave you that? It's a lovely present.'

'I found it.' She resumed her loud singing.

'In some poor bugger's pocket, I shouldn't wonder,' hissed Peadar in his wife's ear.

Little Seamus's eyes were still alight, as if the sound of the singing conjured up a vision before him, whereas his brother had gone to sleep. The coughing volcano was now extinct and Auntie Dora leaned across Sinead and Padraig and tapped Peadar on the arm. She motioned him to open his hand and when he appeared reluctant, took hold of it and pressed something into it, crushing Sinead and her sleeping baby in the process. Peadar looked from the lightly bearded old face to his hand - a tin of Ogden's Juggler pipe tobacco.

'One of my lost lambs left it on my parlour table,' she nodded reassuringly, the voluminous hand fanning the air.

'I cannot accept tha . . .'

'Sure you can, husband! The tide's washed your way, hasn't it now?' She laughed at his confusion as another damp sneeze broke over Padraig's head.

The bitter, black frost was not the only enemy in the wretched streets that night. In the smoky closeness of the Oddfellows' Arms, elbows soaking gently on the puddled bar, slouched three founder members of the High Rip Gang. Their sport was to stalk working men on their way home on a Friday evening and to 'roll' them, relieving them of their wages. Though the motley membership varied, one or more of these buckos always participated or, as upon this icy evening, worked together, without hangers-on to reduce the shares of swag. They were not regulars at the Oddfellows' but they were recognised as associates of the late Brad Kelly, hanged in 1911 for robbery and murder. The gang's victim might only be a casual worker with little more than a day's money on him, paid at no higher a rate than the docker's tanner, it was all the same to them in the dark, the tussle brought short by a sharp cudgel whack to the head or cheek. The Echo had raged impotently in lurid articles, presaging the 'total collapse of law and order in Liverpool's streets' yet still the victims bled into the gutter and, occasionally, died there.

The stale air rang with slurred shouts, sea shanties and snatches of Irish folk songs and the the windows ran black. Men laden with glasses of ale, rubbing shoulders in the crush and treading sawdust, agreed it was 'too cold to snow.' The three men at the bar observed but took no part. One was a lath-like youth with a cough and a look like that of a starved dog. The man on his left wore what resembled a shiny, black engine driver's cap, placed sideways on his head, the peak down over his right ear, a stubby, nicotine-stained home-made cigarette stuck to his lower lip. The third man, to the right of the youth, wore a jacket that must have been several sizes too small for his body, thereby squeezing the blood to his florid face and causing him to gasp as he paused from his ale, exposing a row of black teeth that looked ready to fall out, if only to escape. The landlord, dabbing his shiny pate with a scabby handkerchief, enquired tentatively whether his three visitors would be staying all evening, insisting that of course that would not present a problem but . . .

'Staying all evening? Staying all evening, asks landlord.' The black grin flickered while the landlord pulled his wet shirt from his clammy back, forcing a smile.

'Good Catholic men should be across the road at St Anthony's any road,' wheezed the youth, 'not cavorting in ale houses.'

'Not in ale houses, landlord, not in ale houses,' said the black grin, poking a finger into his collar to relieve the pressure.

'I believe most of my patrons to be God-fearing,' said the landlord.

'So you're disagreeing with me and my friend?' goaded the lath, staring into the face of the bewildered landlord.

'Disagreeing, are you, landlord?' said the florid face, still grinning like a nervous affliction.

'No, no, not at all, gentlemen! Perish the thought! I just meant to assure you . . .'

'Just meant to assure us,' came the echo again.

For the first time, the third man began to speak, gazing straight into the landlord's face like his colleagues: 'Our kettle's got six patches on it made from cocoa tins.' and he nodded twice for emphasis, waiting for a reaction.

'There!' said the youth, as if, for him, that closed the discussion altogether. The landlord edged away, polishing a glass furiously, and they immediately lost interest in him.

The man with the patched kettle nudged his two friends and nodded towards a solitary drinker, who appeared to be spending plenty of money.

'I'll wager he's a docker, mate,' said the youth.

'That copper dome on the Dock Board Offices must be worth a

bit,' said the man with the engine driver's hat, as if in a dream. The other two glanced at him with continued admiration, then turned their attention back to the wealthy drinker.

Six eyes followed every tilt of his head as the Greenall Whitley Champion Pale Ale went down, as the froth was sucked from the upper lip, as the money was counted in the palm of the hand then thrust under the grey muffler into the inside jacket pocket, as the striking check cap was taken up off the bar and flicked on to the ginger head at a rakish angle and as he turned and left.

'Time to go, gentlemen,' mumbled the youth, coughing into a rag.

'Time indeed,' grinned the echo.

'Eight years they've been building that proddy cathedral,' the engine driver meandered. '1904 they started. Bleeding slow.'

The other two turned to him, amazed, then as if choreographed, left in step, one behind the other.

Sean Finnegan stepped out into the cold and paused to listen to the snatches of *Adoremus in Eternum* from St Anthony's, his breath wreathing round his cap. As he clomped over the tramlines, dodging one of the new Ford automobiles and a horse and cart stacked high with tables and chairs, the singing grew stronger. He stood in the night, asking himself whether he should be there beside Peadar and his folk. On an impulse, he readjusted his cap, its former tilt hinting at disrespect. The singing quietened his head from the clamour and odour of the ale house. Still he stood, eyes wide in the lamplight, yet blind to the slouching trio loitering upon the kerb on the other side of the road, lit yellow by the light above the entrance to the Oddfellows'. Not before he reached a hand to pat the wage money inside his jacket was the spell broken and he made off down Chapel Gardens with a spit and a whistle. Striding now down Robsart Street he paid no attention to the phlegmy cough behind him, stopping to chat with one of his workmates, who had come out to empty a tin bath, complaining that it overflowed the kitchen sink.

'Wish I was coming with you, Sean Finnegan, but the auld dear . . .'

'Sure you don't, Michael, with your home and all.' But still he felt a little privileged to be out and about with nobody but himself to spend his money on.

By the Netherfield Road, he was trying to remember the rosary but somehow the words would not come - only bits of songs by Annie Downey at the music hall. Still, there was always time to make amends later. And was it such a sin to spend his hard-earned wage how he chose, doing no harm to anybody? Peadar Grogan's money went into the collection basket, his went to the dog men, but it would all be swept up into the pile somewhere, in somebody's pocket, good money and bad money together.

And still the dark shadows of the three men flickered over the flags a few paces behind.

To shorten his walk, he began to take the back alleys across the Netherfield area, Copeland Street terraces on one side and a school yard on the other. Apart from the rhythm of his boots, there was no sound now and no light, as he made his way towards Heyworth Street at the far end of the ginnel. It was then that he became aware of footsteps behind him and wondered whether they had been there for some time in the margin of his attention. They were not quite normal steps, but somehow light and hurried, and not one person but more than one, moving together, as if with a single goal in mind. He stopped and turned.

'All right, lads?' he called into the blackness.

No answering greeting came, which was strange. He put a hand to his inside pocket and tried again as the steps continued to advance towards him: 'All right, there?'

He backed against the wall of the school yard, heart pumping. Clouds of breath surrounded him. He could smell ale.

'Your money, wacka, if you please,' came a hoarse voice, choked off by a rattling cough.

Sean Finnegan stared into a sunken, cadaverous face, a sick face, a face grown old before its time. He guessed at a weak consumptive frame. He tried defiance, willing his knees to hold up, telling himself he was a bloody docker, not some nancy boy from college.

'You'll not knock me down without some damage, mates.'

'The Titanic went down in April. You'll go down tonight,' came a deadpan monotone from another man, who had a dead dog-end fused to his lower lip and his cap on sideways. Had he not been so macabre in his gormless erudition, this man would have been uproariously funny.

'Down now,' came the hideously soothing tones of a shiny-faced weasel, jerking his chin in Sean's face, both to threaten him and, apparently, to struggle for freedom from his restricting collar. The shine on his face was sweat.

Three of them, then, thought Sean, and one of them clearly deranged and volatile. He made his move, the last move he was to make. He pushed as hard as he could against the scrawny individual directly in front of him and made as if to break away.

As he did so, a truncheon crashed down upon his head with such force that his cranium split and he was dead before his body thumped into the hard, frozen mud, his cap rolling away into the darkness.

Seamus fell ill again just as Christmas was in the wintry air.

''Tis the catarrh and bronchitis plagues the poor mite.' nodded old Mrs Kennedy, stroking the stubbly head, while Sinead coaxed the hot Bovril down what she called 'Red Lane' to the boys.

It made her so sad to listen to the wheezy, tortured breathing through the long night and to see the muck he fought to cough up, fit to choke an adult, let alone a child barely more than two years old.

'He was even sick over Corpus Christi last year in the blazing sunshine,' she said to her neighbour. 'If Peadar and I had the money, Mrs K., I'd take him to to where the rich folk go to take the sea air. I fear he'll take really bad and die one winter in these terrible streets.'

'Don't you distress yourself, Mrs Grogan. That stuff there will set him right. And I hear Mr Morrison's working again now?'

'That's right. Working on the new Cunard building as a labourer. Covered in fancy carving, Peadar says it is. Quite extravagant, I shouldn't wonder. There. All gone down 'Red Lane' now. What shall I do with him, Mrs Kennedy?'

'Make him a little bed in front of the fire with a blanket and pillow and lie him down so he can see out the window to the sky.'

The two ladies sat up to the kitchen table, talking and drinking tea, while Seamus lay wrapped in his old blanket, his head propped up on the pillow , gazing out through the parted curtains at a little patch of blue sky over Oswald Street.

A shaft of misty golden sunlight cascaded into the room and fell upon Seamus, the sparkling dust dancing in the cold light of late morning. For all his suffering, a soft smile grew in the corners of his mouth and spread across his pale face as he lay back, seeing far beyond the meanness of the courts of Oswald Street, places that Sinead could not even guess at as she glanced from time to time at the small wan bundle, the tiny rattling chest heaving to force the poor sooty air into its tubes. The gilded smile and big luminous eyes gave the appearance of a babe old in years, whose body barely kept it lingering in this world, a fleshly anchor. Sinead would smile at him and he would smile back, an uncanny smile, as if it were he who wanted to reassure her. Nor was his reverie broken by the sudden arrival of Padraig, his grey goo-goo dangling from his hand, never out of reach, even these days, bored with his top and desperate for reassurance and attention.

He ran to his mother's side and tugged at her skirt, whining, 'Ma! Ma! Ma!' Now and then he would go quiet and stare at Seamus with fascination, as if he had never seen him before. Although his brother was lying on the floor within easy reach, Padraig would not approach him. He would walk round him, regarding him with something akin to respect, but would not interfere. Padraig, himself rarely ill, seemed to feel that illness bestowed special qualities on his twin, which he did not possess, a sort of power and privilege which emanated from infirmity, something from which robust children were excluded. He would spend long minutes listening to his brother's laboured breathing and follow the rise and fall of the little chest beneath the blanket, knowing that this was his brother, yet wondering at it.

Seamus lay suffering and weak whilst his namesake in the bowl continued to enjoy the life of Riley after more than a twelvemonth. Peadar said it was the Lord's cruel sense of humour, but Sinead insisted that a drowned man fed the starving fishes, so that a sense of justice could only be gained by trying to take a broader view.

'Like that old baggage Auntie Dora, you mean?' would fly the rejoinder.

So Seamus lay, pinned beneath the sunbeam, more golden than the goldfish, which floated in light on the window sill, and Sinead sat and sipped and worried, unaware of the little glowing icon, panting in his blanket by her fireside.

Padraig's anxious little mouth compressed into that determined line, that straight line of lips, that line which was bent on receiving notice and which only relaxed into normal lips when a kiss was planted on the cropped head and a light pat from mother's hand sent him off to play again. He scampered to and fro through the shaft of sunlight, his prickly head dull in its beautiful auburn light, bobbing in and out of it, leaving his brother transfixed, burnished.

When their da came home from the docks, bringing the cold and the smell of the outside into the room with him, he would yank Padraig off the floor and hold him high above his head, bellowing, 'And what mischief has this little scally been up to today?' and while Padraig was still shrieking with delight, his da would kneel down to the prostrate Seamus, as if doing him reverence, and murmur, close to his ear, 'And my little Seamus, how is he doing today?' and his heart would warm to see the big smile and calm, glowing eyes, like his mother's eyes when she was just waking.

When the news came to Peadar, he was humping great bags of china clay on the windy quayside. He lay his bag down on to the wet concrete like a baby, straightened and lifted his cap to ventilate his pate and to reflect.

'Sean? Dead? Are you sure?'

'In the *Echo*, mate. Found in a back alley with his head stove in.'

Peadar crossed himself and looked out across the angry waters of the dock to the bobbing barges and lighters and two more clay boats queuing to unload. Clay for the Potteries, horrible stuff, got up your nose, in your mouth and all over your clothes and the feel of the huge brown paper sacks set your teeth on edge.

'In his late twenties, he was, Eamonn. Hardly started out in life.'

'Aye, mate. I've seen many come and go in the last twenty-five years. Y'know, it was schooners brought the china clay into Liverpool in them days. It still came up from Cornwall but it took a lot longer.'

'Why would somebody do that to young Sean, eh, Eamonn?' said Peadar angrily. 'He wasn't a rich man and had only his wages.' He kicked the bag of china clay, sending a puff of white dust into the wind.

''Tis no worse now than it was then, mate, if you ask me, the violence.'

'It's got to be worse, Eamonn. Killing a young working man. He had nobody, nobody in this world and he died in the darkness, on his own.'

Eamonn placed a fatherly arm round the younger man's shoulders, seeing him so distressed.

'I started in Waterloo Docks as a 'runner', to earn a bit of extra when work was slack. The docks was full of emigrants, desperate to get to America on one of the Cunarders. The poor bastards had to wait as much as ten days in Liverpool just to get a berth, so they needed lodgings. I'd guide them to a boarding house and take a commission, so to speak, from the landlord. If he refused or began any sort of argument . . .' Eamonn smacked his left fist violently into his right and raised an eyebrow to check that his meaning was clear.

'That's not the same as robbing or murdering, though!'

'This is a hard place, mate. It's got tough rules. One of them is: you don't go down dark alleys on your own.'

'But some swine has cut poor Sean's life short for his docker's tanner! Bastards!' He spat twice as Eamonn patted him gently on the back.

'Aye, it's sad, young Grogan, so it is, but what's meant to be is meant to be, I suppose.'

'No! I cannot go for that, Eamonn! It wasn't meant to be, as you put it. He was cut down on a whim by a bunch of rollers. I'd like to meet the man who did that to Sean Finnegan.'

'Don't go scheming revenge, for no good will come of it. They suspect the High Rip again. They're murderers and you have a beautiful wife and two little boys.' He watched Peadar as his clouded face softened.

' Oi! Grogan! Fahy! Will you two shift yourselves and do some work!'

The charge-hand with the big moustache and bulging waistcoat was picking his way over the chaos of ropes, hawsers and sacks like an overweight ballerina. He might have looked comical, but one word from him to the gaffers and someone's earning days could be over for ever.

'Right away, Mr Carey. Sorry, Mr Carey, but we was mourning the untimely and violent demise of handsome young Finnegan of our gang, sir.'

'Well, kindly do it in your own time, Fahy, and not in work time.'

'Certainly, Mr Carey, sir. Apologies, sir.'

'By the by, Fahy, I've been meaning to speak to you for a while. Come with me if you please.'

Eamonn touched his cap to Mr Carey and followed in his wake, slightly stooped from years of heavy lifting and hard labour. Peadar watched them disappear round the corner of the storage shed and wondered whether Eamonn and Sean might have something in common in a strange sort of way.

When Peadar brought the news to Sinead, her hands flew to pat her hair round her ears, then clasped themselves together as she turned to stare wide-eyed at BE STRONG IN THE LORD.

'Mary and Joseph and all the Saints!'

Peadar could see the tears coming as she turned back to him but did not speak. She rarely spoke when she was shocked, just waited and waited for the news to sink in, as if expecting some kind of explanation to be whispered in her ear, something that would place it all in perspective, something that would make it all right. At length she murmured, ' Still, if it is the good Lord's will.'

Peadar, furious, tore his cap off his head, leaving the hair sticking up at the back as if someone had run a flat iron up his neck.

'How can the Lord have willed Sean Finnegan's violent murder, woman? Or if he did will it, how can you call Him good?' To emphasize 'good' he flung his cap down and watched it roll away into the dark corner by the sink and the perambulator and the large mouse trap.

'Please don't take on, love, though I know you're upset.' She paused before adding, 'Come and fill your pipe, for there's cow's heel stew on the boil.'

He shed his muffler and moved grim-faced to the fire where, to Sinead's relief, he began to fill his pipe.

'These weren't just casual dippers, woman, I can tell you.' he groused, placing the pipe firmly between his teeth with an audible click, 'not just some jug troupe out to pick a pocket. No, this was the High Rip. Professionals.'

He turned to her, where she stood behind him, toying with her apron in her nervousness. 'And you really believe we must say it's all for the bloody best, part of some plan, roll with the bloody punches, is it, eh? Eh?'

'What else can we do, Peadar? And please stop that language indoors. You never used to swear indoors in the Old Country.'

'Maybe I had less cause to.'

'You'll wake the babes. God knows I had enough bother getting them off tonight, what with the curtain and all.' She jerked her thumb towards the faded green curtain on its slack wire, which tonight only curtained off the bed itself, hanging there in a heavy bunch, whereas normally it would be drawn across the whole of that half of the room at night.

'Are they all right?'

'Seamus is still wheezing.'

'I'll fix the curtain after,' he said more quietly, drawing on his pipe for a few seconds, looking at Sinead, wondering whether to talk about his other piece of bad news.

'They sacked Eamonn Fahy today.'

'Oh, my God! Not Eamonn?'

'Yes, my love, Eamonn.' He blew out a cloud of smoke.

'You've worked with him since you started at the Stanley. But why in the world?'

'Because he's too old!' He gave a joyless laugh.

'Too old? He's not forty, is he?' She tried the stew from the spoon.

'Forty next birthday. They say he's had a good run. A good run! I ask you! That doesn't leave me many more years, now, does it? I'd be hard pushed to roll with that kind of a punch, that's for sure.'

Sinead paused, the spoon motionless beneath her chin.

'It's his bad back makes him slower in the winter. He cannot lift as much. The gaffer offered him a job in the office, but he knows the poor devil can neither read nor write. Eamonn! Eamonn, who started out loading the sailing ships!'

'Peadar, Peadar, I tell you, my love, it's all part of the Lord's plan, which it's not for us to know or understand!'

'You have gravy round your mouth, wife.' He was peering round the room to see how far his cap had rolled. 'I think God is terrible cruel, then.'

'No, Peadar, it only seems so when you look at one corner of your own life. My poor Ma used to say you could crush half an ants' nest while running to put out a fire.' She dabbed her mouth and chin with her apron.

'So there's no such thing as a tragedy, according to you and your poor Ma?'

'Oh, I'm not clever enough to know, husband. But with your attitude, you're just banging your head against a brick wall.'

'With your attitude, you're making believe the wall doesn't really exist! And build up this fire, for I'm starting to see my breath in this room.'

There came an outbreak of wailing from behind the bunched up curtain, as the few coals in the grate shifted and slipped even lower.

Easter and Pentecost came and went as 1913 became middle-aged and at last even the Oswald Street courts warmed to the sun of Corpus Christi. The Thursday of what Sinead called the 'real Corpus Christi' was soon followed by the Sunday of the procession down Scotland Road, Thursday being just an ordinary working day.

Now the Abercromby and the biscuit works were silent and the air was clear above the Vauxhall chimney. Siobhan had dropped her sister a line from Boston, Massachusetts, at the start of a new life. The O'Neills were spreading themselves across the globe.

The housewives were scrubbing their struggling children that morning with the gusto that they would show their fire irons in the evening scrub out. Two of the Morrison boys sloped off to the dinner-house in Portland Street to plague the welldoers and cause disruption in the long queue. Beyond Great Homer Street, the Orange people were still abed. The slogan across the front of the Homer Cinema was now half washed off, leaving only ' . . . to the Papists.' Peadar's best shoes stood shiny atop an article from the *Echo* about D.H.Lawrence's shocking novel, *The Rainbow*. A large jam tart stood ready for tea. Above the Grogans' heads, poor Mr

Casey was laid out and visitors traipsed continually up and down the stairs. The busker with the stringless fiddle was being stoned by three buckos from Dryden Street until old Mrs Kennedy came out and threw a bowl of suds over the lot of them. The day so far was not exceptional, except that the gutter ran thin and smelly and one of the urchins from opposite had found a farthing in it and was holding it aloft, out of the reach of his unsavoury mates. One or two children were beginning to appear in the street in their Sunday best, two girls even in white for the procession. Both of them had fathers who were charge-hands at the gasworks in Eccles Street, so folk would say it was ' all right for the likes of them.' Some of the boys wore grey trousers and white shirts. The smarter children had been warned not to get dirty, so they stood around self-consciously, arms dangling, simpering at each other. A group of men of the Confraternity in waistcoats and caps stood smoking, talking about the new diesel oil engines which were replacing the coal-fired engines in some of the ships. As they sounded off, they would stretch their braces to lend gravity to their predictions and warnings.

Inside No. 8, Peadar was behind the curtain, soaking in the tin bath and smoking his pipe. Sinead was wrestling with Padraig in the sink, wondering which was more slippery, the soap or her son. Padraig always managed to get soap in his eyes. Seamus, on the other hand, seemed to revel in being washed, as if it were a complete cleansing, not just the dirt. He stood like a naked little statue, eyes tightly shut, smiling at nothing in particular. When Sinead ordered, 'Hands, if you please', he would stretch forth his chubby little arms like a sleep-walker. Sinead's apron was soaked but she was content. Sometimes, while she was bathing the babes, she would reflect how poor Colm would now be five and poor Dominic seven, had they survived. But they had not and no good was served by dwelling upon it. She herself was but two years away from thirty and where were the days going and were her child-bearing days coming to an end? Peadar still cursed the murderers of Sean Finnegan, who remained unavenged. Birth and death - what mysteries!

Still the sun shone as the procession moved down the Scotland Road all the way to St Patrick's. Hordes of school children led the way, grouped into cadres according to their school, followed by the adults, the men in their confraternities. At the end came the canopy, supported by four men bearing poles. Beneath the canopy was the priest, bearing the monstrance which contained the Blessed Sacrament.

As the canopy approached Dryden Street corner, where the Grogan family waited, the excitement mounted as did the heat and the crush of bodies. Padraig had thrown a tantrum and left his mother in no doubt that he had no interest in the procession. He tugged at her hand and pouted and stamped his foot, because he could see nothing at all, which was, presumably, what he wanted. Seamus sat on his father's shoulders, his face alive with anticipation. Now and then he would spur his father on, as if he were riding a horse, his little legs opening and closing. Rarely was Seamus more animated than his twin.

The priest's heavily embroidered cope seemed to Sinead to belong to another world, perhaps even to Heaven itself, so impossibly beautiful was it. The sunlight glinted painfully on the monstrance as if it had no substance but was itself made of light, as only a holy thing could be. The tiny portion of the Blessed Sacrament inside its glass bulb made Sinead feel quite overcome, something that was of Christ Himself, moving along here, only feet from her own door. Her faith was vindicated. Her daily toil had a purpose. Christ lived!

As the canopy moved on, Peadar felt Seamus relax and become somehow heavier. His little cropped head had followed the priest, his eyes turning with the canopy as it moved, his head turning in concert with his mother's head, the two of them similarly focused. Peadar simply felt uncomfortably hot and turned to see the man next to him loosening his collar with a dirty finger, and then grimacing with relief, revealing a mouthful of ugly black teeth. As he straightened from putting Seamus down on the ground, Peadar felt sure he had seen the man somewhere before. And what about his cap? Peadar looked at the man's loud check cap, which certainly did not suit him at all. The man glanced sideways at his observer, aware that he was being looked over. Peadar struggled to make sense of what he was seeing: a cap like that belonged to some swaggering bucko, not a scrawny miserable-looking character like this man. Even so, scrawny or not, none of his clothes appeared to fit him. Everything he wore looked as if it were intended for someone else.

The man had had enough of being scrutinised and was moving off through the crowd, his cap bobbing up and down, further and further away. Then the light dawned in Peadar's head. The distinctive cap - of course poor Sean Finnegan!

'Hey, you!' yelled Peadar.

'Peadar, what on earth is the matter?'

'Hey! Wait!' he ignored her, brushing aside a protesting youth. He battled his way in the direction of the bobbing cap, which had now disappeared, some of the people around him jabbing him angrily. He stopped. It was hopeless. He could hear Sinead calling him. He turned back.

'Peadar, we could have lost Padraig and Seamus! You just simply left them! What possessed you? Did you see the Devil himself?'

'Aye, I believe I did,' he murmured.

'What are you on about?'

'It was just a wild idea. Nothing definite.'

'Well, be definite about your responsibilities with these boys, will you, please?'

Yet by evening she felt aglow. She had been within feet of her God. It was somehow more powerful than Mass, because it was more unusual, more special, and that conferred mystery on the whole occasion. She sat back from the cluttered table, her hands at rest in her lap. Seamus squatted on the floor, toying abstractedly with his brother's damp goo-goo. Peadar leaned back in his chair, his head against the wall, his eyes closing slowly. He was drained. So was Padraig. He had exhausted himself and lay on his back, asleep.

As Sinead turned her head to look into the darkening room, she caught Seamus's eye and knew he felt much as she did, clean and somehow elated. It was at that moment that she felt sure that he would cope with life, whatever tribulations were cast his way. His smile was not the same as his da's. Peadar's smile was one of masculine charm. It showed he was in control, or wanted you to believe that he was. Seamus's smile came from a light within him. It was always there and always would be.

While Nurse McEwan was supervising the carrying downstairs of poor Mr Casey, she had confided to Sinead, 'Your little Seamus is a saint, Mrs Grogan, a saint,' though Peadar had assured his wife it was the milk stout talking.

'For the laying out of a corpse she receives enough drink to re-float the Titanic!'

The next day the *Echo* announced, 'Scuffles between Catholics and Protestants mar Corpus Christi Celebrations.' That, and the sure knowledge that the week's rent was due that day, started Peadar on about Sinn Fein in Ireland and the slow progress of the Liberal Government's latest Home Rule bill. He sounded off less and less these days and only when he was worried or frustrated, for he rarely drank to excess.

'Four years we've been over here now and back home the bastard Ulster Volunteer Force is out training in the open, if you please!'

'Don't go on, love, and don't curse in front of the babes. Go off to work while you've still got work to go to.'

She glanced across at BE STRONG IN THE LORD. On Corpus Christi, for the first time that she could remember, it had not needed adjusting all day. But today, there it was, crooked again. She knew better than to fuss with it while Peadar was there, so she waited.

'Maybe we should go back, Sinead, back to the Old Country. I could join Sinn Fein or that Republican Brotherhoood and fight for full independence.' He slapped his cap on.

'And maybe you could give up a good job here and maybe you could get shot and maybe your wife and children could starve! How would that suit you?' She watched him suck on his dead pipe. Knowing that she was winning, she pressed home, 'If you feel that way, why did we come here in the first place? You've done all right. Better than in Armoy, I'll wager.'

'Aye but we're Irish, wife, not English, and we're of the Faith.'

'Well, I am, husband, I don't know whether you are!'

'Sure you sound like Nurse McEwan!' He was almost smiling now, at last.

'Peadar, everyone here is of the Faith.'

'But it's an enclave, that's all it is.' His hand was on the door. Soon she would be able to straighten that embroidery.

'Oh? And what's an enclave, pray?' Her head was inclined for a goodbye kiss.

'We're surrounded by heathens. The English toffs don't want Irish Home Rule.'

He came back and kissed her quickly but she held him back. The second one was longer, much longer. When at length he drew away from her and put his cap back on, she patted her hair into order and said, 'No more procession watching for you, Peadar Grogan.' And she meant it.

Once he was gone and the twins were presentable, and the place was tidy and the mountain of washing was loaded into the perambulator, it was time to go along to No. 12 at the blind end of the street next to the Abercromby with its din and smells, like a voracious monster that was devouring something unspeakable behind its wall, and there was Mrs Kennedy, waiting to take the boys in for a couple of hours.

'Don't talk pennies to me, Mrs Grogan! Just do these few things for me and I'll be made up.' And another great pillow-slipful was dumped on to the sinking pram. Because the sun was shining, the two ladies tarried at Mrs Kennedy's door, watching the twins scampering up and down her steps.

'Civil war in the Old Country, they do say, Mrs Grogan,'

confided Mrs Kennedy, crossing her big arms and nodding all her chins.

'Don't let my husband know. He's hot-headed enough. I've had enough of Sinn Fein and its history to last a lifetime, Mrs K. This country's been good enough to us, so it has.'

'Sure enough, Mrs Grogan, sure enough, but the good Lord must be on the side of the Irish Catholics back home if there's any justice at all for the having.' She looked up and down the street as if addressing a public meeting and nodded at the tall factory wall.

'Oh, Mrs K., I think the Lord loves all humanity, not just a small part of it. His people should try and agree together.'

'Easily said, my dear! I maintain that God is a Catholic.'

'If we abandoned ourselves to Him instead of fighting, I'm sure this world would be a better place for these boys to grow up in.'

'That evil UVF has over a million pounds saved up and is ready to start a war, so a man told Auntie Dora at Mass. Orange devils, pah!' She spat over the railings on to the paving stones.

The boys ran down the steps to see where the spittle had landed. Sinead told them to come away.

'You mark my words, Mrs Grogan, next year will be the year of civil war, 1914.'

'A civil war, that would be terrible, Mrs K.'

It was about a year later that Peadar and his gang arrived at the Stanley to find no work, which was unusual for a Monday morning. Having been told to report back that afternoon to the pen, they had split up and gone their separate ways, apart from Peadar and Tom Downey, who were strolling in the sunshine between the warehouses down Great Howard Street. These days there was too much traffic for ambling along the road itself or between the tramlines. Tom had just been into Flynn the barber's on the corner of Upper William Street to place a couple of bets. The warm sun and pleasantly cool air were an invigorating and seductive cocktail. Peadar felt these were days in which anything could happen and had been sad to learn of the death of Eamonn Fahy, just two years after he had left the docks to do odd jobs at the market in Juvenal Street.

'The poor sod died of boredom,' said Tom. I blame Mr bloody Carey.'

'Aye, a man's finished at forty, I've got about four years to go, Tom!'

Peadar laughed uneasily. The boys would be starting school next year, among the precious few from Oswald Street that went to school at all. None of the many Morrisons had had any schooling. Larry was soft on that sort of thing, having had none of it himself.

''Tis the Walker's Pale gives me my learning!' he would chuckle toothlessly to Peadar on the landing. Larry and his wife had barely a tooth between them.

'The Old Country is fit to erupt, Tom.'

'Aye, I believe it is, Peadar.'

'Would you care to have my Echo, Tom?'

'Anything in it today, is there?'

'No, mate. Some Austrian's been shot.'

'Who would that be, then, Peadar?'

'Hold on and I'll tell you,' for he knew full well that Tom was not a good reader and preferred to have the news read aloud to him.

He read out the article about the assassination in Sarajevo of Archduke Franz Ferdinand of Austria and his consort in their automobile by a bunch of students.

'Anything about our pay in there, Peadar?'

'Can't see anything, mate. Apparently that shooting could have international effects.'

'How's that, then? And where is Australia?

'Austria. Not Australia.'

'Well, where is Austria?'

'I don't rightly know.'

'Well, any road, the troubles will come from Ireland, Peadar, not from bloody Australia!'

'Austria, Tom, Austria.'

1915 - 1923

Losing the Faith

*But as for those who treat our signs as lies, we shall gradually bring
them down by means of which they know not*

The Koran

Peadar's decision to go to war had really been made on the first rent day in August 1914. Monday 3rd August it was and Stanley Dock lay sweltering in the clammy heat. Mr Carey's tiny office was almost unbearable that afternoon and the commingled odours of his sweat and his cologne hung, heavy and dense, trapped within its confines. Peadar breathed in this atmosphere very discreetly as he ducked through the low doorway into the gloom, his soft knocking having been answered by, 'Come in, Grogan, for Christ's good sake, instead of mucking about out there, tickling the door!'

He stood in front of Mr Carey, twisting his cap in his hands, his springy brown hair matted with sweat. Mr Carey sprawled, creaking, in his chair, using both hands to part his walrus moustache before attempting to speak, his vast stomach apparently on the point of firing a salvo of buttons into the heavy air.

'Well, now, Grogan,' he began, reaching behind him with unexpected grace and precision for a sheet of paper, 'how long have you been working at the Stanley now?'

'Getting on five years now, Mr Carey.'

While Peadar's stomach churned with foreboding, Mr Carey continued to run his eye over the sheet of paper.

'Five years, eh?' he echoed, absently, and read for a while, the heat pressing down on the dingy little room.

'Yes, sir.'

'Happy years, Grogan?' He looked Peadar up and down.

'Very happy, sir.'

'You're a good worker, Grogan.' He was watching Peadar over his paper now.

'Thank you, sir.' Peadar was in agony now, wondering what this was leading to.

'Since my promotion, Grogan,' said Mr Carey, leaning back and pressing his thumbs into his waistcoat pockets, thereby stretching the material to an almost impossible extent, ' I've been meaning to ask you whether you fancy some . . .' he paused, his hands open, palms up, 'some slightly lighter work.' The word 'lighter' he gave heavy emphasis.

Peadar took a small step forward, his voice feeble, 'Oh no, sir, no, I'm still fit and strong and I . . .'

Mr Carey raised a fat index and frowned. 'No, Grogan, no! That's just it, I'm afraid. You're getting slower. How old are you, man?'

'Thirty-six, sir,' he almost whispered.

'What? Speak up, Grogan! I can't hear you if you whisper!'

'Thirty-six.' Peadar felt himself sagging, as if under a great weight, a weight far heavier than that of any sack of china clay. He saw the face of poor dead Eamonn Fahy, the face of poor murdered Sean Finnegan with his loud check cap. The only original member of the old gang not dead or put out to grass was Tom Downey.

'Thirty-six is a good age for heavy dock work, Grogan. A man's back can't be what it was and his breathing . . . .'

'I'm sound in wind and limb, sir, so I am.' He licked his upper lip and tasted salt.

'Face it, man, you're slowing down. It's quite natural, going on forty.'

It seemed funny when Sinead pulled his leg about it but it certainly was not funny now. Peadar knew what the next question would be and held his breath.

'Can you read and write, by any chance?' There it was - the writing on the wall, in fact.

'I can read quite well, sir, but I cannot do the writing.' He tried to pitch his voice up, to sound positive, hopeful, but it rang in his own ears like a knell.

'No writing. That's a pity, that's a pity. I taught myself, you know.'

'All the men take you for a well-instructed man, Mr Carey.'

'Quite so, quite so.' Mr Carey crossed his fat legs with surprising ease and steepled his chipolata fingers. 'I want you to consider lighter work, Grogan. The rate will be lower of course, but you will find it easier going.'

'But I can manage the work, sir. It's no bother to me.' He licked the sweat away from round his mouth, which was dry and tasted foul.

'You don't understand, man. The job is changing. We need a smaller number of fast, fit men. We can then save on wages and still get the work done in the same time.'

'I can still be fit and fast, sir, no problem about that.'

Mr Carey put his sheet of paper down behind him and took up a copy of the *Echo*, which he brandished in the thick air.

'You say you can read. Well, have you read today's paper?'

'No, sir, but I keep up with the news. I know the Russians are making ready for a war with the Germans.'

'Ancient history, Grogan, ancient history! That was last Thursday! You know, no doubt, that all the British officers and men of the armed forces have been recalled from leave and that all the coastal defences are being manned?'

'Yes, sir, but how does that affect the Stanley, with respect, sir?'

Mr Carey rubbed his eyes in mock disbelief: 'How does it affect the Stanley?' he squeaked, regarding Peadar through his fingers. 'Last Friday, the London Stock Exchange closed for the day. Today, Germany has declared war on France and has threatened to march into Belgium tomorrow. There's going to be a war, Grogan, there's going to be a bloody war!'

Peadar stared at him but could think only of the Golden Syrup tin on his mantlepiece, sitting on the green baize next to the photographs of poor Dominic and Colm, empty. Empty because his gang had not been called from the pen for several days until today and Peadar's earnings were smaller than in any previous year.

'The port of Liverpool, Grogan, will almost certainly deal with the shipping of all the motor transport and all the frozen meat to feed the troops.'

Peadar looked up from the grubby linoleum. 'Then surely more dockers will be needed, sir, not less.'

'Grogan, we shall want fit young men, not men coming up to forty!'

'But what when the fit young men have all gone to war, sir?'

'Fit young women perhaps.' Carey smiled to himself but Peadar found his whole line of thinking ridiculous. The very idea of female dock labour!

Over by Christmas, Tom Downey, had said. Over by Christmas. So the whole shennanigan was hardly going to affect his own life. Just three or maybe four months of it. Still, he'd got to do something. He could see his present job disappearing fast before his very eyes. The overpowering little office and the whole of Stanley Dock Depot, and the noise from the saw mill across in Lightbody Street all began to fade. He could feel Sinead's eyes upon him for guidance, little Seamus beaming trustingly and fidgety Padraig struggling from his arms to forage for food. Peadar knew he himself would soon be stacking empty crates and boxes for a fraction of the docker's tanner and trying to do deals on the side, selling firewood to the likes of the Morrisons from the debris of the broken boxes. Even then he would be competing with the box boys and barrow boys of the wholesale market in Juvenal Street. Here were his thanks for years of back-breaking labour! Even Sinead would have a difficult task explaining the meaning of this in God's plan, what with her ants' nests and her oceans of life and her daft ideas of justice. It's the Golden Syrup tin that really matters in this world and the next life will have to take care of itself!

Or maybe his decision had not really been made firm until the following Friday, 7th August 1914, when the advance parties of the British Expeditionary Force were beginning to leave from Southampton, bound for France under the command of Field Marshall Sir John French. Peadar had seen many newspaper pictures of him, looking handsome and dashing on horseback. But still it was a far cry from the Stanley Dock that afternoon, as Peadar's gang sat among heaps of empty sacks, piled up like mountains between two of the big mooring posts on the hot quayside, the tobacco warehouse behind and the flat black water before, sucking and slapping half-heartedly a few feet below them. A couple of clay pipes were alight, and the Ogden's Juggler smouldered in the bowl of Peadar's new cherrywood which he complained still tasted a little like charred newspaper.

'You'll never beat the clay,' the others would assure him. 'Men will still be smoking the clay in a hundred years' time.'

Peadar watched the trams rumbling along Great Howard Street and the omnibuses weaving in and out, their flanks clad in huge advertisements for Pears' Soap, Walker's Pale, Bovril and Mazawattee Tea, and he wondered how long there would be Grogans at No. 8 Oswald Street.

On that Monday night, Sinead had sat on the edge of the bed, patting her hair down nervously and trying to be 'strong in the Lord'. At first she had whispered, 'Jesus, Mary and Joseph!' crossing herself, and drawing the curtain back to look at the faces of her sleeping boys, top-to-tail and nearly four years old. This was exactly what had happened to poor Eamonn Fahy. First there was the so-called 'lighter work' and then there was no work at all. In any case, Peadar's gang had been earning less and less nowadays. It sounded to her as if they spent as long kicking their heels in the pen as actually being given work on the dockside. Some of the other gangs seemed to do all right. Perhaps they were just younger.

And then there had been the death of Mrs Kennedy at No. 12, with her note left in the drawer for Sinead, dated just after the old dear's stroke:

'My dere Mrs Grogan, in the event of my deth, me having no kin just take eny of my few chatels that you wish and I will be more than happy. God keep you all. Marjorie Kennedy.'

Sinead had had no idea that the old lady could write, nor could she imagine what to do with Conal, her vicious, scrawny Alsatian, adopted as a stray six months earlier. Noisy, anti-social Conal had been neglected during Mrs Kennedy's short illness and stood guard at the door of No. 12, looking hungry and barking at anyone foolish enough to venture near the steps.

Nurse McEwan came on a Tuesday morning to lay out the body and invited Sinead round to pay her last respects. Sinead said she would get the boys ready and be round directly and five minutes later the three of them emerged into the drab wetness, Padraig leaping ahead down the steps and Seamus blinking and smiling into the thin, soaking rain, as if he could see the sun right through all the cloud. Sinead, bringing up the rear, drew her shawl anxiously about her shoulders. Corpses would always remind her of her two dead babies. Turning to haul the big street door to, she called to Padraig, noting the thinness of her own voice, 'Don't go inside till I get there, now will you? I don't care that Nurse is inside and may call you. You wait for me.'

She could hear the commotion coming from Dryden Street where all manner of horses, lorries, omnibuses and automobiles which had been requisitioned by the authorities were being lined up, before being driven away. Peadar had been awakened early by a big fight over there, something to do with one of the automobiles, so folk said.

Padraig ran straight into Conal. The Alsatian lunged at him with a growl which exploded into furious barking. Panic-stricken, little Padraig stumbled backwards, lost his footing, which was normally very sure, and sprawled on the wet flagstones with a shriek of terror. For a second, Sinead stood rooted at the foot of her steps. Conal, his coat matted flat with rain and filth, stood over the boy, growling with outrage, his steaming body shaking.

Sinead screamed, 'Leave him alone you devil's creature, he's just a baby!' and she made as if to run to her son, but Conal turned towards her and growled, very quietly, his eyes burning. She held back, her hand to her mouth. It was tiny Seamus who, still smiling, toddled without hesitation right up to Conal, talking to him all the time, just as he used to talk to himself, 'Conal! Conal!

Here, boy! Here, boy!'

'Seamus, come away, come away!' whispered his mother, wringing her hands.

Conal looked up. He gave a little yelp. Seamus squatted beside him so that the dog towered above his close-cropped head.

'Here, Conal! Here, Conal!'

The dog turned to Seamus and sniffed him, losing interest in the small, prostrate bundle lying in the rain beneath him. He began to lick Seamus's face, sending the boy into fits of laughter. Conal scampered round Seamus, flicking rain everywhere and treading all over Padraig's legs. As Sinead drew near, her eyes fixed on Padraig, the dog's attention never wavered from Seamus who was kneeling in the wet. Conal followed every move of the little hands and face, his long tongue dangling sideways, eyes alert as if waiting to be entertained. Padraig clambered to his feet, while his mother still held back, now watching Seamus, just as the dog watched him and the rain fell all around. Then Seamus stood up, turned his back on Conal and started up the steps to No. 12.

The street door stood ajar. Seamus scampered up towards the darkness within. Sinead was too late to bid him wait again. She took the hand of Padraig, filthy as the hobs of hell from head to toe. Both hesitated on the top step, wary of the presence of death, fearful lest it be contagious. Sinead crossed herself. Padraig pressed his wet face into his mother's shawl. Seamus had disappeared. So mother and son, holding hands like a pair of waifs, advanced into the unknown.

In the front parlour the curtains were closed and no light burned. All the furniture had been removed so that you could make your way cautiously round the open, rough wooden coffin which lay on the table.

'She's all ready, Mrs Grogan,' came the voice of Mrs Morrison from the back scullery, amid noises of vigorous hand-washing. You can pop in and see her now, love.'

Sinead and Padraig tip-toed closer, amazed to behold little Seamus on the far side of the coffin. He had pulled up the one and only chair in the room, left there for the more fragile mourner, and was kneeling on it, elbows on the edge of the coffin, smiling down at the cadaver within.

'Seamus!' whispered Sinead sharply. 'Come away!'

The little round face looked up, puzzled, at his mother. 'It's only Mrs Kennedy, Ma. Nurse says she's sleeping.'

'You mustn't lean over the . . . body like that, son. It's not nice.'

'It's just Mrs Kennedy,' protested Seamus's piping voice as he looked across the coffin at his mother, astonished.

'All the same,' she drew near with Padraig's hand gripped tightly in hers, and craned her head tentatively over the side of the coffin.

Old Mrs Kennedy lay in her best dress, buttoned up to the throat, her hands clasped over her chest, the rather severe expression on her face which she had never worn in life, made the more so by her blanked out eyes, a penny placed over each. She looked blind. Her scant, grey hair was brushed silver, her veiny blue nose like a piece of black pudding. Her vermilion lips were somehow sucked back into her mouth as if she were expressing disapproval of her situation. Sinead began to pray quietly, unaware of Seamus's wandering hand which reached down into the coffin where he toyed with the strands of silver hair and stroked the cold cheek.

Padraig was cold, wet and fidgety. He had no interest in the coffin and no desire to be lifted up to see within.

Mrs Morrison came and whispered in Sinead's ear, 'I'm away now, Mrs Grogan, and I'll be baking some funeral biscuits. Auntie Dora's helped out with the ingredients. Such a Trojan, that woman!' Then she hobbled away, out into the greyness.

Nurse McEwan told Sinead that Mrs Morrison had done nearly all the preparation of the corpse. All she herself had had to do was to help with the lifting. 'And Mrs Morrison is precious near to being a corpse herself, poor soul.'

And so it was that Peadar's wage became smaller and less predictable than ever. Sinead tried to earn some extra at home by doing a bit of rag-picking but the stink of the rags made them all feel ill and Peadar told her to chuck them on the fire or into the gutter. She then tried sack-making but the work was insufficient and the money even worse. The matchbox-making lasted the longest but you had to keep the paste warm all the time and the smell of it was terrible in that one room in which they all had to live, eat and sleep. Moreover, the lock on the street door was faulty and they would often go out in the morning to find that the smell was aggravated by the drunken vomit left by dossers who pushed their way in to the hallway.

The hour of 'calling on' at the Stanley was half past eight and these days Peadar and Tom would often wait for work until half past eleven or even later, crushed together in the pen with perhaps a hundred men.

Then, when a contractor or foreman came to the gate, they would all surge forward, even standing on each other's heads and shoulders. Peadar had only two more weeks of this before his new lighter work was to begin and he began to wonder whether he would live to see it.

The day Sinead fully understood his line of thought was the day she stood outside Lionel Hunt, the grocer's on the corner of Great Homer Street and Rachel Street. The two ladies standing with her both had husbands who did a bit of casual at the Stanley or at the Prince's when the coal-heaving went slack, though neither man had ever been a 'royal' or a regular like Peadar. The shop was no more than a converted end terrace house with a narrow pavement separating it from the cobblestones of Rachel Street and a small-paned bay window almost blanked out by a vast advertisement for Fry's chocolate, gummed on the inside and fading to an almost uniform pastel yellow. Equally weathered was the wooden sign above the open door, 'L. Hunt, Grocer.' Because Mr Hunt traded from his own home he was considered a 'dishonourable' trader, hated and mistrusted by larger, wealthier grocers and the butt of their insults when he had the front of his house knocked out and converted some years before, on his retirement from the Vauxhall

Distillery. He now stood just inside the door, hoping the ladies would step inside but appearing to examine the slate-grey sky for signs of more rain.

Dominating the conversation was a tall young woman known to everyone simply as Clodagh. She stood with her long hands clasped together as if about to sing a song or make a speech, her long brown dress falling almost to the tips of her clogs on to the cobbles, a grubby apron about her front and a greenish shawl around her shoulders and pulled up over the back of her long, brown hair. She was a handsome woman, probably in her late twenties, but wild. Her friend, Mrs Murphy, who was older and wrapped up mainly in patched-up black, seemed to be happy to nod and agree with whatever Clodagh announced in her long, nasal drawl. Sinead and Mrs Murphy, who had kept to the pavement, now appeared to be almost pinned against the front of Mr Hunt's shop by Clodagh's animated discourse. Though she had both feet in the street, she still stood head and shoulders above her attentive audience. Her talk these days was all about the King's Liverpool Regiment, the pride of Kitchener's New Army, and how her husband had joined up.

'Of course I shall miss the bugger, Lord love you, Mrs Grogan, but 'tis regular money, so it is, and 'tis also the travel to foreign parts.'

'But what about your babes, Clodagh?'

'Better to have some of his army wage coming in than just his useless body about the place!'

Sinead laughed with her and Mrs Murphy nodded and smiled.

'And when will he be leaving for France, Clodagh?'

'Soon, Mrs Grogan, soon. He's been kitted out and had his medical. The doctor told him he was fit!' Here she leaned back and roared with laughter, 'I could have told him that myself!'

She and Sinead laughed and giggled together, while Mrs Murphy continued to nod and smile.

Suddenly, Sinead saw the Golden Syrup tin in her mind's eye and then her embroidery in quick succession. Then she appeared to see them side by side and knew all at once that Peadar would eventually be marching away too. She crossed herself, feeling a small, cold chill on the back of her neck.

'Are you all right, Mrs Grogan?'

'Thank you, Clodagh, I'm all right.' She patted her hair down at the sides then asked, 'Do you think the world is going to be turned upside down with all this war?'

Clodagh laughed again and took Sinead's hand in her own: 'Lord love you no, Mrs Grogan! It's just a few months' good steady money, that's all it is. They all say it'll be finished by Christmas. Pity, if you ask me. My Mick will be back to casual money after it's all over.' Mrs Murphy nodded again. 'And do you know what?' Clodagh went on, hands now back on her hips. 'They've given him a bloody gun!' She roared again. 'Only a bloody gun! I ask you! He'll kill his bleeding self before he kills any Germans!'

These raucous carryings-on brought Mr Hunt, resplendent in a starched white apron and grey alpaca jacket, on to the doorstep, his pale jaundiced face looking like one of his pats of butter.

'Now, are you ladies come here to do business in my emporium or just to use my bit of pavement as a place for your own bawdy gossip?'

'Go and drown yourself, Lionel!' laughed Clodagh, tossing her head back. 'We'll come inside when we're good and ready, won't we, girls?' Sinead was embarrassed and Mrs Murphy nodded vigorously at Mr Hunt who tutted and raised his eyes to heaven, as he shuffled back indoors, giving vent to his feelings with a muttered, 'By that time I shall have closed the shop.'

Clodagh stepped up on to the kerbside and leaning towards the open doorway, called, 'And what's your opinion of this war then, Lionel?'

There was a long pause, during which they watched a long convoy of commandeered omnibuses smoking down Great Homer Street, their colourful peacetime finery removed, the top deck loaded with equipment and the lower deck boarded up with planks. From one of the top decks a tommy who might have been about thirty, a typical 'old sweat' yelled out to the three women huddled on the corner, 'Ladies, it breaks my heart to go!' and he whipped off his cap and pressed it to his chest.

Without hesitation, Clodagh lifted her skirt right above her knees and shouted, 'Well, here's something to remember us by, my darling!'

Sinead turned away for shame, but not before she had spied a little tattoo just above Clodagh's left knee.

The soldier whistled and waved his cap, then was soon gone, engulfed in smoke and noise.

'I have always been infirm, Miss Clodagh. My feet, you know,' came the response from within. 'And I was too old for the African War, of course.' Clodagh smiled. Mrs Murphy nodded and the three of them traipsed into the shop. There were two rickety chairs placed by the counter. Clodagh chose to stand, while Sinead and Mrs Murphy sat and rested their arms on the polished wood surface.

'Today, ladies, I have some beautiful Cheshire and Lancashire cheeses.'

'How about a nice glass of stout for the three of us to begin with?' leered Clodagh, towering over the counter, clearly unnerving the waxy Mr Hunt. She brushed aside the opening syllables of Sinead's protests with, Don't you fret, Mrs Grogan, love, he's got gallons of the bloody stuff at the back, haven't you Lionel, you little tinker?'

Mr Hunt jerked back to avoid being tickled under the chin, and shuffled off to the back of the shop. While Sinead was still wondering how to engage Mrs Murphy in conversation, Mr Hunt came shuffling back into the shop bearing a tray with three glasses of stout, which he set down rather heavily, so it seemed to Sinead.

'Where's your glass, Lionel?' crowed Clodagh. 'Aren't you drinking with us girls, then? Aren't we good enough for you?'

'It doesn't come cheap, you know,' protested Mr Hunt weakly.

'Tight-fisted old turd!' laughed Clodagh.

'For pity's sake!' hissed the grocer, quietly, his gaze roving desperately round the shelves.

Clodagh was, however, determined: 'No, there's only us here, Lionel, so don't you worry, dear heart!'

Sinead was now very uncomfortable and Mrs Murphy's nodding was becoming more like a nervous tic. It did appear strangely as if Clodagh had come here merely to wage war.

They made their few purchases, with the exception of Clodagh, who clearly had no intention of handing over any money for her butter and sugar. Mr Hunt, repeatedly wiping his sweaty hands on his apron and in a state of visible terror as to Clodagh's next move, stood limply behind the counter. Sinead held her breath, wanting no part of it. Clodagh, leaned forward over the polished surface and made an exaggerated pout at Mr Hunt, her one hand on the counter and the other placed provocatively on her hip. 'Put this lot on the slate, will you, Lionel, darling?' she cooed menacingly, putting heavy and knowing emphasis on the word 'slate' and raising her eyebrows to check comprehension.

Mr Hunt squirmed between anger and fear: 'Of course, Miss Clodagh, with pleasu . . .'

'I do hope that is no bother for you, Lionel?'

' No bother, Miss Clodagh, I do assure you!'

'After all, Lionel,' she licked her full lips slowly, relishing his growing anxiety, ' it's really still you who owes me, isn't it?'

His face paled from a butter pat to a bag of flour. 'I . . . I'm not sure I fully understand what you . . .'

'Oh, yes you do, you little tiger, Lionel!' She had snapped the smile off and her eyes were blazing. 'Shall I remind you why you owe me, in front of these ladies?'

'No, that won't be necessary! I recall clearly now. Yes, you are indeed in credit, Miss Clodagh.'

'Well, next time, I'll have payment in advance, you bastard!' she whispered, straightening to her full height.

Mr Hunt mopped his forehead with a corner of his apron, and Mrs Murphy nodded, blank-faced. Sinead made a mental note never to go to the shops with these two again.

But late summer 1915 found her in a dilemma beside which this and all previous dilemmas paled into insignificance. The boys were long asleep behind the curtain and Peadar and Sinead sat by the big, open sash window, the tattered net curtain stirring in the warm twilight. The fire was pale and low and made no noise. Sinead sat on the left, her elbow resting on the table, the aroma of cold scouse still in her nostrils, though supper was over. Peadar sat square to the window, thinking how this could all be quite romantic, sitting in the evening, no light burning and the kids abed - romantic under other circumstances, for he was about to change the course of their lives.

'That rat, love, that was in the trap by the sink this morning, did you ever see a bigger one?' No response.

'And did Father Castlereagh talk to the boys about school?' Still no response.

'And does Father think I should go back to the clay pipe, does he?'

He forced a smile in the fading light. A very long pause, during which they both listened to Seamus's wheezy snoring.

At last, Sinead turned towards her man's handsome silhouette, the same face she had looked up at in the warm lane near Armoy in the summer of 1903, and now, as then, she felt her blood race. He had covered her face with kisses and said he would love her for ever and then he had knelt down by the side of the lane and had run his hands slowly up her legs, panting into her belly, while she stroked the top of his head, knowing full well that this was the right time and that she wanted him now.

'So, you're going to war, Peadar Grogan?' Now it was his turn to be silent.

' Is it because I can have no more babes?' She saw him shake his head slowly.

'Is it because I'm an old cow of thirty, not the slip of a country girl you married?' She knew he was smiling without trying to look at him.

'Peadar, you said yourself that this was an English war. Your wonderful Sinn Fein and your beloved Irish Brotherhood are campaigning against it: 'England's War', they call it.' Both stared ahead for a while.

'The Hun is at the gate, my love.'

'What? Where did you hear that one?'

'That poem by that Rudyard Kipling. It was in one of the papers last year. About a year back. Tom Downey knows it by heart. Part of it goes: "The Hun is at the gate."'

'Oh, I know! The same Tom Downey whose brothers back in the Old Country are out leafleting for Sinn Fein against the recruitment!' she scoffed quietly.

'The Old Country's a mess. See what happened at the Curragh last spring. There's nothing to be done in Ireland yet. Ulster couldn't be forced even by the Brits to join a united Ireland. The proddies are too strong. There'll be no Home Rule while this war is on and other countries are joining in, and it goes on and on. All over by Christmas, wasn't it they said?'

'It wasn't just "they" who said it, Grogan. It was you too who said it.'

He nodded sadly. She reached out and laid her right hand lightly on his knee and he then covered her hand with his own, a hand so big and warm, she felt protected by it. But could it protect itself? And though her hand was warm, there was that little chill on the back of her neck again.

He sucked on his unlit pipe and scratched his head. 'This new work is no good. It's not regular and the money's too low. We can barely pay the rent these days, even with your stinking matchboxes. I hardly notice the stench now. I'm used to it. We're all used to breathing that muck in.'

'Do you think it's bad for Seamus's chest?'

'Well, it can't do the poor mite any good now, can it?'

She shuffled the chair closer and lay her head on his shoulder.

'I'm working alongside riff-raff now. They've no pride in their work and they steal a lot of stuff from the dock. All the good men, the men that I've always admired, are joining up. It seems the good and decent thing for a good and decent man to do.'

'Like who, for instance, Mr Good and Decent?'

'Like Fletcher, the landlord's agent, and Riley, his assistant. You know, the man with the beard like the king.'

Sinead nodded in the thickening dusk and asked, 'What about that weasel McGrath? Has he joined up?'

'I don't know about him. He's probably working for the Germans!' They both laughed softly, Sinead nestling into Peadar's neck.

She said, 'I wonder what you'd look like in uniform,' and kissed him playfully on the cheek.

'All the ladies will adore me!'

'Oh, will they indeed? That's the sort of tittle-tattle I picked up from that shameless Clodagh. The men do say that for an army cap badge or a belt they can have as many French girls as they want and as much wine as they can swallow. Is that the loud trumpet call from France, husband mine?'

'I've never drunk wine in my life, woman!'

She smacked his left thigh and took the scruff of his neck in her hand: 'The new knocker-upper told me that Kitchener is fed up with the Irishmen, because they're not coming forward fast enough.'

'True enough,' said Peadar. 'He cannot fill the Irish Division of his New Army and he says he'll draft men into it from England and Scotland. A lot of workmates of mine, Irishmen like me, want their own Irish units.'

'Will that happen?'

'I don't know. Some high and mighty bigwig has branded us all "slum-birds from the big cities."'

'Well! And you want to go to war for the likes of them!'

'There's the promise of new skills and new opportunities especially when it's all over, which can't be long now. I can send regular money home, travel in France, make new friends . . .'

'Spoon with French whores!'

'Away with you, woman! You could give up the matchboxes and concentrate on the boys. It's schooldays soon.'

'Army pay won't change us into millionaires, Peadar.'

'Well, at least it has to be better than what I'm bringing in nowadays, when I bring home anything at all.'

'So, your mind's made up, my love. What will you do? Will you sail away and leave the three of us just like that?'

'Sure I will not! First I'll be down the recruitment queue and see what's cooking down there.'

'They'll probably tell you you're too old, I hope.' She blew into his neck and his arm slipped round her shoulders and his fingers played with the wisps of fine hair at the the base of her neck, so that she shifted her legs and drew in a slow deep breath. His grip became firmer about her. She whispered to him, 'Take your coat off the hook and spread it down here and be quiet about it.'

She heard him tip-toe to the door and unhook the coat. She rose and placed both chairs under the table, pushing aside the strong temptation to light the lamp and clear away the scouse. It was all but dark. Peadar padded back and there was a rustling as he spread the coat out on the cool floor.

'I reckon you'll reek of that old pipe,' she whispered, looking down at him as he made himself comfortable on the coat.

'Please yourself, woman,' he smiled, opening his arms towards her, 'if my smell offends you!'

'Oh, I dare say I can put up with it,' she said, as she lowered herself beside him, and he reached for her, rolling her way. The fire dropped further down in the grate, a couple of drunks went past the window, shouting, Seamus coughed, then all was quiet.

She brought her knees up and drew her feet back and the big, warm hand slowly pushed her dress up to her knees and paused and paused and, oh! it seemed to wait there a long time. She listened to his breathing for a clue and it was still steady. Then the hand moved again, easing the dress down the slope of her thighs, down, down, then stopped.

'Why, woman, you're naked! Have you no shame, Irish hussy?'

His chuckle was hoarse and laboured. She had read the signs all right!

'When you went to fetch the coat, I took them off. They're over the back of the chair. I'll put them back on, if you want.' She felt his finger over her mouth.

She eased her legs open as the hand slipped down between them and fondled the moist tangle of hair, where she was all slippery now, like the underside of a piece of soap left lying in the sink, but warm, very warm. He wondered whether all women were like that. Poor Sean would have been able to tell him.

He entered her gently, gently but at an angle, so that a soft farting noise came out of her, as the warm air was pushed out from inside her to make way for him. She breathed out from between her legs to let him in. Was there anything she would not do for him? God, how he would miss moving between these thighs! Surely no other woman could be like Sinead! As he moved up and down on her he thought of that loud check cap bobbing up and down in the Corpus Christi crowd, that day before the war. It so reminded him of Sean, Sean whose cap was never found, Sean whose cap had gone the way of his wages. And he himself, Peadar, would he be braver tomorrow than today? Was this a soldier inside Sinead now? Was there a soldier inside himself?

When Sinead opened her legs to him, it was no gesture of submission for her. No! She felt she was using her legs to entrap him, to stop him going away. When he was upon her, she closed her legs tightly about his waist to hold him to her. He was in her power! Each of his pushes was a move towards her instead of away from her. She was in control! Perhaps if they made love all night and all day she would be able to keep him there, away from the outside world, so cruel, so unjust.

Then all at once, Peadar began his death rattle and his movements became jerky and she could have cried, for she was losing him, even as he flooded inside her, still she was losing him. She could feel him going away from her.

The vicious click of the big trap by the door, about three paces from where they were lying, came like the slamming of a door inside her head.

'I think we have another Orange boy!' whispered Peadar, delighted.

She heard him stand up and adjust his clothes, then the striking of a match to light the lamp on the table amid the supper debris. Still lying on her back, she rolled on to her right side to face the door and beheld, gazing straight back at her, the wide, dead eyes of a trapped rat. It seemed to stare at her malevolently. It loathed her, not only because of its violent death, but because of all she stood for, all her foolish and unrealistic hopes. Instead of screaming, she began to weep.

'There, there, love! It's only an Orange boy! I'll go and chuck him in the gutter where he belongs.'

The door of the neat little terraced house in Cazneau Street opened and out came the dapper, suited figure of Eberhard Holz. He sniffed the keen damp air of early morning and tucked his brown cow gown under his arm. He trotted off on his stubby legs, round the corner into Collingwood Street, smiling into the breeze that met him there. Two minutes' walk and on the left was St Nicholas's church and adjoining Roman Catholic school, the main football rival of St Anthony's. The caretaker of St Nick's school had gone over to France, so a couple of volunteers, John Lyle, proprietor of Roscommon Street dispensary, and Eberhard Holz, shovelled the coal and lit the fires in the classrooms five days a week during term time. Advancing down the street towards him, from the direction of Great Homer Street, where she still rented her rooms above Vogel's, steamed the formidable Clara Orrett. Holz hardly knew her but prepared to raise his trilby.

'Good morning, Miss Orrett.'

Her head was down, wreathed in steamy breath. She could not have heard him.

'Good morning, Miss Orrett. What a nice fresh mor . . .'

'Don't you speak to me, Kaiser Bill!'

Holz thought he must have misheard her. 'I beg your pardon, Miss Orrett?'

She stopped and turned to face him, all gin breath and warm armpits. 'You heard me, Kaiser Bill. Bleedin' German. Sunk any passenger ships lately, have you?'

'I - I don't understand.'

'Lusitania! Understand that, do you? We won't forget that round here. This being a port, like, we don't greatly appreciate folk who drown innocents!' With that, she spat on the pavement and stormed off, head now high. Holz stood for some time before walking on.

The following Sunday, while Mrs Holz was scrubbing out, her fire irons all about her on acres of newspaper, a brick came through the window.

Eberhard held her shuddering shoulders tightly to him, helped her dab her piggy little eyes on her apron and murmured, 'Nanu, nanu, nanu!'

But it was the white paint daubed along the wall in the market in Juvenal Street that really did it: 'German spies', it said, in big white letters all along the wall. Business had been slack and pilfering on the increase for some time. Eberhard said it was because people were starving, but their friends, the Gerlachs, also Berliners, had been arrested and taken to Knockeloe internment camp on the Isle of Man. What was to be done?

Monday morning was thick, yellow fog in Oswald Street, fog that smelled of smoke and tasted of sulphur. Seamus was playing with Conal on the steps of No. 12, now occupied by a man from the Abercromby and his wife. They had adopted Conal together with a few sticks of furniture. Padraig sat on the steps of No. 8, watching from a safe distance. He still did not trust the big lumbering dog with the smouldering eyes.

The fog shrank the world to three sets of court steps, bounded by a shifting yellow curtain, through which came only the muffled sounds of the factory at the end. The boys' breath and the dog's breath hung, motionless, around them. Then they heard footsteps from the Dryden Street end and all three stopped still and peered into the fog. A plump silhouette came into view, gradually taking on colour as it waddled nearer, a grey shawl held tight by one hand, over the head and round the shoulders, a brown skirt down to within an inch of the boots, and a lot of puffing and blowing.

'Why! Padraig and Seamus! Ich such' eure Mutter. Is Mam at home?'

Padraig nodded and moved aside, as Mrs Holz clambered up the steps to No. 8, using the hand-rail to thrust herself forward in a series of jerks.

Inside it was warm and cosy and smelled of smoky coal and soapsuds. Sinead turned from the fireplace, putting her little crucifix back on the green baize of the mantlepiece and patting her hair into place. As soon as she had heard her name being called in the hallway she knew who it was.

Mrs Holz bustled through the door and staggered over to the chair which Sinead had pulled out for her. Mrs Holz sat down on it like the collapse of a great building. She dragged the shawl from her head and gasped for air for a few seconds.

'Liebchen, those boys are growing, or else I am shrinking, nicht wahr?'

Sinead smiled proudly.

'But where is your man, Mrs Grogan? Has he found work now?'

Sinead put the big black kettle on the hob. 'No, he's at the army recruitment office in the Volunteer Drill Hall. You know, St Anne Street, by the timber yard.'

Mrs Holz nodded, her breathing easing. And you don't like it, eh, Liebchen?' She slapped her thighs for emphasis, screwing up her little piggy eyes. She gave a mirthless laugh, like a man's laugh, deep and resonant.

Sinead shook her head and turned to the window, listening to the shrieks of the twins and the excited yelping of Conal, coming from the almost invisible street. 'You've had more trouble, haven't you,

Mrs Holz?' Sinead had parted the net curtains and was gazing out into the fog.

Mrs Holz shuffled her chair nearer the fire. She stared wearily into the coals. 'Yes, we have had more trouble. Eberhard can't stand much more of it.'

'How long have you been at the market?' She could see that Padraig led all the games and that it was he who had all the ideas. She wondered whether it would be the same story when they were both at school.

'Since 1900, when we first came to England. We just changed one big city for another big city.' Loosening her shawl as she warmed up, she leaned forward as if to search the fire for some kind of explanation.

'I'm so sorry,' Sinead murmured. Conal and Padraig still treated each other with great suspicion and occasionally the dog would race across to the other side of the street and vanish momentarily from view. Then he would reappear, as if by magic, emerging from the swirls of fog like some legendary beast. He always ran straight to Seamus, whereas his brother took a step backwards whenever the animal came near.

'I suppose we shall have to think about going back to Berlin.' She was rapt in contemplation of the red hot coals.

'I wish we could help in some way.'

'We are not wanted any longer. It is the way of things. The city is like one person, one enormous person, a person who has a boil on the body. What was healthy skin yesterday is poison today. And Eberhard and I are that poison.' Sinead turned from the window to protest but Mrs Holz, without looking round, waved her protest aside with a gesture, and went on: 'I am not afraid for myself. I am afraid for Eberhard.'

Sinead smiled down at her. 'Do not fear the big city. Simply learn its ways.'

'Did I say that, Liebchen?'

'You did. Your wise words have helped me so much over the years, especially when we were new from Ireland.' She placed a hand on the old woman's shoulder and knew that it comforted her.

'Well, now it's our turn, Eberhard's and mine, to be re-shuffled. This terrible hostility is only local inflammation. Once we are gone, it will all die down. The boil will heal. The skin of the city will close over us as if we never existed.'

Sinead shuddered. She thought of the ants' nest. Then as she moved to the hob to make the tea, she said, ' You know, Peadar would want to go out and get hold of the culprits and teach them a lesson they'd never forget.'

Mrs Holz turned to her with a face full of peace: ' Justice is the Lord's, Mrs Grogan. You know that as well as I do. If folk need to be punished, then they will be punished, but in God's own good time. Perhaps your husband does not believe that.'

'He certainly does not!' she smiled into the teapot as she stirred the leaves round. 'I wonder who's right, Mrs Holz?'

'Those who believe, of course! Someone who believes in nothing cannot possibly be right. Such a person knows the price of everything and the value of nothing!' And then she made her piggy eyes bulge again, as she used to, to amuse Sinead, who fell into fits of giggling. In her mind, however, she knew that things were not as clear as they once were and that she could not see her way ahead as once she could and that the fog was both inside and out.

'Seamus Grogan, are you part of this lesson?' Sister Anne's voice rang out beneath the high ceiling of the boys' classroom. As all the cropped heads swivelled round to look at Seamus, so his own head jerked back to the forward pointing position. His mouth hung open.

'Well, Grogan, are you a part of the lesson or apart from the lesson?' all carefully stressed to convey the meaning and the irony, all totally wasted on Seamus and his colleagues in their long rows, two abreast.

'No.'

'No, what?'

'No, Sister Anne.' Anyone who could have seen Seamus's face, turned to the window, would have realised that he was not really watching the cows being driven past the classroom towards the dairy, but was staring out beyond the street, out into nothingness, an expression of peace upon his small features. The intervention of Sister Anne had come as a genuine shock.

It had been Padraig who had poked him and pointed at the passing cows. Seamus was slow to notice when he was being watched. The cows had been his springboard to infinity. His eyes had rested on their passing flanks momentarily then up high above their heads into the off-white sky. For a few private seconds he had been far away from St Anthony's school and this classroom with its sooty fire and frighteningly garish crucifix.

'Follow your brother's example, Grogan!'

'I was pointing to the cows, Sister Anne,' Padraig piped up.

'Nonsense! You're just trying to protect your brother.'

And that was that. Nobody argued with Sister Anne. She was the first person any of them had heard speaking without an Irish or a Liverpool accent. She came from somewhere else, maybe 'over the water', beyond the Mersey.

In the narrow playground, shadowed by its high wall, Padraig kept a watchful eye on his twin, so often prey to strolling bands of bullies who wanted him to play a Hun in their war games, so they could knock him down and tread on him. Padraig was a new force to be reckoned with, alert and unafraid of other boys, always ready to put his fists up.

Seamus most loved morning prayers, usually taken by Father Castlereagh, or occasionally by Mr Callaghan, the headmaster. Each successive word of the Our Father, or the Hail Mary, or the Glory Be fell like a warm pebble into a still pool inside him until he was filled with it all as if he had eaten. He was sated. It even kept the cold out. Padraig usually fidgeted all through the prayers, chafing to be more active, rolling his brown eyes in impatience at his brother's involvement and wondering what he was gaping at, what he was seeing, when there was nothing there to be seen except a large wall map of the world, and Jesus covered in blood on the cross.

Peadar queued in the fog, astonished at how many other men wanted to volunteer for war. He was well to the back, right round the corner in the alley by the servicemen's club. All about him was the pot-pourri of unwashed bodies, ale and cigarette smoke, ahead of him an undulating sea of caps and mufflers, in his ears several different conversations and the scraping of clogs on cobblestones, frequent coughing and spitting. The front end of the queue, round the corner in St Anne Street, was lost in the fog, together with the clang and rumble of the trams. He had the uneasy feeling that, on reaching the front of the queue, he would find not the recruiting office but the 'dinner house' on Portland Street, that this was, after all, a long, long soup queue. Many of the men here seemed, to judge by their comments, to confuse His Majesty's Army with the League of Welldoers, poor starving bastards! He recognised a lot of dockers here too, and one of the many Morrisons, a shoe-black by usual trade, hobbling on his rickety young legs up and down the line of men, trying to sell second-hand adventure magazines, the *Rover*, the *Champion* and the *Chips*. To advertise his wares, he had pinned copies of the comic papers all over his filthy coat, drawing shouts of 'Here comes the Illumination Tram!' A grotesque sight, hopping and limping through the yellow fog, he made Peadar feel as if he were being welcomed into Hell by some twisted gremlin. He turned up the collar of his coat and clicked his cherrywood between his teeth. The close walls of the alley ran thick with damp and drizzle, like blood.

'I'm going for the girls, me!' said a voice behind him.

'And the red wine. Don't forget the red wine!' laughed another.

'Since when did you ever taste red wine, Mick Rafferty?' came from further back.

'Since when did he ever have a girl?' from just in front of Peadar, leading to more laughing and nudging. Some of the men were in a more sombre mood, weary of poor conditions and constant strikes in their own trades, the railways, the boiler-making and the cotton industry.

And so the queue, like the days and nights of Peadar's lifetime, receded into the unknown. Sinead would have anticipated coming to the head of the queue, planned for it, prepared herself for it with great conviction, whereas he drifted along with the others, all like cattle to the slaughter.

'It's not what happens to you that's important, it's the way you see it and the way you feel about it,' she always said.

The real cause of the birching of Ciaran Cassidy was probably Conal, the dog, from 12 Oswald Street. Ciaran, urchin son of James Cassidy, coalheaver, of 'back of Wilbraham Place', joined the Grogan twins on Scotland Road every morning and they hopped and skirmished their way to school together. One bright frosty morning, the ragged Alsatian simply refused to let the twins go to school without him, so that stout little Ciaran found the dog loping warily behind the two boys, along the road towards St Anthony's. Ciaran, bursting with pride at having the huge dog padding along with the three of them, became proprietorial towards it and gave it sharp commands (which it completely ignored) letting everyone know he was of the exclusive coterie of this beast. On their arrival at school, faces shining like lanterns in the icy light, Conal steaming like a brazier, they caused uproar. Conal barked at any ragamuffin who came too close to any of them and the children cheered and shouted. Inevitably the commotion brought Sister Anne out into the small playground.

'Whose dog is that?' she shrieked above the barking and yelling. 'Send it away this instant.'

This had no effect whatever, so she circulated among the boys, asking who knew where the dog came from.

'Please, Sister, it came with the Grogans!' chorused several sneaky voices, and a hush came over the chaos.

Conal stood panting, puffing clouds, tongue dangling, looking around suspiciously.

'Oh it did, did it now?' growled Sister Anne, hands on hips. 'Is it your dog, Padraig and Seamus Grogan?' She fixed them with a threatening stare, sufficient to curdle milk.

'No, Sister Anne,' piped Padraig.

'Then why in God's name have you brought it into these premises? Get it OUT!'

Ciaran Cassidy stepped forward, one chubby hand gripping the dog's knotted mane for support, still proud of his new friend who attracted so much attention.

'Please, Sister, the dog's doing no harm.'

She rounded on him, glaring down at his round sticky face. 'And what business is this of yours, Cassidy?'

'He's my friend, Sister!' He beamed at his eager audience who cheered and laughed.

Sister Anne, however, was not laughing. 'How dare you make light of this? Get the dog out of this yard at once!' She stamped her foot, but the young Cassidy was adamant.

'But, Sister, the dog's doing no harm. I want him to stay.'

Her eyes flashed and the spittle flew: 'Don't you dare argue with me! Do as you're told!'

The dog looked at Ciaran and Ciaran looked at the dog. Ciaran appeared to reflect for a moment, then replied, 'No, I'm not sending him away.' He looked her square in the face as if to say, 'I'm not scared of you anyway. After all, you're only a woman. My Ma's like you and my Da kicks her round the parlour!'

Sister Anne was white with rage. 'How DARE you, Cassidy? Get inside and wait to be punished!'

He patted Conal with deliberate slowness, so that Sister Anne had to wrench his hand away and shove him bodily towards the classroom door. Seamus, with Padraig supervising, then escorted Conal to the squeaky iron gate and shut him out There came a few barks, then silence.

The classroom was too hot and smelled of coke fumes and carbolic. Known as the 'babies' class', it contained boys aged from five to eight years. There were nearly forty of them, all either with prison-cropped hair or completely bald with the scalp painted purple because of ringworm. They all realised something was going on, something out of the ordinary, when Mr Callaghan came in, escorting Ciaran by the upper arm, together with Sister Anne and Miss Heap. At Mr Callaghan's command, the class rose and was instructed to remain standing. Mr Callaghan took up a position at the front of the class, clearly intending to address them all, still grasping the cowed and cringing Cassidy, who stared at the wood block floor but whose eyes were still dry, a detail noted with admiration by his fellows. The two ladies stood on either side of the headmaster, Sister Anne starched and severe, Miss Heap willowy and full of permanent cold, her impossibly small handkerchief fluttering under her raw, red nose, her eyes those of an albino rabbit.

Padraig and Seamus were by the far wall, away from the window and right in the front of their row, so that both should have had a good clear view of the proceedings, except that the low, morning sun was shining directly into their eyes so that they could not see properly and had to squint.

The headmaster gave a long homily about obedience and courtesy and then an outraged account of how little Cassidy had shown neither quality that morning, and further, of how he had been rude and hostile to one of his teachers. With much regret and a heavy heart, Mr Callaghan was now saying, it was now incumbent upon him to uphold the disciplinary standards of the school by birching Ciaran Cassidy. The effect of these words was electric and there was an audible intake of breath.

Cassidy was made to face the front wall with his back to the class and to place his hands on the wall above his head. He wore a grubby grey shirt and braces, trousers to just below his knees and clogs with no socks. Miss Heap appeared to be holding his coat and cap. Sister Anne then held his dimpled hands together at the wrists against the wall and Miss Heap, depositing the coat and cap on the nearest desk and tucking her handkerchief into her sleeve, knelt to hold his ankles apart.

All the heads turned for a second as Father Castlereagh swept in and stood at the back, then all the attention was focused upon the imminent drama at the front.

Padraig was terrified. Seamus felt only sympathy with Ciaran. After all, it was he and his brother who had caused the dog to come to school in the first place. He raised his hand. Padraig felt as if he were about to faint with fright. Had his brother gone mad?

'Please, Sister Anne.'

'What is it, Grogan?' She twisted round, maintaining her grip on Ciaran's hands.

'It's not his fault, Sister, it's mine.'

Padraig knew that by 'mine', the implication was 'ours'. Why couldn't Seamus pipe down and let it all blow over?

'Ciaran Cassidy was impolite, Grogan. You were not. The punishment is for insolence, not for bringing the dog into school, although that was very foolish.'

'I should be punished as well.'

Padraig swallowed hard. The whole room held its breath All ears listened. It was Father Castlereagh who spoke. 'An admirable gesture, Seamus Grogan, but out of place on this occasion.'

There was a pause, then Mr Callaghan said, 'Let us proceed.'

Seamus now felt resigned. Punishment had to follow crime. It was part of the order of things. He waited to behold man administering the justice of God.

Padraig felt only his pounding heart and his dry mouth and his bursting bladder. He was still painfully dazzled by the sun and not fully able to witness the proceedings. As the vicious bunch of birch twigs swished twice on Ciaran's backside, Seamus felt two simultaneous pangs of guilt whereas Padraig felt flushed with a warmth of gratitude that the punishment was not his that day.

When they arrived home that afternoon, Mrs Morrison was telling their mother of the disappearance of Mr and Mrs Holz. They must have fled during the night, leaving everything behind and their door wide open on to the street.

The recruiting sergeant looked every inch a soldier. In his late thirties, sitting ramrod straight on his chair, lean and moustached and with thinning fair hair, he looked up at each volunteer as if the man's every weakness were known to him. Any notion of larking about evaporated under this man's blue-eyed scrutiny. It was clearly not going to be a charabanc outing after all. Peadar immediately felt a reluctance to meet the man's stare, an urge to stand to attention. Could this be right for a son of Antrim? But what else had he, apart from his heritage? His roots would not fill the Golden Syrup tin! The Old Country had half starved him. England had given him a wage, then taken it away from him. He simply had to look this man in the eye and see a new tomorrow. Sinead would be taken care of and so would the boys' school fund at St Anthony's. That God-awful stink of glue could waft away along the gutter of Oswald Street and be gone for good and all! Glue, carbolic and chimney smoke! He wondered what France might smell of. The sergeant's weathered skin must have cured beneath some exotic sun - perhaps in the Transvaal. His own city pallor could be transformed too. What would Sinead say then? He would come home the conquering hero, suntan and all! Bunting, ribbons - and a mention in the *Echo* . . . .

'Name?'

'Grogan, sir.'

'Christian name?'

'Peadar, sir.' He spelled it for him, his voice cracking with nerves in front of the other men in the queue.

'How old are you, Grogan?'

'Late thirties, sir.' He looked straight ahead.

'How late, Grogan?'

'I'm just thirty-seven, sir.' He waited to be told to leave.

'Address?' Peadar could not believe it.

'8 Oswald Street, Liverpool, sir.' He was still being interviewed!

'Have you a trade, Grogan?'

'Docker, sir.' He still looked straight ahead, sweating profusely.

'In employment at the moment?'

'Casual, sir.'

'Are you a family man, Grogan?'

'Wife and two children, sir.'

'Religion?'

'Roman Catholic, sir.'

'Are you a Republican, Grogan?'

'I do believe in a free Ireland, sir, yes sir.' He swallowed, assuming that about finished his chances, but on this issue he would not lie. A thirty-seven year old Republican! Now he met the sergeant's stare, adding, 'Sorry sir, but there's no point in lying to you.'

The sergeant remained impassive. They looked at each other.

'Grogan, why do you want to fight for England and the King?'

'The Home Rule can wait, sir, while the little nations take up the sword together against the oppressors.' He really believed this but he had also learnt it by heart, having heard it at a propaganda rally at Walton Park.

'All very commendable, I'm sure. Have you ever been active as a Republican? In the Sinn Fein, say?

'No, sir, I have not.'

'We can check, Grogan.' The penetrating blue gaze searched his face.

'You may check, sir.'

At this point, the sergeant sat back in his fold-up chair with its canvas seat and took a long, hard look at Peadar Grogan. He told him that he believed he was straight and honest and said he liked that. Peadar nodded and mumbled his thanks. There followed a few more questions until finally he was told to sit over in a corner with a group of about a dozen other men and wait to be called for a medical examination.

He sat on a long bench against a wall, only a couple of paces from another recruiting sergeant dealing with another queue of men of all ages. Before the sergeant at that moment stood a youth of surely no more than fifteen years. Peadar heard the sergeant bellow, 'What's your age, boy?' and the youth replied, 'Sixteen, sir.'

'Then go out of here and walk around for five minutes, lad, and when you come back in, you might be a bit older!'

'Yes, sergeant!' beamed the youth, striding off, full of hope.

Peadar knew the army was going to take the boy. He was not sure what to think. Was it right or wrong? Had the fog got right inside his brain? He knew with no doubt at all what Sinead would say about a young lad being allowed to take his chances at the Front but what else had life to offer him apart from cold, damp, poor food, cramped rooms, disease and death before he was fifty?

After Peadar had watched a few more men go through, he was struck by a man now at the head of the sergeant's queue, who was clearly too short to be a soldier. After a few preliminary questions, the man was asked, 'How tall are you, Duffy? You look a trifle short-arsed to me!'

'Five foot one, sergeant.'

'Take this Bible, Duffy,' said the sergeant, grinning broadly and handing him the hefty tome.

'What's this for, sergeant? I've told you the truth.'

'I want you to stand on it, Duffy.' He smiled at him as an alligator might smile before clamping his jaw down upon his hapless prey.

Duffy stood shakily on the Bible, using his outspread arms to steady himself.

The sergeant bawled across the room to one of his colleagues: 'Sergeant Mayall! Over here, if you please!'

A rotund bully of a man in uniform came and stood next to Duffy, eyeing him with fierce amusement.

'Sergeant Mayall, how tall would you say this man is?'

Sergeant Mayall walked round poor, shaky Duffy several times, scratching his chin. Then at last he said, 'He's about three or four inches shorter than me, so that'd make him five foot-five or -six, at least. Got to be.' He patted Duffy on the back so that he slipped off the Bible and stood beside it, noticeably reduced in height.

'Got to be!' beamed Sergeant Mayall.

Duffy was delighted and leaned forward to grasp the recruiting sergeant's hand. The fog which now filled the hall seemed to Peadar to have further confused him and made him unsure what to feel about it all.

He watched Duffy walk springily away, to be quickly swallowed up in the throng of men and the invading fog.

After a long wait, he found himself in front of the Medical Officer, who measured his height and his chest, checked his vision in no more than thirty seconds and finally weighed him. Peadar moved silently from one stage to the next, feeling like one of the cattle plodding down Addison Street towards its doom. As the tape measure whisked about his chest, as figures were written down by his name on a piece of card, figures relating to his own body, he was touched by a mild panic, a sensation of loss of control. He had made this decision and now events were running along at their own pace, faster than he was able to take in. However, most of the other men were younger than he was, so he tried to affect a tough nonchalance, nodding and winking to youths who looked terrified, yet tensing helplessly whenever his name was shouted. Taking the card he was given, he reported, as instructed, to another sergeant, which meant yet another queue. While he waited, he listened to what the others were being asked. They were being offered a choice of units, cavalry, artillery or infantry. The majority were opting for the infantry. One asked which would involve the longest train ride as he had never set foot on a train, while others asked for a unit by the sea, since they had only seen the Mersey and they believed that the sea was much bigger.

Once told which unit they would be joining, the men were told to report back in seven days to pick up their documentation and to be inoculated, when their army clothing and weapons would be issued to them.

One man asked whether the clothing was free or whether he would have to pay for it as he was unemployed. The sergeant yelled at him, 'It's buckshee to you, my lad, but it costs His Majesty a lot of money:- twenty-eight shillings for a greatcoat, twelve and six for a jacket, eight and ninepence for trousers and eighteen shillings and sixpence for pantaloons. All right, boy? Any further bloody stupid questions?'

The youth, almost in tears, shook his head. Peadar shuddered. All his decisions seemed to end in the unknown, in slowly moving queues which led into fog.

The clothes were free, the journey to the unit was free and even the trip across to France, a trip normally way beyond the likes of Peadar Grogan, was free.

Sinead said that nothing in this life comes without a price label on it, nothing is really free. Yet these things really were free, weren't they? For once he was going to enjoy things that he wouldn't have to pay for. Sinead, bless her, couldn't always be right about everything.

Peadar was now next in the queue. He tugged his handkerchief, something he rarely used but which Sinead had forced upon him that day, from his trouser pocket to catch the dew drop on the end of his nose. In so doing he emptied one shilling and twopence halfpenny on to the floor. He heard nothing in the surrounding din of voices and he could not have hoped to see the coins rolling and spinning among the forest of legs and shoes.

With old Mrs Kennedy dead and gone and the boys at school, Mondays were just not the same. Shortly before eleven, Sinead was in a fever to clear her matchbox junk away before Father Castlereagh arrived. She hoped the stink of glue was not too bad, since she herself could not smell it at all any more. She stacked the sheets of matchwood and blue paper in the corner by the sink, then straightened with a sigh to pat her hair into place as she looked critically in the little oval mirror. The sheets of sandpaper, for the striking surface of the matchbox, the handling of which always set her teeth on edge, she shoved under the bed, noticing in passing that the trap under the bed needed emptying of its fat victim.

'Orange boy,' she muttered to herself, stacking the glue pots, brushes, scissors, knives and other tools between the bed and the sink. Then she drew the curtain across. 'Out of sight, out of mind!'

She straightened the embroidery BE STRONG IN THE LORD, knowing full well that no adjustment was necessary, just as none had been necessary five minutes earlier. She touched the rosary with one hand and poked the fire with the other. The rosary, in its place on the green baize on the mantlepiece, was cool to the touch. Did the power to calm her flow from it, or did it somehow absorb her troubles into itself? Or did both of those magical things happen at once?

Conal's barking announced the arrival of Father Castlereagh. Sinead drew the net curtain aside to behold the Alsatian standing at the foot of the steps shaking bodily with the violence of his indignant barking and the poor priest hesitating a few feet away by the gutter, looking helplessly towards her window. She threw open her door and marched out into the hall, where she struggled with the handle of the street door. The door opened suddenly, so that Sinead almost fell on her back in the hall. She patted her hair with both hands as, red and flustered, she came down the steps.

'Be off with you, Conal! Go sit on your own steps!' She smiled apologetically at Father Castlereagh, adding, 'At least he keeps the vagrants away!' Father Castlereagh ventured forward as the dog withdrew, sulkily, towards No. 12.

'Good day to you, Sinead! Thank you for saving my bacon! Why that beast is like something out of Revelations, to be sure!'

'Good morning, Father. I'm so sorry. He isn't ours. We cared for him for a while, and I suppose he's never forgotten it. He's very protective.'

'He was hungry and you gave him food. Don't reproach yourself. 'Tis the wearing of the black cloth he took a dislike to. Animals don't take kindly to it, you know.'

She showed him inside and sat him in Peadar's upholstered chair by the fire. She drew up a kitchen chair for herself. Grey light fell upon Father Castlereagh, a man in his fifties with cropped, silver hair and a contrastingly ruddy complexion. As he gathered himself together in the chair, he resembled a rook preparing to roost. When the creaking and rustling had died down, he clasped his hands together and looked expectantly at Sinead. She, however, sat and looked down at her hands in her lap. She was thinking of how the priest's very presence in the room sanctified it. Here was a direct link with the Lord and Our Lady breathing the same air as she, about to mull over her own private worries! She felt closer to God at moments like these.

Father Castlereagh belched softly: 'Porridge oats! I do apologise. They unfailingly fill me with enough wind to part the waters of the Red Sea!' He patted his belly and said, 'Quiet in there now!' beaming at Sinead, who felt more warmth coming from the fire by the minute.

'And where is Peadar now? Surely he's not already gone to the Front, is he?'

'No, Father, he's at the training camp. He's there all hours but he has to come home every night, because they can't accommodate all the volunteers.'

'Training camp, is it? And where might that be?'

'Walton Park, Father. He goes off in his khakis and looks such a fine figure of a man.' Her eyes filled with tears, tears from nowhere. She had not the faintest idea why she felt like weeping. She dabbed her eyes on her sleeve: 'I'm so sorry, Father.'

'Don't distress yourself, child. Talk to me while I'm here. I'll give you what comfort I can, you know that.' He leaned across and squeezed her hand, then sat back waiting, while she sniffed and cleared her throat.

'He's joined the Third Liverpool Pals. I think their proper name is the Nineteenth King's or some such. Part of Kitchener's New Army.'

Father Castlereagh listened, and watched the fire. The coals heaved and sighed, as though they were listening too.

'In the thirtieth Division, they are, under a Major-General called Shea.'

'Sure you do take a laudable interest in your husband's doings, child! And, you know, Shea sounds like a good Irish name, now does it not?' He leaned forward and smiled.

'Indeed it does, Father.'

'And which of the so-called Armies is Peadar's Division in now, can you tell me that, eh?' He sat back, still smiling, as if posing a teaser to a young girl.

'The Fourth Army, Father,' Sinead answered proudly.

'Ah, yes, indeed, indeed, under the command of General Sir Harry Rawlinson, known to his friends as Rawly, I do believe.'

'Why, Father! You do know quite a bit more about the military than you let on!'

'Well, maybe I hide my light under a bushel, child, I don't know. But I do know that the brave Sir Harry has his HQ - that's army jargon for Headquarters - in a big castle, miles behind the lines.'

'Father, I'm so impressed.'

'Don't be, Sinead. I should think the louder bangs must be quite audible from the castle.' Father Castlereagh looked into the fire with pursed lips, knowing his last remark had gone straight up the chimney.

Sinead searched his face, then asked, 'Father, is war wrong? Is Peadar wrong to want to go to war?'

'Our Lord told us that He came not to bring peace but a sword. He gives us the means to wage war on our fellows. What we do with it is left to us.'

'So Peadar has to search inside his own heart?'

'That he has, that he has.'

'He thinks about giving us enough to eat. That's what drives him. And he understands a fight for freedom.'

'And what does his heart tell him over and beyond money and food and fighting?'

'I'm not sure, Father.'

Conal started barking outside the window again. Sinead glanced apologetically at Father Castlereagh, who said, 'Tell Peadar that I'd like to see him and to chat to him before he finally goes off to France.'

Put that way, it almost sounded as if he were going away on holiday without her. For a moment she wished she could be going with him.

Conal was now growling, something that he rarely did. Then a stone was heard skittering across the cobbles, followed by some shouting. Sinead and Father Brendan sat and listened.

'Be off, you bastard, or I'll have you put down, damn you!'

Sinead jumped to her feet and parted the net curtains.

'Oh, no! It's that awful Mr McGrath come for the rent. All the other collectors have gone to the Front. There's only him left. I'm pleased you're here, Father. That man makes my flesh creep.'

Hardly had she finished her sentence than the street door was kicked violently open and a heavy knocking shook her own door. Father Castlereagh rose and turned to face the visitor who had come inside before Sinead had had the chance to invite him. Outside, Conal continued to growl his protest.

Almost swaggering into the room came a man who hardly resembled the awkward, clumsy figure of a few weeks before. But this was the first time he had called without his 'colleagues', as they used to describe each other. He walked slightly stooped, so that he gaped up at the world from beneath his loud, check cap. His waistcoat, collar and trousers appeared to be several sizes too small, making him struggle to breathe, which he did with audible effort, drawing back his lips. All this, together with two rows of black teeth, gave the impression of a malevolent gargoyle. He fixed his eyes upon Sinead, who stepped well back to let him come forward, and a grimace of delight broke on to his face.

'Good morning, little lady!' he cooed breathlessly, giving a little bow but never taking his eyes off her. The voice from the still figure standing by the fireplace took him completely off guard:

'Upon my soul, Sean McGrath his very self!'

McGrath stopped in his tracks as if frozen. His beady ferret's eyes darted fiercely beneath the peak of his cap. Suddenly his features relaxed into an almost coy little smile: 'Father Castlereagh! Well, well! This is a most welcome surprise!'

'Mr McGrath will be here for the rent, Father,' Sinead whimpered, backing away towards the fireside.

'The rent, Father,' McGrath whipped off his cap, nodding deferentially in the priest's direction and making feverish adjustments to his collar.

For her part, Sinead glanced at the Golden Syrup tin, knowing that only half the rent money lay inside it.

'Yes, indeed, Father, the little lady's rent!' He stood in shadow, twisting his cap around in his hands, his laboured breathing the only sound in the room, though Conal was still growling outside.

Sinead was quite relieved that Father Castlereagh knew this man but felt far too timid to enquire into the circumstances of their acquaintance.

'And how are you keeping, Sean? Treading the straight and narrow, I see.'

'The straight and narrow it is, Father!' He bobbed and nodded several times as he spoke, still wringing his cap as if to strangle it.

'That's good, Sean, that's very good. So now you're a rent collector?'

'Ahem, more of a landlord's agent, Father, if I might correct you there.'

'Quite so, Sean, quite so.'

Sinead stood transfixed by the figure in the semi-darkness, unable to move. Then Father Brendan, his hair glowing silver in the poor light, broke the silence.

'Well, you carry on with your business, Sean. Mrs Grogan and I were just talking. Her brave husband is training to go to the Front.'

McGrath who had been looking humbly down at the floor now glanced up to cast a furtive eye at Sinead. His mouth twitched as he rapidly looked her up and down, then flicked his gaze aside to Father Castlereagh.

'One week's rent is now due from the little lady, plus arrears totalling two pounds, three shillings and threepence ha'penny.'

Trembling, and cross with herself for her weakness, Sinead took the tin off the mantlepiece, prised off the lid with her finger-nails and held out some coins to McGrath. He craned his neck forward out of the gloom to try to see how much money was being offered. Sinead made no move towards him so McGrath was obliged to take a step forward, still staring into Sinead's open palm. Sinead closed her eyes as he took another step towards her. Now he was looking down into her hand. He glared, looking from her hand to her face, and then back again.

'This ain't enough, lady!'

Sinead looked helplessly at the priest whose ruddy face shone like a warning beacon to McGrath. Sinead quavered that it was at least one full week's rent.

'One full week!' leered McGrath, his eyes darting round the room, as if evaluating all of its contents. Then he sniffed. He sniffed a second time, a long, suspicious sniff.

'Funny odour in these premises, lady.' His eyes continued to rove over every detail in the room.

Sinead thought she might faint.

'A sort of gluey odour, wouldn't you say, Father?' He gave another shallow bow in the direction of Father Castlereagh.

'I'm sure I can soon get rid of it, whatever it is, Mr McGrath,' she said.

'Just so long as you're not carrying on a trade or business on these premises, lady.' McGrath smiled a crooked smile, looking hard at her now, from head to toe.

Sinead was at a loss. She could not lie before the priest, and she could not tell the truth before the landlord's agent. She wanted to die, to disappear.

Then Father Castlereagh stepped forward, clapped McGrath on the shoulder and beamed, 'My, my, Sean, what a suspicious fellow you are, to be sure! Is not this little family a sober and hard-working family, Sean?'

He nodded, speechless.

'And are these not good tenants, who keep the place clean and pleasant to live in?'

Again McGrath nodded unwillingly.

'And don't they always pay landlord something, however small, even in the bad times, eh, Sean?'

McGrath glared at the floor. Father Castlereagh laughed and patted McGrath on his arm, making it clear that he considered the matter closed. Sinead flinched as the coins were snatched from her hand.

Father Castlereagh, clasping his hands together before him, almost as if in prayer, looked appraisingly at McGrath. 'Are you yourself not away to the Front then, Sean?'

McGrath thrust the coins hurriedly into a leather pouch attached to his belt and swallowed several times, like a man who had just been sucking a distasteful cough lozenge.

'I would be so keen to join the army, Father, but my poor back excludes me,' McGrath almost sobbed at his ill fortune and put his hand to his side with a grimace of pain. 'I've always been a martyr to my back.'

Sinead had never heard Conal continue barking for such along time, barking and growling in turn.

'Well, Sean, I've no doubt you'll need to be getting on your way now, a man of business like yourself.' Father Castlereagh saw him preen at these words, then added, 'And one with an infirm back too!' The preening ceased, as if cut off by a switch.

'Indeed I must, Father. And I shall see the little lady next week.' He flicked an ingratiating smile at Sinead that made her reach for the back of a chair.

Conal threatened to go berserk as McGrath re-emerged into the street. Several stones were heard rattling across the gutter with, 'One day I'll do for you, you see if I don't!'

Sinead and the priest sat facing each other in silence for a while. Conal was now silent and little blue flames could be heard lapping around the coals.

Sinead smiled weakly and whispered, 'Oh, Father, I cannot bear that man near me! Can you not come and visit me every Monday at this time?'

He laughed and leaned forward, patting her hands, which were fluttering in her lap: 'Sinead, that man is a sad, weak soul. Do not fear him. I first clapped eyes on him in a house for derelicts. He has fallen by the wayside at times, it's very true, but it now seems he's earning honest money. But there we are!' He laughed again, adding, 'And I should not let on so about Sean, I know, but I cannot go away from here knowing that you are in fear of such a pathetic soul.' He fought to stifle another belch, which rattled down his nose. 'Quiet in there, I told you!' he bellowed, patting his belly. 'Porridge oats, that's what it is, porridge oats!'

Peadar, Dearest Husband,

I am so pleased you arrived safely and were not sick on the boat from Folkestone. I know I must not go on about how much I love you and miss you and wish the place was thick with your pipe again. I still keep taking your cap off the hook and holding it against me. I slept with it last night after Seamus finally went off to sleep. The separation allowance has come through at last - one shilling and a penny per day and twopence per day for each of the boys. Are you sure you can give us half of your own pay, my love? That is one shilling a day and would make such a big difference. Padraig is shooting up and getting very big. Seamus not so much, poor soul. The matchbox work is over now. The men have gone to the Front and it's all done by machines.

I know you may be cross but I've been down to Maguire Street where a shell-filling factory has been opened in the old malthouse there, almost opposite the back of the mortuary. I can get work there and when the boys aren't at school, Conal's new family, the O'Briens, of old Mrs Kennedy's place at No. 12, will have them. Mr O'Brien, such a nice man, works at the Abercromby as you know, but they've all gone on short time because of the war. A lot of factories have shut down and a lot of people cannot pay their rent. Some poor souls are starving. But we are well, my darling, so do not worry yourself on our account.

Over here the prices are going up something dreadful and some of the men's families have been paid no separation yet. I am so sorry for them. To get the allowance I had to buy our marriage lines and the boys' birth certificates at sevenpence apiece and post them to the Army Paymaster. What a rigmarole, but it was worth it.

Now take good care of yourself and eat all the food they give you and keep warm and dry. The boys send their love as do I.

God keep you safe.

Your loving wife,

Sinead.'

'Eh, boys! Is Wilbraham Street down here on this side?'

Seamus and Padraig looked the woman up and down. She must be delivering the letters because she was wearing the same uniform as Mr Flynn did and she was carrying a heavy brown bag. Padraig stepped forward and looked at her.

'Where's Mr Flynn?'

'Gone to the Front, my love.' She smiled but was clearly exhausted.

'Are you doing Mr Flynn's job?'

'I'm doing my best, love.'

'But you're a lady!'

She laughed. 'And so are the people digging this road up further down towards town, and so are a lot of bank clerks and the tram conductors!'

'Our Da worked at the Stanley. He's at the war too.'

'Ah, the docks!' Again she laughed. 'The dockers have refused to take on any women. What do you think of that?'

113

Seamus and Padraig did not know what to think. The idea of a lady delivering the letters was quite strange enough to be getting on with.

They walked with her to Wilbraham Street but were held up on the corner by a crowd of some thirty or forty people, mostly women it seemed, who were involved in some sort of scuffle. The post lady said, 'They've got a C.O. I'm off to deliver the rest of this little lot,' indicating her bag. With that, she disappeared. The boys stayed, fascinated.

'What's a C.O.?' asked Seamus, half in a world of his own.

'I don't know.' Padraig's eyes shone with interest. He took his brother by the hand and led the way towards the noisy fray.

In the middle of the crowd was a young man in his twenties. His cap lay trampled on the cobbles, his jacket was torn along the back seam and one of his boots was missing, so that one foot was bare. He had dark hair, was clean shaven and looked terrified.

The air was thick with cries of, 'Coward!', 'They'll probably shoot you!', 'My husband had his leg shot off for the likes of you!', 'My son's gone to the Front and he's got a bad chest!'

Each time the man lunged at the circle of women to try to break free, they would push him back into the middle. His own swearing at them was drowned out by their shrieking and cat-calling.

Seamus tugged at his brother's sleeve.

'I want to go home. I don't like it!'

'It's fun. Stay by me. You'll be all right.'

Suddenly the man was down on his back, a woman sitting astride him, pinning his arms to his sides. The woman's long, wild hair covered her victim's face, though his shouts of 'Get off me!' were just audible. The woman turned her face towards her eager audience. 'Shall I kill the bastard?'

Piercing screams of approval deafened Seamus who clasped his hands desperately over his ears. Padraig's attention remained riveted on the ugly scene.

'Kill him, Clodagh! Kill him!' yelled the women.

Clodagh drew her right arm slowly back, paused, then sent her fist flying into the side of the man's face. He squirmed beneath her.

'What has he done wrong, Paddy?' Seamus was still struggling.

'I don't know.' Padraig's eyes never wavered.

Clodagh straightened and looked scornfully down upon the man beneath her. She drew her long brown dress up above her knees, still sitting astride him.

'This is the closest your kind will get to a ride with me, sunbeam!' The man turned his head aside. The crowd roared with laughter. Clodagh took his face in her hands and forced him to look up her dress. 'There, take a last look and a good long whiff!' She hit him so hard in the face that his head snapped back against the cobbles with a thud and he lay still.

Seamus began to snivel. 'He's dead, Paddy! She's killed him.'

One of the women knelt to Seamus. 'No, love, he's not dead. He's just out cold, but he'll live, even if our own men don't.'

'What did he do wrong, Missis?' asked Padraig.

'He's a C.O., chuck. He's a Conscientious Objector.'

'Is he a murderer?'

'No, but he's as good as.' She sounded very angry.

Seamus was pulling at his brother's jacket. Perhaps it would be best after all if they asked their Ma.

'Well, Mrs Grogan, and aren't you the early one?' Auntie Dora looked up from the trestle table set up on the pavement outside her terraced house.

'Good morning, Auntie Dora. I've got myself a job. I start this morning.'

She looked at the round, old lady , hoping for encouragement.

She was disappointed. Auntie Dora readjusted her gigantic hat and tugged moodily at the grey curls escaping from beneath it: 'Disgraceful, isn't it? Seven of the morning and already I have eight lost lambs queuing for my soup.' She pointed sadly to the straggle of women standing in the rain.

'Who are these ladies, Auntie?' Sinead nodded, embarrassed, to the ladies, who nodded glumly back.

'How are those two big schoolboys, Mrs Grogan?' Auntie Dora scratched the grey stubble on her chin.

'Thank God, they're hale and hearty! They're with my neighbour, Mrs O'Brien, who will get them off to school. Do you know the O'Briens?'

'These here ladies, Mrs Grogan,' Auntie Dora indicated the group of sodden women, shuddering and coughing as they waited, ' these here women are waiting for the Medical Mission Hall to open its portals, when it's good and ready, if they aren't all dead by then!' She raised her eyes and crossed herself.

'Is it for the loan money they've come?'

'Half past eight it opens. You don't need to whisper, Mrs Grogan.'

Sinead smiled weakly at the ladies, who nodded again.

'That's right, Mrs Grogan. The loan money, because their separation allowance still hasn't come through.'

Sinead knew she might well have been in the same predicament herself. 'That's a godly thing you're doing there, Auntie!'

'Pawning their innocent souls to the Soldiers' and Sailors' Families Association, so they are.'

'Have you made sure they know how to apply for their allowance, Auntie?' Sinead still felt a little intimidated by her.

'Have you still got that devil's hound, Mrs Grogan?' Sinead opened her mouth to reply, but Auntie Dora cut her off: 'They ought to tell them about all that in the Mission Hall. Mind you, Mrs Grogan, the SSFA has to be paid back in full when the army money comes through but fortunately -' she paused theatrically '- I give all my food and services free - free in the service of the Lord and Our Lady!'

She raised her fat arms to the heavens and the ladies clapped wearily but, Sinead could see, sincerely. 'They couldn't pay me anyway. They've probably popped every stick of furniture in their place, poor souls.'

The ladies nodded.

Sinead looked again at the eight faces and said to them, 'Still, girls, we must hold up our heads for our menfolk, mustn't we now?' Again they mumbled agreement and forced a smile.

'You'll be along to work then, Mrs Grogan?'

'That I will. At the munitions factory in Maguire Street. Are you going to wish me luck, for there's no more matchboxes to be made at home?'

Auntie Dora squinted at her through her tiny spectacles, then, apparently forgetting she even existed, picked up another bowl and bellowed, 'Next, please!' banging the bowl on the table.

As Sinead walked away, she heard Auntie Dora saying to the lady she was serving, 'Nice woman, that Mrs Grogan of Oswald Street, but she keeps a dreadful dog!'

The first thing Sinead noticed was the smell. Even half way down Maguire Street you could smell it, and taste it. She paused before going into the factory building and sniffed again. It made her feel slightly sick. Still, she'd probably get used to it. It wasn't much worse than the matchbox glue. She squeezed her hands together and breathed in, thinking about a pound a week plus overtime. She would be able to reduce the arrears on the rent so she would not have to worry about that weasel Mr McGrath, and she could bring the boys' school fund up to date.

Wading through the mud, which she noticed to her surprise was yellow, she stepped into a dim, disorderly office, where an elderly man with purple lips told her to wait while he found a charge hand.

Bunched on to an inadequate number of hooks were countless overalls and mob caps, possibly black originally but now all shades of yellow.

From the shop floor came a lot of loud noise - machinery, shouts and screams -   and that awful smell, now so powerful it was making her eyes water and her nose run.

Then the elderly man came back, supporting a young girl of eighteen or nineteen who appeared about to pass out. To Sinead's horror, she saw that the girl was covered from head to foot in a yellow powder. Even her face was a mask of yellow. As she struggled weakly to pull off her mob cap, it became clear that her hair too was yellow.

The old man bundled her outside, where she sank to the ground just outside the doorway. The sound of retching was heard.

The man craned his head back round the doorway and called, 'If you're quick, you won't get your pay docked. If you keep leaving your station, they might fine you.' More retching prompted Sinead to move outside to see if she could help the poor girl but the old man restrained her.

'You can't waste your time with every yellow girl that gets sick!'

'Yellow girl?'

'Aye, yellow girl. That's what you've come to be, isn't it?'

'What's a yellow girl?' Although it was painfully obvious.

'A TNT girl. A shell filler.'

They were interrupted by the arrival of the charge hand. He was so tall he had to duck to come into the office. Broad and with a mop of wavy, grey hair and a full beard, he looked to Sinead like the giant in the *Jack and the Beanstalk* story that Seamus so loved to hear.

'Where's our new yellow girl, then, Mr Slater?' he growled, looking straight at Sinead and grinning, as if a tray of food had just been set before him. He took a cap and overall from one of the untidy heaps and held them out to Sinead. 'Here, put these on if you know what's good for you!'

'Do you provide any gloves?' asked Sinead, timidly.

'Gloves are available, my lady,' he jeered. 'They have to be available, but nobody wears them.'

'Why is that?' She was determined not to appear as frightened as she felt.

'Why is that? Why is that? Tell her, Mr Slater!' The charge hand continued to smile at Sinead, even when he was not addressing her.

'It slows the work down, that's why,' grumbled the old man, puckering his mauve lips. 'This isn't a government factory like the Woolwich Arsenal in London, you know. We have to make a profit or we won't have no job.'

'Come with me now,' beamed the charge hand, indicating the way to the factory floor, 'and get that cap and overall on!'

She fought to get them on as quickly as she could while the giant strode off towards the din. When she caught up with him, he was standing at the head of a very long bench, which was surrounded by about thirty women aged from eighteen or nineteen to thirty or forty. Not one of them looked up from their work. Mustard yellow from cap to boots, they resembled fantastic figures from some penny dreadful.

'These here women are topping and tailing,' he shouted above the noise, his voice deep and powerful.

'Topping and tailing?' she screamed, her eyes streaming.

'The shells!'

Sinead nodded.

He guided her over to the left and she felt his big, warm hand on the small of her back. She stepped out a little so as to avoid it. They arrived at a place where the heat and fumes were really overpowering. Sinead put her hands to her nose and mouth. To her horror, the charge hand took her by the waist.

'Now, don't go fainting on your first day, will you?' He squeezed her and laughed. Some of the women gave them both a knowing look, clucked their tongue and turned back to their work.

'The TNT is brought here as a powder. These ladies here melt it down, add some nitrate and pour it into a shell case in the form of a liquid.' The yellow powder was blowing all round the factory, as were the fumes from the hot liquid. 'The shell cases then go to be topped and tailed, as we saw over there.' He pointed to the right, still holding Sinead by the waist.

'You, my lovely, will start here.'

It was as she had begun to dread. She supposed that the topping and tailing was a more coveted job, because it was away from the worst of the heat and the stench.

'Is it dangerous?' she shrieked.

'We have the odd little bang now and then but the bloody building's still standing, so don't you fret!'

'I mean to the ladies' well-being, Mr . . . .'

'Jabez. Call me Jabez. A bit of skin irritation. No danger to life. The Medical Inspector of Factories hisself said so. Now, the money, the important bit! You'll be paid on 'time-rate', as we say, at one pound a week plus output bonus. You work a twelve hour day with overtime available. Seven in the morning till seven in the evening.'

'And what about food, Mr . . . ?'

'Jabez. Call me Jabez! Food, you ask? This is a place of work, my hopeful yellow girl, not a guest house for the well-to-do!'

His deep, loud guffaw could be heard above all the factory noise, and again Sinead felt his big, warm hand on the small of her back, moving around slightly but not quite a caress, the finger-tips probing and guessing at the outline of her waist. He leaned towards her to shout in her ear and she smelled pipe tobacco on his breath and in his beard and her thoughts turned to France for a second and her stomach turned over. He steadied her as she stumbled and she realised he could easily have picked her up bodily, if he had had to.

'Steady there, yellow girl! Now, as regards food, if you bring it you can consume it between twelve and one at your work bench. You may sit on a bench to do so, but I must pretend not to see you, if you follow?'

Sinead indicated groggily that she did follow, at the same time realising that she would be expected to stand on her feet for more or less twelve hours a day in this stink, in the knowledge that, at any moment, the whole factory could be blown to kingdom come.

'The other - arrangements - your workmates will tell you.' For the first time the giant appeared embarrassed.

'Arrangements?' screamed Sinead, coughing and weeping.

'Er, should you be taken by a call of nature . . . ,' Jabez turned his large grizzly head aside, his eyes downcast.

Sinead thought to herself, 'He's happy enough to feel my body, but the idea that I have to go for a pee is too much for him!' She nodded understandingly. He looked relieved.

When Peadar Grogan landed in France in Summer 1916, it bore no resemblance at all to his pipe dreams. Life was harsh for the Liverpool Pals, so harsh that the minor discomforts of their training camp at home now seemed insignificant. The 'old sweats' took the newly arrived units in hand, taught them a few 'wrinkles and wheezes' and buoyed up their flagging morale. On the ground were heaps of fallen fruit going rotten and in the fields unharvested crops. The Pals were grossly overloaded with outsize packs and staggered, bent double, rather than marched. The only French people they had seen since leaving the coast were women, who seemed to be doing all the work, and very old men. The few exceptions had been a handful of mutilés de guerre, no longer fit for military service. They had had a sobering effect on the Pals and had silenced their singing for a while. This was an aspect of war that none of them had given a second thought to in Liverpool. On their second day, one of the sweats took off his pack, sorted the essential from the 'trimmings', as he put it, and handed out the unwanted items to a band of verminous children, who were delighted with their new acquisitions. The other men followed this example and were able to march away a few minutes later, heads high and spirits soaring.

The Pals had a long march. They were to position themselves at the southern end of the line with the rest of the Thirtieth, next to the French Sixth Army. Those men actually on the Front Line looked out over No Man's Land and the German trenches, with the small village of Montauban beyond and to the left and patches of woodland, some almost totally devastated by war, directly ahead. They were to undergo a further period of rapid training, while getting accustomed to life in the trenches and to come to know the drudgery of 'fatigues'. This was hard unskilled labour and any infantry unit out of the line, either resting or training, could be called upon to do it. It consisted usually of digging holes and trenches, filling sandbags and carrying heavy loads.

The newly arrived Third Liverpool were divided into groups of fifty men and escorted to the line for training in trench warfare, first the officers and NCOs and then larger and larger parties. Peadar soon came to realise that most of his days would consist of either fatigues or sheer boredom and that the glorious heroics of war occupied about five days in a typical year.

The trench system in which he and his 'muckers' were to live, eat and sleep was reached by an access trench some way back from the lines. That led to three zig-zag lines of trenche - first, the reserve line, the farthest back, then the support line in the middle, and finally the front line. Each straight section was called a 'bay' and communication trenches joined up the three lines. Peadar had expected to live in a dug-out, some of which had lighting and some crude furniture, but these were only for officers and senior NCOs. He and his pals had to spend hours scraping holes in the sides of a bay where they could crouch for shelter. The fortunate ones got hold of canvas sheets to cover themselves when it rained. The trench floor was slatted wooden duckboard, a lot of which was damaged, so that your foot could slip through, scraping off the skin and filling the wound with mud and splinters.

'Who needs bleedin' Jerry?' the men would complain. 'You can kill your bleedin' self in your own trenches without ever clapping eyes on one!'

And so it was, in the pre-dawn darkness of late June, that Peadar and his platoon were given the routine order to 'stand to'. Having by now been moved forward to the front line, this meant manning the fire step in case of an early German attack. Shivering and coughing under greatcoats and blankets, they got ready to peer over the top. It was a sight already etched upon their mind - a few hundred yards of No Man's Land beyond the rolls of barbed wire, then the Boche trenches protected by their own wire, then an old brickworks, black and ragged against Bernafay Wood, and Montauban to the left, about a mile away - only a mile but it might as well have been back in Blighty.

Then, all of a sudden, 'morning hate' would break out, always to the irritation of the platoon commander Lieutenant Ronnie Hebden. Countless rounds of rifle and machine-gun ammunition would be fired off by both sides and Lieutenant Hebden would yell above the detonations, 'Rifle cartridges cost over a penny each, you bastards!' Heads were kept down and the noisy exchange was so far completely harmless, just a symptom of nervous tension.

Then both sides kept an unofficial truce whilst breakfast was cooked over small fires. Water would be lugged along the cluttered bays for washing and shaving. Columns of smoke from the enemy side told of a similar routine. A quiet day would follow, during which Peadar and his pals slept fitfully, woken by somebody falling over their legs or by an officer coming to inspect their trench. At dusk they were called to stand to again, followed by hot food arriving from the rear and a tot of rum, unless Lieutenant Hebden forbade it, which he did when he insisted he could 'smell a Jerry attack in the air.' So far, he had been mistaken each time, earning himself the nickname 'Clanger'. Sometimes the Germans used to serenade them across the darkness and they would pipe up in return with something suitably raucous and suggestive. After that they might not see or hear a German for days on end.

Peadar's platoon stood to one morning with one more day left of its eight-day stint in the trenches before retiring to the billets in the rear to recuperate. The platoon, sixty men strong, was divided into four sections of fourteen men, each section under a lance-corporal. Peadar's closest mucker in his section, Diarmuid

O'Rourke, said as he did every morning, 'Another day, another bob', although the soldiers were paid in francs. Because of this, Diarmuid was known as 'Bob' O'Rourke. This unfortunate man it was that gave Peadar his first experience of sudden and violent death.

'Morning hate', more vicious and prolonged than usual, was in full swing. The grey light of dawn was improving and a fine day looked certain. However, the promise of good weather was not a major consideration for Peadar's platoon, because, that morning, Jerry was firing shells as well as the routine small arms fire. Peadar and Bob were standing to on the fire step, heads down, eyes screwed tightly shut as a barrage of fifteen-centimetre shells burst all around them with ear-splitting detonations and thick black clouds of acrid smoke. Peadar's stomach churned with each long shriek, which heralded the arrival of each shell. Earth and stones were flying everywhere and Clanger Hebden was weaving frantically up and down the bay, shouting orders which his men could not hear. The nearest Lewis gun, which took six men to operate, had just jammed for the fifth time. Two sappers who had spent the night tunnelling under the German barbed wire and laying explosive, were now visible, flat on their bellies about fifty yards out in No Man's Land, unable to move any closer.

The after-taste of his pipe was now soured in Peadar's throat by fear. How could men do this to each other? Were these the same breed that crooned *Lili Marlene* and *Keep the Home Fires Burning*? Now they grieved at the gulf between themselves and their loved ones at home, now they deliberately blew their their fellow man's body to pieces, leaving his limbs to soak, bloat, rot and stink in a sea of mud and debris. Peadar's religion taught him respect not just for his own body but for that of his fellow. Here, half-buried in the remains of some French field, he could see what a vain hope it was, all wishful thinking, not based on the real nature of man at all. Why had dear sweet Sinead never understood? Because she had never set foot in this place.

Bob O'Rourke yelled in Peadar's ear, as he pointed into No

Man's Land, 'Peadar, those sappers are going to die! We've got to do something, mate!'

He grasped Peadar's jacket and his grip convulsed with each explosion, both men feeling the fire step shudder beneath their boots.

'What do you reckon, Bob, with all these Jack Johnsons falling all around us, eh?' Bob looked at him, his eyes wide.

Peadar went on, 'One of them will send us to Glory-be!'

But Bob was clearly torn. He peered over the top. He looked back at Peadar. Then he let go of Peadar's arm and rose to his full height, standing tall on the fire step. He waved his arms at the sappers, shouting, 'Over here, lads! Over here!'

They did not seem to respond. Peadar put his head down again and noticed Bob's legs buckle, very slowly, as if he had decided to sit down and rest after all. He raised his eyes to congratulate Bob on seeing sense, then blinked in horror. As Bob slumped slowly backwards, Peadar saw that his head had gone. For a few seconds dark red blood pumped from his severed throat and splashed all round the sides of the trench, covering Peadar's trousers and boots. The body hit the duckboards and rolled over twice.

Peadar sat on the wooden slats, his back against the side of the trench, his legs splayed before him, eyes glazed. Strangely, all he could think of was, where the hell had Bob's head gone? He had to find it. How could a man die without his head?

Clanger Hebden found him when he stumbled over him in the smoke and tumult. Peadar was crawling around the bottom of the trench, on all fours, covered in blood from the waist down, looking for something. Clanger at first thought Peadar was wounded and that the blood was his. He knelt and took him by the shoulders.

'It's you, Grogan! Are you all right, man?'

'Bob's head, sir. Bob's lost his head,' said Peadar, gazing at him as if in a dream.

The lieutenant helped him to his feet, while the whole trench shivered and lurched with each explosion. A couple of men glanced in their direction, then at the headless corpse, then busied themselves with their own survival.

The din died away to a whisper in Peadar's ears. He desperately fought to take in the fact that normal, ordinary men were actually doing this to each other, and on such a massive scale. He had seen death before: the stuck pigs in Armoy, dangling, bleeding to death, upside down. But that had been for a purpose. That was for folk to eat, folk who had few of the good things in this life. He had seen dead people lying at rest. They had been released from some fearful sickness or had simply come to the end of their years. He had seen some horrific accidents at the Stanley Dock - young men gone to an early grave. But this! Suddenly he felt faint and a wave of nausea swept over him. He signalled the officer to release him, whereupon he sank to his knees on the duckboards. As he leaned forward to retch, there, staring up at him from beneath the slats was the chalk-white face of Bob O'Rourke.

Rent day. Sinead, her fourteen-hour day at last over, plodded up Scotland Road, her yellow hair like a pantomime wig in the dying light. Earlier that day they had had a small explosion. One of the 'nitrate girls' had lost a couple of fingers. Jabez had laughed at the girl. Sinead had never heard an explosion before. Nor had she seen someone lose part of her body. No-one had known she was crying uncontrollably, because her eyes watered all the time, as did everyone else's and her nose streamed like a tap. Still, two hours' overtime would go a long way and Mrs O'Brien would have some change to give her back from the rent money. So kind of her to pay the man every Monday, while Sinead was at the factory.

Clodagh nodded to her as she strutted by, counting money in her palm and whistling *It's a Long Way to Tipperary*. Clodagh's new, dark blue skirt swayed like a pendulum, away over the cobblestones, her tune dying as she minced into the twilight, her long shadow rippling behind her like a dark train.

Sinead wondered why the Almighty had led her to toil in such a frightful factory. She accepted her bad cough and her night sweats as the penalty for earning good money. You had to pay for good fortune. Our Lady paid for being the handmaiden of God. She lost her Son. Sacrifice was part of life, to be endured with cheerfulness and resignation. She herself had two sons and a loving husband, so why should she complain? She would have to break Padraig of that habit. He was ever hungry or thirsty or bored. Still, his brother made up for it. Seamus smiled through his bronchitis and chest pains. His world was always right for him. As for Peadar, it was his gradual loss of faith that worried her most. It worried her more than his safety, for if he had faith, as she did, his safety was of secondary importance. Peadar had begun to rail at the will of God. It came across in the letters he struggled to write, or in those he got a friend to write from the Front. He would ask, how could God do this, or how could God allow that. Heaven alone knew the horrors of the war at the Front, but it must all still be part of a much vaster plan. It had to be, otherwise it was all meaningless chaos and there was no point in living. She patted her hair and it felt dry and thin.

She turned into Dryden Street and covered her head with her shawl. A gust of wind eddied dust and litter over the cobbles. She turned her head aside and screwed up her eyes. It was growing darker. She thought, even if you don't know the street you're in, you know more or less where you're going. You believe it all leads somewhere.

By the time she got to Oswald Street the light had almost gone. She shuddered. The room would be empty and cold - no man, no boys. Only faithful Conal would be sitting, waiting, on her steps. Mr O'Brien always kept the boys late at No. 12, regaling them with stories of the African War. They would wave to her through the window when she came down the street, but would not come home till the fire was lit and the room warm. Then they would bound through the door, bursting with Mafeking and Ladysmith, and she would still feel sick and try to wish it away like making the pavement seem to slide backwards as she walked along it. Oswald Street was silent. The biscuit factory and the Abercromby were on short time and had shut down for the day hours before. The courts stood black against the sky. Up at the far end, on the left a light burned at No. 12. She crossed the road briefly to the opposite side, so as to wave and see the boys' faces in the window more clearly. There was Mr O'Brien pointing her out to the boys and encouraging them to give their ma a wave. She stood, wrapped in her shawl in the chilly darkness, with the sudden strange feeling that she was waving goodbye, instead of hello. Why was she waving goodbye in the dark? Who was going away? Was it the boys? Was it herself? As she stood and smiled up at the bright window, waving feebly, she felt that Oswald Street was growing wider, that No. 12 was moving away from her, that she was on a quayside. Oh, how sick she felt! Reaching out to steady herself, she found the warm soft muzzle of Conal, patient, faithful Conal. He had come to squat beside her, searching her face for inspiration. She patted him absently, fumbling in her bag for her key. Instead, her fingers first closed round her little crucifix, which she squeezed, as tears welled in her eyes.

The room was cold, even after a long, fine day. Sinead went wearily about her routine tasks, filled with gratitude, as ever, that Mrs O'Brien had had the goodness to lay the fire for her. Every match Sinead struck reminded her of the stink of the old glue, and, what was worse, as she knelt at the grate, she flinched nowadays when a match flared into life, in case of an explosion.

The thought of having to prepare and cook food nauseated her. Her own appetite was waning and she was growing thinner. Her breasts were flatter and seemed to collapse and slide to either side of her body when she lay on her back in bed - like underdone fried eggs they were. Peadar had used to juggle them in his hands and laugh with delight at their fulness, and she would have to pull a face in order to look down at herself and see what he was about, and chide him for his roughness with her.

Feet on the steps. The boys were back already! A knock at the door. Why would they knock? She wiped her hands on her apron and went to the door. As she turned the knob, it was twisted violently so that it slid round in her hand. Her fingers fluttered to her mouth.

'Good evening, little lady. I trust I find you well?'

Her mouth was open but no words would come. McGrath grinned at her, his teeth so black as to be almost invisible. He eased himself round the door, whipping off his check cap, but keeping his eyes on her face. Then, without turning, he pushed the door softly to behind him.

'Mr McGrath,' she began.

'Sean, please, dear lady. Sean's my name.'

'Mr McGrath, the rent money's at No. 12 as always.'

'No. 12, dear lady, I know. But I have been unavoidably detained and now come here directly.'

Sinead was trembling: 'But I haven't got it here!' It sounded abrupt and now she was afraid she might upset him. Oh, where were the boys? McGrath stepped tentatively forward. Sinead stepped back. A growl from Conal outside made McGrath's eyes flicker and he cursed under his breath, leaving a blob of spittle on his chin. Again he moved forward, until he had Sinead more or less pinned against the corner of the kitchen table. He pushed a finger into his collar to ease his fitful panting. Could she smell cologne on him? She thought it most unlikely.

'Please go to No. 12. Mrs O'Brien will pay you there as usual.' She was pleading now. He put his hand to his leather pouch, as if he were molesting it, and jingled its contents.

'No need, little lady. Someone like yourself doesn't need to worry about money.'

She was confused. She looked at his sweaty face. Yes, sure there was a waft of cologne. On such a creature! He looked as if he wanted the toilet, she thought. She was quite unable to read his barely contained desire.

'What do you mean? Of course I need money!' She kept her voice low, still anxious to appease him.

'We might perhaps come to some little . . . ,' he scanned the room, then the ceiling, ' . . . arrangement.' She thought he was going to blackmail her because of the matchboxes.

'I don't work here any more. Only at the factory.'

At that point his face changed and he hissed, ' I don't care about any matchboxes, you stupid cow!' His change of tone shocked her. She reached out for the back of a chair.

'What? How dare you talk . . . ?'

'Talk!' he butted in. 'Enough talk! Help me, and forget the rent!'

His breath was catching noisily in his throat and he grasped the crotch of his trousers. Then at last, as the truth dawned bright inside her head, he took her by the shoulders and snatched her towards him. Her legs were turning to jelly and she almost stumbled as she tried to free herself. He caught her round the shoulders and clamped a hand hard over her mouth. She smelled that unmistakeable tang of coins.

She felt guilty, guilty that she had given this man the impression that she was so easy, guilty that she was not fighting and kicking, guilty that she could not scream, guilty that she had not been able to give him the rent and get rid of him, guilty because she went out to work and neglected her family. Now she was reaping her just reward. It was all her own stupid fault. She was indeed a stupid cow!

Suddenly, instead of the corner of the table it was this man's fingers pushing brutally between her cheeks while he feverishly covered the back of his own hand with kisses for he dared not remove it from her mouth. The oddest thoughts came into her mind, as her dress was tugged up at the back and she felt a hand running over the seat of her drawers. First she thought of how the food was going to be late. Then she worried about the state of her underwear, which she had stood up in all day. She heard her own faraway voice whimpering, 'Don't! Please don't.' Then she wondered what her dreadful yellow hair must look like. And there was Conal growling outside again. McGrath's breath was so foul that she had to draw breath herself in the few seconds when he pressed his face into her hair. She seemed to have lost the use of her arms and legs. He bore down on her until she was on her back, her outstretched arms pinned against the floor, head to one side, her hair a gilded halo. His weight was upon her legs.

'Queen of the May! Don't you dare move or make a sound or I swear I'll kill you.'

He taunted her and slapped her face from side to side, while Conal growled like thunder in the street. Soon she was naked below the waist, feeling the chill of the floor on her legs and behind, showing places only her own man had ever seen. In a dream she felt him enter her like a spear, for she was dry like a sheet of her own sandpaper. She heard him cursing from far away as he roughly withdrew from her. Her eyes were tightly shut. She knew he was kneeling over her and felt him make a lot of little jerking movements, followed by a gasp. The she felt a succession of lukewarm blobs of liquid pattering on her legs and running between them to her backside, where it went cold. Only then did she find her voice and a scream she barely recognised as her own tore out of her throat.

The street door crashed against the wall like a cannon shot and then something thudded into the door of Sinead's room so hard that it flew off its hinges and was hurled sideways into the room. Within a split second McGrath was flailing beneath Conal, his trousers round his ankles. The dog had him by the throat and shook him effortlessly from side to side, so that the man's head was dashed repeatedly against the chair legs.

'He'll kill me!' gargled McGrath, his face now bloody.

'Stop, Conal!' The dog let him go.

Man and woman lay and stared at each other, breathing heavily, both half naked on the floor. The broken door lurched and shifted but no-one stirred. Conal eyed the man with disdain and sniffed scornfully at his spindly legs and shrivelled penis.

'Get him away from me!' whimpered McGrath, drawing his legs up to his chin and struggling with his trousers, not daring to try to stand. For long seconds she did not look at him. She looked at the legs of the bed and reminded herself to smear some vaseline on them, otherwise the bugs and cockroaches would climb up there and creep all over the boys while they slept. Every couple of weeks she recoated those legs. Then, still lying on the floor, she pulled her drawers back on, very slowly, her face burning, while Conal stood over McGrath.

'Go from here and don't you ever come near me again. If you do, I shall tell my man what you did when he comes home on leave and he will find you. He may not kill you but you will wish that he had.'

Slowly McGrath rose and reclothed himself, setting his cap shakily on his head. Sinead called the dog over to her and got up and stood by him, holding his shaggy mane for support.

The man tottered backwards to the exposed doorway, turned and fled. The last sound Sinead heard of him was coins jingling in his leather pouch as he ran down the steps outside.

At about that same moment, hundreds of miles away in north-east France in the town of Amiens, four British soldiers on a forty-eighter were settling down at a table at Chez Lucienne. The small dingy bar, thick with the cigar-like smoke of many Gauloises, boasted half a dozen round tables and a narrow bar counter at the far end. The place was packed and conversation difficult, because of the shouting, singing, clinking of glasses and occasional outburst of cursing. The khaki uniforms well out-numbered the local berets and labourers' blue salopettes. From one table came the drunken rendering of *Mademoiselle from Armentieres, parlez-vous* and from another in national defiance, *C'est la Java Bleue* or a pidgin version of *It's a long Way to Tipperary* or *Goodbye Dolly*. But what Peadar had not expected was the girls.

Lucienne, the patronne, was a loud blancmange of a woman. When she clapped her dimpled hands, the long beaded strands which hung down over the back entrance to the bar were parted and in trouped four scantily clad girls. The furious applause and cheering of the men and the strong, heady wine made Peadar smile in spite of his confusion.

'What's all this, mate?' he shouted to Alf Targett, one of his closest muckers.

'Those are what are known as girls, my mate,' Alf roared back, slapping Peadar on the back, so that he had to put his drink down. 'Shows we've done too long in the trench if you've forgotten what them there are!'

'Trench fever!' laughed Private Alan Conlon, known as 'Whizzbang' because he had been buried alive for several minutes when a whizzbang shell had almost killed him.

'But I came here for a few drinks, Alf.'

'Peadar, we're all a bloody long time dead, mate,' and Alf waved one of the girls over to their bottle-strewn table, to the accompaniment of further applause and a few lines of *Hush, here comes a Whizzbang!* sung in honour of Whizzbang Conlon who had risen, knocking his chair over, and making vigorous masturbatory gestures.

Peadar ran his fingers through his thick springy hair, pulled out a louse and stared at it: 'I'm a married man, Alf, a family man.'

'So are Whizzbang and Soper here, my mate. So was poor old Bob O'Rourke.' He crossed himself and so did Peadar. 'Now, our wives are a long way away. We might never see them again. These might be the last girls you and I ever see. Ever think of that, eh?'

Peadar shook his head and tried to think of Sinead back home but the noise and the smoke kept distracting him and he felt rather dizzy.

The girl, who could be no more than seventeen or eighteen, swayed across to their table and placed her foot on the edge of Alf's chair, sliding her flimsy pink dress up to her knee.

'I am Sophie,' she smirked, stroking Alf's neck. 'What is your name, Tommy?'

Alf introduced himself and his muckers, who nodded and

grinned to her in turn. Peadar reached for his glass but missed it and clutched the air. Sophie saw this and laughed, 'Oh la, I think this poor Tommy is drunken soldier!' She released Alf and moved round to Peadar, stroking his head.

'I'm a married man, Sophie.' He indicated the second finger of his left hand.

'So what, Tommy? I don't want to be your wife! I just like to boum boum with you!'

The table erupted. Sophie covered her ears for the din. The dizziness which Peadar felt was like the dizziness far away Sinead had felt. It was not just the wine he had drunk but the dim awareness that a whole way of life was about to pass away for ever.

Sophie decided to sit on her victim's lap, straddling his legs and facing him, nose to nose. She pouted into his face, hitching her dress up to her thighs. Peadar fought to conjure up Sinead's eyes and mouth and smell but the taste of the rough red was upon his tongue and the perfume of fresh-washed hair and cologne were in his nostrils. For the first time he asked himself whether he was thinking of going with this slip of a French girl. Would he and could he? His hands moved down and rested on her flanks. Gingerly his thumbs began to stroke through the thin dress, though his fingers remained still. Then the tips of his fingers slowly circled, describing lazy wheels on Sophie's thighs. She shifted upon him so that all at once his hands were touching warm, smooth, living flesh. No-one was taking any notice of his guilty fumbling. No-one was watching his furtive hands. No-one appeared to bother when his palms slid slowly up the warm softness, until he practically cupped the girl's buttocks in his hands, for she wore nothing beneath her dress. In the din of the place no-one heard his long, slow intake of breath, like that of a man about to dive underwater.

'Talk to the girl, Grogan!' roared Soper, gesticulating to Lucienne for another bottle of vin ordinaire. Lucienne clapped her hands, shuddering the generous flesh of her exposed upper arms. The beads parted again, to reveal a pretty young brunette clasping a bottle of wine to her well-defined cleavage. Sophie turned to Soper with a smile: 'Tommy and me, we don't have need to talk, do we, Tommy? Our bodies can make all the conversation, n'est-ce pas, Tommy?'

And with that she pinched Peadar's cheeks with both her little hands and shook his head from side to side, so that his bewildered expression very much resembled that of McGrath when the dog set about him.

'Oh, I don't know about that!' slurred Peadar with a diffident smile, trying to avoid Sophie's eyes, which scanned his face. She leaned forward and sniffed his hair.

'Your hair, it smell very strange!' She sniffed at it again.

'Addison's Pommade,' mumbled Peadar.

'What is that?' she laughed.

' It helps to keep our hair clean. Army issue. We get it free,' he said lamely.

'How do you mean, Tommy?'

'The bastard means it's supposed to kill the lice!' bawled Whizzbang, winking at Sophie.

'What is lice?' she pouted, kissing the tip of Peadar's nose.

'It's like "puce",' squeaked the voluptuous Adrienne, the wine bearer, who was standing behind Soper, massaging his neck. Sophie gave a little scream and ruffled Peadar's hair playfully. She cooed into his ear, 'Then I shall have to wash it for you, before we make boum boum!'

Again there followed more laughter, applause and long swigs from the most recent bottle which was being passed round the table. Adrienne wagged her tiny index at Sophie: 'Take it easy with him, Sophie! He has to go back and fight the Boche after you have finished with him!'

'Up you go, Grogan, my old mate!' Soper pointed to the ceiling with one hand while the other helped Adrienne on to his lap. 'Don't just serve King and Country, go up and serve Sophie as well!'

Peadar turned aside and grinned foolishly.

'Give her a whizzbang from Whizzbang Conlon!' yelled Conlon, thumping the cluttered table and rattling the glasses and bottles.

Dimly he recalled mounting the bare wooden stairs. He remembered how Sophie had helped him up, stair by stair in case he fell, and how they had laughed together as they collapsed heavily on to the narrow, squeaky bed. Peadar stared at the low, yellowish ceiling, hardly aware of Sophie who was tugging his trousers off, and waited for the small voice of conscience to come and trouble him. It was there but so very faint. He thought it was the voice of little Seamus.

'Get off to bed, son, for your ma, there's a good lad.'

'Who are you talking to, Tommy? There is only you and me here.'

He looked up to see Sophie standing over him, stark naked, and his mind sank to his crotch. As she clambered gently upon him with great concentration, he felt himself falling through the mattress into a bottomless abyss, where there were no voices and no sounds but his own gasps and moans.

'Are you OK, Tommy?'

'Peadar. My name's Peadar! Private Peadar Grogan, Third Liverpool!'

'As you wish, Tommy.'

'Tell us again about the robbers, Ma!' piped Padraig, eager, bright-eyed, bouncing on the bed.

Seamus was downcast. The whole episode had upset him. He had hardly left his mother's side since the robbers had crashed through the door and threatened her. Fortunately they had had no time to take anything. Good old Conal!

'But why would they rob off us, Ma? We've got nothing to rob anyway.' Seamus was perplexed, cross-legged on the floor.

'Leave it, both of you, please!' Sinead patted her hair back from her ears and glanced at her framed embroidery, wondering whether to straighten it up again. No, it didn't need any more attention.

'Is Conal a hero dog, Ma?' Padraig asked.

'Yes, I suppose he is. Don't break the bed.'

'You should tell a policeman about the robbers,' Seamus mumbled.

'Seamus, love, please do stop talking about it.' Sinead put down her foaming scrubbing brush and her wet, red hands fluttered to her mouth.

'Sorry, Ma,' Seamus went quiet and sat very still. Padraig began to growl like a dog and waved his hands about like claws, dancing up and down on the bed.

'Paddy, stop. Ma says stop.'

'Mind it, you!' sneered Padraig.

' Stop! Both of you, stop.' She dropped her hands to her apron and stared forlornly at the scattered fire irons. Seamus looked up and saw the tears patter on the newspaper, which was spread all over the table.

Sinead leaned forward over the table, supporting herself shakily on her hands, which she planted among the fire irons. She yearned for the sound and smell of Peadar. When Mr O'Brien had come round to mend the door for her, just the sight and noise of a familiar man about the place had made her feel warmer inside.

'Are you crying, Ma?' Seamus asked, catching his breath.

'No, love, I've got something in my eye.'

'Is it some of that T ten T from the factory?'

'TNT, you soft lad!' Padraig jeered, still bouncing.

'I expect it is.' She shook her head to drive away the tears, took up her brush again and applied herself with vigour to her task, feeling Seamus's concerned little face pressed into her back. He tried to embrace her but she knew that if she turned to him she would break down completely.

'I hope me da's killing lots of German soldiers!' shouted Padraig, now in combat with an imaginary foe. Sinead concentrated hard upon her scrubbing, because each separate movement filled up another second of her time and stopped her from thinking. She cast her watery eyes around the neat dim room while she scrubbed. Sometimes those four dingy walls seemed to imprison her. Today they made her feel secure, secure with her boys. It was a kind of imprisonment, yet one which made her glad. Perhaps nothing in this life is all good or all bad, but is touched with shades of both. In this room she saw all that she needed. All her few poor things were around her, within reach. The factory at Maguire Street could be a figment of her imagination - until she stopped scrubbing for a moment and held up her hands to the light filtering in from the street. There they were like dabs of haddock - red fading into yellow. But there was the friendly smell of cow's heel stew, warming quietly, filling the room. She did not feel too bad today and she had soaked her hair before combing it through, which made it darker, less yellow.

Padraig leapt on to the floor and scrambled under the bed.

'I found another 'roach, Ma!'

'Oh, not another one! I thought I'd rid the place of the filthy vermin. The locust bean boat is in port again and all the courts are crawling. Your da' would have been able to warn us in the old days.'

Padraig paused: 'Is that the boat that's full of 'roaches?'

'That's where the big ones come from.'

His response was to grab the empty shell case from under the old pram and brandish it, as he crawled back under the bed.

'I'll fire a shell at it!' came his muffled cry.

'You watch yourself, son! Don't do any damage now!'

'No, Ma!'

Mr O'Brien's brother had lost a leg and gained a shell case at Gallipoli the year before. Sinead had not wanted the thing in her place at all but Padraig had pleaded and pleaded. She stood and watched now, as he caught the insect, kept it still with an index pressed down upon its tail end and crushed its head with the base of the shell case. With great care he retrieved the squashed head, which had become completely detached, and held it aloft for his mother to see.

'Look! Its head came right off! Do you think that happens to soldiers in the war?' He beamed with excitement.

Sinead shuddered: 'Wash it away down the sink!'

The episode with McGrath had knocked her for six. She was already flimsy and full of cold all the time. Just as those shells killed the Germans, so they also killed their own in the factories that made them. Sinead nodded. She reckoned it was God's own justice at work. Maybe she was dying for the cause too, like the soldiers. But now, on top of the endless hours on the factory floor, to come home and be attacked like that! Was that God's justice, too? For making weapons of war and neglecting her own fireside? She had told no-one what had happened. She was so ashamed. In any case, McGrath would not be the first rent collector to collect more than the rent. She was like one of her own Orange boy rats caught in a trap, one of her own ants in her ant-hill, of no consequence, part of the unstoppable march of God's universe. What was the use of complaining? Did the stones complain when she walked over them to get to the street?

'Is that nasty rent man coming tomorrow, Ma?' whispered Seamus, tugging at his mother's apron.

'No, son, he won't be coming tomorrow,' she said in a faraway voice, gently unclasping his hands.

' But it's Sunday today and it's Monday tomorrow. Aren't we going to pay the rent?' Seamus's face fell with anxiety.

His brother, flicking the headless cockroach across the floor, piped up, 'No we won't pay no rent! I'll shoot the nasty rent man with my Lewis gun!' and he made loud machine gun noises.

Weakly, Sinead raised her hand: 'Yes, I shall pay the rent. I'm not refusing to pay the rent. We've got enough to worry about without the landlord pitching us out into the middle of Oswald Street.' A stray wisp of yellow hair fell over her eye and she left it there.

'So, what will happen, Ma?' Seamus was still worried.

'Are you going to take the rent to the landlord?' To Padraig it was just a guessing game.

'No, my love. I don't know where he lives. He might not even live in Liverpool.'

'What, then?' Seamus was almost in tears.

'Well,' laughed Padraig, 'If the nasty man isn't coming, and if Ma isn't taking the money, that means we'll be having a new man for the rent, don't it, Ma?'

'Yes - a new rent man tomorrow.'

'Ma, you've got some hair in your eye. Do you want me to . . . ?'

'No, Seamus, no thank you. I don't want to be fussed.'

The rumour that something big was going to happen came to Peadar and Whizzbang Conlon from a mucker in the divisional artillery. Reggie 'Whacker' Pope helped to man a fifteen-inch howitzer several trenches behind the Third Liverpool Pals. This was their last of five days' recuperation in the transport lines, well to the rear. Tomorrow all three would be back at their stations. Seven hours' fatigues over, they stretched on the warmth of the white chalky soil of Picardy. Observing high overhead, a German sausage balloon floated languidly.

'The Manchesters are off training near Amiens,' yawned Whacker.

'Training for what?' Peadar's eyes were closed.

'Something, that's all I know. They've got this big field all marked out with the Boche positions and redoubts. It's a rehearsal for something.'

Whizzbang opened his eyes and squinted at Peadar, 'And think of all the new men flooding in during the last few days. Thousands of them. It must be something pretty important.'

'Every man either a regular or a volunteer,' Peadar said to Whizzbang.

'So what?' Whacker spat into the tufted grass.

'So there's not a single conscript. It's good for morale, Pope.' Peadar rolled over on to his stomach and began to suck on a blade of grass, 'Although Hebden says the top brass have stopped talking about a victory this year.'

'Oh, top-hole, old thing,' came from Whizzbang. 'So now it's scheduled for 1917, is it?'

'That's about it,' came Peadar's muffled voice.

Whacker Pope pretended to take pot shots at the receding balloon.

'You know my mate Bernard, the Frenchman, the bloke we go to Lucienne's with?' Peadar went on, not bothering to see whether they were listening, 'Well, he's with the French Sixth Army, as you know, just down the line from us, and he told me that the French have almost had it at Verdun. They want the Tommies to show their flag a bit and give them a break.

'They won't send us in to Verdun,' Whacker spat sagely again. 'It's not our sector. We're about as far as the Brit front reaches. All the rest of the Western Front is French, right down to Switzerland, three hundred miles of it, and the frogs are bloody welcome to it!'

'What do you reckon then, Whacker?' Peadar turned on his side to study this fount of knowledge, this man who fired a howitzer over their heads time and again, deafening them.

'Pozieres.'

'What?' laughed Conlon.

'Pozieres Ridge. You can laugh, Whizzbang. It runs all along the rear of the Boche lines about ten miles.'

'I know it bloody does. We all know. We spend most of our life looking at it.'

'High ground, my lad, high ground. A strategic advantage.' Whacker Pope winked knowingly at his audience.

'Pozieres Ridge is Boche, Whacker!' Conlon stared at him in disbelief. 'To take the whole of the ridge would mean pushing our Front, at least eighty-five miles of it, at least ten miles forward!'

'That's right!'

'None of us would live to see it, mate,' said Peadar. 'We'd all be dead. The Front's been where it is for ages. It's like a wall. It won't be moving anywhere. Fritz is well and truly dug in.'

'You wait and see if I'm right, Grogan.'

Two days went by. The trench was quiet. The midday sun beat down on Peadar's bay, known as Morecambe Bay. Smoke rings of Ogden's Juggler, a supply of which had come with Sinead's letter, rose slowly, expanding and thinning. Peadar watched them until they had completely disappeared, then blew several more. Now they all knew, all the man, though unofficially. The first day of July was to be the start of the 'Big Push'.

The Tommies now out-numbered Fritz by seven to one. Peadar and his platoon had been for their rehearsal near Amiens and knew what was expected of them. They had watched the crowds of new artillery men and their big guns being moved in. At the briefing by General Sir Harry Rawlinson they had been told of a five day bombardment, which was to bring to an end the trench warfare, the weeks and months of attrition, and avoid another winter in the trenches. The cheering went on for several minutes, while Rawly smiled indulgently. Some of the younger men had wept openly. The old sweats had just nodded and spat between their boots. But for now, all was quiet. Whacker Pope was probably smiling to himself and patting the barrel of his gun.

Even the Germans' cat-calling across No Man's Land had stopped: 'Hey, Tommy, your Kitchener has gone to the devil!' because the unfortunate man had drowned a couple of weeks earlier. Their other war-cry was 'Hey, Tommy, remember Jutland! You lost fourteen ships! You will now lose the war!' Soper had been bawled out by Clanger Hebden for holding up his placard with 'BOLLOCKS' painted on it and waving it towards the German wire.

Peadar's platoon had been assigned to dig a new trench system for the new arrivals. They had had to bag every grain of the chalky soil for secret dumping at night. He and Whizzbang had unearthed several British corpses in the process and now did not even bother to gag when the familiar foul stench floated on the warm air. They had also helped to lay water pipe-lines from newly sunk wells and to stack up great mountains of horse fodder, ammunition and rations. They had all stopped asking about the mammoth excavation project behind the transport lines. It was rumoured to be a mass grave in anticipation of the British dead. The sheer size of it reduced even the chirpiest soldier to silent contemplation.

Peadar thought less and less about life and death and what they might mean. He regarded both as attainable by throwing a switch - now someone is born, now someone is dead. Now a man is alive and running, now he is dead in mid-stride, no mystery, no fuss. Moreover, his remains stink until they are dried out, nothing sacred about any of it - a bag of corruption that smells even worse dead than alive. When we are alive the smells are mainly internal, secret. When we die, the smells are obvious to everyone still living. The latrine bucket and the foetid cadaver - similar contents, similar smells. Sinead could go on believing we are all sacred, belonging to God; her little nose had never been thrust against a bucket of shit or a body half-devoured by rats. The collapse of Peadar's faith was silent. It all collapsed from within without a sound.

It interested Peadar not one jot that his reasoning was unoriginal, that the disgust he felt, the disillusionment, were well-known reactions to the human body. He would have expected Father Castlereagh to reassure him that it was this very foulness of the human flesh and organs that made it so miraculous, because this bag of gas and slurry aspired so high, aspired even to cast off its mantle of flesh at its death. But all round Peadar were men who aspired only to go on living, they cared not how, they just did not want to be blown to pieces, to be picked clean by birds as they dangled in the barbed wire, letters of love from their family fluttering in tatters from their khaki pockets. Had their souls gone to heaven? He doubted it. They were gone for good. The men shot down in No Man's Land could not always be retrieved. Their bodies stayed there in the sun, rain and snow, day after day and week after week. Peadar could see them when he looked out from the fire step, slowly sinking and shrinking, becoming more and more like part of the ground itself. 'Dust to dust', but where was the 'sure and certain hope'? Gone.

More strongly than ever he wanted to get away from this place, to hide on board an ambulance barge and float away, down the Somme, to drift with the summer breeze in an observation balloon high above the battlefield. A host of British balloons was visible from his trench, grouped around the town of Albert. It must be so nice and cool up in one of those things! Scout 'planes of the Royal Flying Corps buzzed jealously around them, daring the Hun to try and shoot one down!

A letter from Sinead always made him restless. He braced his boots against the dusty duckboard and leaned his back on the warm trench wall, shifting his cherrywood to a comfortable position between his teeth with an audible click. He read and re-read her letter, turning the little crucifix this way and that in his hand. That was the third crucifix she had sent him since his arrival in France. The first had made him cry his eyes out for ages. Bob O'Rourke had had the second one and see where that had got him! Peadar gazed down at number three, a small piece of engraved metal, an effigy of a Roman method of execution. Suppose it were a gibbet instead of a cross - would it possess any more or any less mystic power? He slipped it into his tunic pocket.

Peadar, Dearest Husband,
I do hope the pipe tobacco and the crucifix will be welcome while you are far away from us here in Oswald Street, where all is well and much the same as ever. It did look recently as if all the women at the factory were going on strike. On strike! Did you ever hear of such a thing in all your life?
The reason was the Whitsun holiday. The government was going to cancel it, because of the need for more and more shells for all you brave boys at the Front. In the end, Mr Asquith, whom the girls call 'Squiff', said it could be added on to our August Bank Holiday after all. So the strike was called off, 'a victory for the

workers' our charge hand called it. . . .

Peadar paused. To threaten a strike of munitions because of a day's holiday! Had they any idea what conditions were like here? Ought he to tell her that, in any case, one third of all the shells were duds, because of shoddy or hurried assembly? They simply fell to earth without exploding. No. What was the point, even if he were daft enough to try to put that in a letter?

. . . How lovely, Peadar, my love, to have poppies growing between some of the trenches and even under the barbed wire. That crimson is for our Lord's blood which was shed for us, for us and even for the Germans. . . .

No, wife! That crimson is for the blood of the men sent one after another to their death on the orders of men who stay in castles behind the lines, where the noise of battle is no more than a distant roar, and, yes, for our blood and for that of our enemy who is sent over the top as we are.

. . . The two boys will soon be seven years old. How does that make you feel, my own darling man? Old? Seamus is still a little saint and Padraig the fearless one, though without that lovely soft side which his brother has . . . .

So, Seamus is still a victim, the one all the other children pick on, whilst Paddy is the one who sorts them all out to let the bastards know and remember who the Grogans are!

Uncharacteristically, Peadar did not re-read the closing lines of her letter, but put it with the crucifix in his tunic pocket.

The final briefing was at early morning. The platoon sat round Lieutenant Hebden in a large field. They were three miles behind the lines between the villages of Suzanne to the west and Vaux to the east. The Deccan Horse of the Indian Cavalry had exercised here and torn some of the grass up. Behind them lay a narrow lane, some marshes and then the River Somme. The lieutenant stood among them, as they sat or squatted, for the grass was still damp with dew. He stretched out his arms for silence. The platoon became hushed, as if ready to receive a sermon. Hebden's back was against the morning sun, his face in shadow. The men squinted up at him, dazzled by the light. Peadar believed he ought to be able to feel the spirit of Bob O'Rourke squatting beside him here, but in fact he felt nothing. Bob was nowhere to be felt, nor could Peadar sense any of the other fallen soldiers who had marched here to the Somme with him. He was relieved, not glad, but relieved that he was still living, smelling this moist field, feeling the early sun in his eyes. This was enough for him, from one second to the next. Hebden had promised an extra ration of rum. Perhaps they would have to approach him one after another to receive it. His outstretched arms threw a long, cross-shaped shadow over the platoon. The shadow hung, motionless for a moment, then collapsed as his arms fell to his sides.

Peadar learned that soon the first men to go over the top and open the assault would be named. The date and time would be confirmed, so the rumours would cease. The infantry were to advance to within one hundred yards of the German wire, wait for the cessation of the British bombardment and then rush the enemy. Peadar felt a strange mixture of excitement and fearful nausea.

'General Rawlinson is confident that enemy resistance will be minimal. Our own artillery will have pulverised their trenches and our shrapnel will have been aimed to cut their wire.' Peadar smiled as he conjured up an image of Whacker Pope and his team with their huge fifteen-inch howitzer, firing shells so big that you could watch them as they arced into the air and then seemed to stand still before plummeting to earth, followed by a distant 'crump' noise.

'Just before the attack begins, the cavalry will be moved forward to the front line. If the wind is from the west or south-west, we will not hesitate to use poison gas against the enemy. The infantry, including members of this platoon, will advance across No Man's Land in a series of waves, one wave per minute, at a slow walking pace.' It sounded like suicide. Still, at least Jerry would have received a good pasting first. But suppose he survived it?

'There will be absolutely no cheering, no shouting and no running, for whatever reason.' Tell that to a panic-stricken youth in the middle of No Man's Land! 'You will take no prisoners. That is an order, though you will not see it in writing.' Christ! This was going to be bloody serious! 'Any of my men refusing to go over the top, regardless of the battle conditions, will be shot on the spot by the military police.' They looked at each other out of the corner of their eye. So, here, at last was the real thing, the sort of war Bernard had already fought and survived at Verdun, the sort of war that was wiping out the French Sixth Army. Peadar had mislaid Sinead's letter and crucifix and had an odd sense of guilt about both. That is how he knew for sure that he would be among the chosen for the opening of the attack.

The routine noises of getting up could not deafen the tumult of yesterday's memories. The tumbling rain, the gutter rushing down the middle of Oswald Street, salvos of heavy drops drumming on the grimy window, driven by the wind, and still she was troubled. The bickering boys, the hiccoughing water tap, the many Morrisons stomping up and down the stairs, the lumpy black kettle sighing on the hob, none of it could take her mind off her tussle with Jabez.

'Seamus, Padraig, will you be off to school now?'

'Has me da sent another letter yet?'

'I don't know yet, Seamus, love.'

'Is he all right?'

'Sure he's all right.'

'Last one out in the rain is a nancy boy!' came Padraig's challenge from the open doorway, one little boot in the hall. The rain sounded even louder now. Sinead adjusted their coats, nearly new from Paddy's Market. She stepped back to inspect them, her hands on her hips, a stray lock of yellow hair over one eye. She tossed her head to shift the wispy strand and then tried to blow it aside, but both to no avail.

'You'll do. Now, don't dally in this rain, do you hear me?' They nodded as one. 'Get straight to school. Conal's at home in his basket, I shouldn't wonder. You can go without him this morning.'

The outside door slammed behind them and their shrieks died away, dissolving in the rain. Slowly she pushed the room door shut and drew Mr O'Brien's new bolts across. Then she crossed to the table, drew out a chair and sat down heavily, her elbows on the table amid the breakfast chaos, her chin in her hands, staring straight ahead, though the wall offered no solace, nor the pounding rain. If only Peadar were here! All this surely would never have happened. Is a woman alone such irresistible bait? How old must she be to be left alone? Look at her now, poor scrawny creature, bombshell blonde and yellow in the face and eyes! It didn't take much to stir a man to passion! How many secrets did she have from Peadar now? He risks his life for his country and even for folks who are not his countrymen, and she fills in her time fighting off every Tom, Dick and Harry who takes a passing fancy to her! Oh, but she did fight Jabez off! She might be a guilty woman but she was not a sacrificial lamb. 'Not peace, but a sword,' Father had said, and by God she had wielded it! Mrs Holz would have been proud of her yesterday. 'Do not fear the big city. Learn its ways.'

She and a couple of 'nitrate girls' had been moved to topping and tailing and it was a relief. The regular toppers and tailers were going down like ninepins and Sinead hoped she would not be next. It was either the TNT sickness or typhoid, no-one was certain. The stink was less fierce down this end and the girls were more friendly, probably because you could actually hear yourself speak here and have a bit of a chat. It was generally acknowledged that Jabez had taken a shine to Sinead and her workmate, Ethel, both of whom kept themselves to themselves rather more than the other girls. They did not nod and wink to the men or call out to them across the shop floor. The men, in turn, treated them with more respect than the others. Jabez found any excuse to wander over and inspect their work. He would stand right behind them and tower over them, leaning over their shoulder and breathing into their ear. Sometimes he would put his huge arms around them, in a show of demonstrating how they should assemble the shell, something they knew probably as well as he by now. If one of the girls said, 'They don't need your help, you great lummock!' Jabez pointed to his ears and shook his bearded head, to imply that the noise of the factory was drowning them out.

That particular day, however, was different, because when he came back in at half past one, he smelled of ale. It was a smell she had rarely found on Peadar. He sometimes wafted pipe tobacco from his hair and his shirt but that was a reassuring smell, like his sweat. Ale was somehow a threatening odour, one which hinted at a certain way of life, of a certain attitude towards life. The many Morrisons often left an eddying wake of it behind them in the hallway, Auntie Dora breathed it when she complained she was 'plagued with the bile', and poor Sean Finnegan had reeked of it. It was the smell of broken homes, of the music hall, of street crime, of instability and of loose women, all things which Peadar, thank God, avoided. The fact that Jabez was a giant of a man, added to the discovery that he was a daytime drinker, made him a more menacing figure than before, one capable of excess. A smell betrayed as much about a person as did clothing. It was like invisible but detectable clothing. That was the power of a smell.

'Well, now, my yellow girls, I have here some new gladrags for you from the management!'

Between his hands he held up a dark blue, one-piece garment of coarse cotton.

'This here is a boiler suit made for ladies, the working garment of the future. Very daring, eh, girls?'

Several sickly yellow faces turned to see the boiler suit.

'So you'll be wanting us all in them, will you, Jabez?' came a voice from near a pile of waiting, empty shell cases, plump organ pipes with the tips missing. It was little Edwina, who had to work standing on a piece of duckboarding to reach the bench top. Everything about her was small apart from her voice.

'Not me, Weena, the management,' he bowed sarcastically.

'Figure-hugging, are they?' Weena looked knowingly at the other girls, who smiled back.

'I myself would scarcely take note, Weena!' Several of the toppers burst into raucous laughter. A slant of dusty yellow sun filtered through the skylight, high in the roof girders, lighting the thousands of empty shell cases, standing upright, acres of them, like an outsize honeycomb spread across the floor. Jabez held the boiler suit across Ethel's back but she brushed him irritably aside. Sinead waited with anger for what she knew was coming, the sunlight spreading the sweat across her back.

'Well, my little canaries, one of you has to try this on and show Mr Gardner upstairs,' Jabez beamed, his waistcoat and rolled -up sleeves almost steaming, his off-white apron betraying his arousal. He transferred his attention to Sinead, quiet Sinead, and pressed the boiler suit against her back. She pushed down on the bench top with her open palms and breathed in slowly, head down.

'Get off me, Jabez, I'm warning you!' she said, without turning to look at him.

'She's warning me, girls!' he laughed, tossing the boiler suit on to the bench and clasping Sinead round the waist. She gave a stifled shriek of indignation.

'Leave her alone, you brute!' yelled Edwina, throwing a piece of rag at him.

All at once, Sinead wrenched herself free, spun round and brought her knee up into his groin with all the force she could muster. All the work stopped in that part of the factory as Jabez sank to his knees, clasping his crotch, wheezing, 'Pope Catholic whore!'

'Rent man!' growled Sinead, in a voice unlike her own, and spat a gobbet of saliva in his face.

'Serves you right, you bastard!' Ethel pointed her screw driver at him. 'And that's from a Methodist!'

As Jabez went down, the blob of saliva, glistening like a huge diamond in the shaft of sunlight, slithered, snail-like, down his cheek. As he knelt, head raised, as if in a mosque, the spittle sank into the beard on his cheek, where it disappeared, its peacock hues vanishing. Sinead stood trembling, too angry to cry, the breath catching in her throat. Surprisingly, she thought about kicking him while he was on the floor. Her fury towered above her fear for the first time she could remember.

Peadar had guessed right. He passed a dreadful night. The rat bite on his ankle was going septic, he was infested with lice, even in his eyebrows, and the latrine bucket had been kicked over in his dugout, flooding all over his blanket. By dawn he felt sick and knew he was in for the 'trots'.

Just thirty minutes later he was being issued with his normal packs plus a rifle and bayonet, two gas helmets, two hundred and twenty rounds of ammunition, two hand grenades, two empty sandbags, a shovel, a pair of wire-cutters, a flare and countless other impedimenta - around seventy pounds' worth. None of their training had been carried out with this weight on their backs. Clanger Hebden had told him and the others in the first wave to be grateful, because the men in the following waves would have to lug duckboards, bundles of stakes and great rolls of barbed wire.

The incessant din of the British five-day bombardment was about to cease, although many night patrols had come back with stories of German wire still intact and of German troop reinforcements arriving under cover of darkness. How secret was this action?

Clanger condemned such talk as 'windy' and told his men to light up their pipes and slope arms as they strolled across No Man's Land. Zero-hour, which had been put back forty-eight hours after several summer deluges had flooded the trenches, was now 7.30 a.m. on the 1st July.

Peadar and Whizzbang had no dry underwear so wore their

pyjamas under their trousers, and both men's boots were rotting. They prepared their packs in uncomfortable silence, unlike Soper and Targett, who sang Burlington Bertie in raucous duet. How could they feel so cheerful, unless they were completely stupid? It was said the gunners were exhausted, with blood-shot eyes and bleeding ears after six days of stupefying shell-fire at the enemy. Poor old Whacker Pope!

As Peadar's platoon tried to assemble in Morecambe Bay, the trench was so packed with heavily laden men that forward progress was very slow. Soon there was a complete traffic jam and all the men came to a halt. A red-faced CSM charged past to find out where the problem was and discovered a young officer shouting at a man to wake up and get out of the way. The CSM explained that it was a corpse and shoved it aside.

'Broad bloody daylight! What a time to choose!' moaned Soper, staggering over the broken duckboards. 'I wish I was with Adrienne on that creaky old bed, making Lucienne's ceiling shake!'

'Randy bastard!' wheezed Alf Targett, bent low, picking his way. Some bays were still waterlogged and sewage could be clearly seen floating in it.

Then the Germans began an unexpected bombardment.

'What the hell?' Peadar paused and looked up. 'I thought we'd knocked those bastards out!'

'Apparently we haven't. Move along there, Grogan, or we'll all cop it.' Whizzbang spat into the dark water swilling round his boots.

Because the men were so crowded together, they began to get hit, to be wounded, and to be killed. As the queue inched forward, the men had to step over the half-submerged corpses, ignoring loud and repeated orders to throw the bodies over the edge of the trench. They simply had far too much to carry even to attempt it.

The roar of their own artillery and the German barrage sounded like the end of the world. The whole earth shook continuously and the yell of voices was snatched away by the holocaust. The air above the trenches was thick with whizzbangs and shrapnel. How could any man dare to go over the top this morning? It was sheer suicide, although they were chucking everything they had at Jerry, including shorter range trench-mortars. Zero-hour was approaching. Peadar fumbled for his crucifix, then remembered he had lost it. Now Sinead would be convinced he had lost his magic protection. He would have to take care.

Saturday evening sunlight bronzed the low west front of St Anthony's and warmed its blackened stones. Inside, dust danced in golden shafts that poured against the confessional as it cowered against the far wall next to the statue of the Sacred Heart. As she went in, Sinead felt the familiar cool mustiness embrace her and her shoulders sank, as she gave herself up to it - mouldy books, incense, candles and a whiff of death. She felt better, and looking about her in the comforting gloom, beheld a heap of blackness at the altar rails, which she knew by its hat to be Auntie Dora, apparently saying a full rosary. A flood of sunlight ran along the stone flags, past the soles of the old dear's feet, leaving her untouched, in darkness. Next to her, breathing her penance like a lover's declaration, knelt Clodagh, having unloaded her sins nearby. Her long, slim, kneeling form looked like something folded up against the rails, waiting for further use.

Sinead breathed in slowly, feeling lighter, and wandered over to the confessional, lifted by whispered prayer from every corner.

She knew Father Castlereagh was inside and that he was now sitting alone. Mr Riley had just come out, Mr Riley, the former landlord's agent, Mr Riley with his beard like the King's, who was now a legless cripple, swaying about on crutches, waiting for his new artificial limbs. Mr Riley had left his real legs behind in a shell hole at Ypres.

Her feet now moved towards the dark curtain. She glanced down to watch the flagstones sliding past her boots. Which was really moving, her boots or the floor itself? She drew the curtain back and stepped inside. Closing the curtain again, she sat down in almost complete blackness, an absence of everything, of light, of pain, of anxiety. If death were a bit like this, it wouldn't be too bad. There was a slight movement by the grill opposite and a smell of whiskey.

'Bless me, Father, for I have sinned in thought, word and deed. It's three weeks since my last confession.'

These simple words released a flood of well-being inside her, starting from her toes and welling upwards through every part of her. Gradually this mysterious flood dissolved her, replaced her, so that she became almost a part of the fabric of the building and her sins seemed something separate, apart from her, a sort of detached substance, like when you see horse mess in the road and you want to walk round it.

Father Castlereagh's semi-articulate kindness came mumbling through the grill, though Sinead hardly heard it. She was floating. She never wanted to leave this enclosed place. Then she heard her voice explaining: 'Father, I was set upon and defiled in my own house. At first I did not intend to tell you, my man away and all.'

'Lord above, child! What were the circumstances of this terrible thing?' More whiskey fumes floated through.

'That man you called a pathetic, lost soul, Father, it was him. It was the rent man.'

'Sean McGrath his very own self? Dear God in Heaven! Sure I took him for a poor weak excuse for a man.'

'The fault must lie partly with me, Father. I must have driven him to it, not knowing what I was at.'

'That is something for your own conscience, child. But a man who assaults and violates a woman is a sinner indeed, upon my word he is!'

'If my man wasn't at the Front, sure such a thing would never have come about.'

'Did you make overtures to Sean? Did you encourage him?'

'I did not, Father. I loathe the creature, if you will pardon my expression. You know him. He is a foul person.'

'Did you tell the police?'

'I did not. Why would they be bothered about such a thing?'

'Sure these are terrible times, terrible, terrible times, so they are!' He belched softly. 'Quiet in there!'

'He told me that if I would give myself to him, I would never need to pay the rent.'

'Did he now, did he now?'

'And no, Father, I was not tempted in any way!'

'Sure you weren't, child, sure you weren't.'

'It was awful, awful! I wanted to die there and then!'

'I don't believe that you have sinned, rather that you were sinned against.'

'But I still feel guilty, Father, I do. And there's more. . . .'

'More, child? What on earth do you mean, more?'

'At the factory where I work . . . one of the charge hands . . . took a bit of a shine to me and Ethel, both of us, mind, not just me. Well, he tried to put his hands on me once too often.'

'And what did you do, child?'

'Hit him where it most hurts a man.' She held her breath and waited. There was a long pause.

'And how did the man react? Was he in pain? Was he injured?'

'He was that, Father. Great pain.'

'And you never did anything to inflame him, to light his fires, so to speak?'

'I never did, Father. But I will not have any man mess about with me again in that way. Was I wrong to strike back, Father?'

'Vengeance is mine, our Lord did say, though maybe you were His instrument on that occasion. Yet you still may want to do penance, you say?'

'Yes, Father. I want to do something, Father. I don't feel right with myself. I have a gap in me like my boys' front teeth.'

'I don't follow, child.'

'Seamus and Padraig have no front teeth at present. They have

155

a big gap at the front.'

There was a pause while Father Castlereagh fought to digest this information. Then: 'And you feel some sort of penance will . . .'

'Make me strong in the Lord, yes, Father!'

'We will say an Act of Contrition together, then you will say an Our Father between two Hail Marys. There! How does that sound?'

Relief swamped Sinead. Now she could go on.

At six minutes to Zero Hour, the British barrage was reaching a shattering climax. From somewhere the order was passed along the trench to move off. Peadar struggled up the ladder and followed Alf Targett, Whizzbang and Soper single file through the British wire. As soon as he stood upright at ground level, he felt exposed and immediately crouched low. The noise, smoke and fumes were far more intense up here, and he found himself reaching forward to grasp hold of Alf's tunic for direction. Alf glanced briefly round with a mixture of fear and excitement on his clumsily shaven face. All Peadar wanted now was a good shit in quiet and privacy. To think how the Morrisons banging on the lavvy door had used to upset him!

The men began to spread themselves out in long lines as they had been briefed, and flattened their bulkily laden bodies against the thirsty white soil - long straight lines of khaki, motionless, waiting. The Boche trenches offered little return fire. They were apparently being pulverised. So far so good. Peadar lay with his fingers in his ears for relief from the aching noise. If he had found the crucifix, he would surely be squeezing it now. He started to pray in a whisper, inaudible even to himself, but he could not find the words. He could not make himself believe that a magic formula could protect his soft flesh from bullets, shells and shrapnel. Where was his faith? Where had God gone? Had God deserted him? Had he deserted God? If God needed a person's faith in order to exist, then maybe Peadar had slain God, at least within his own self. Amidst all this slaughter, God was just one more casualty. Perhaps God's death had coincided with the blowing of the first, huge British mine a few minutes before. Perhaps the next nine remaining ones would finish him off. Dimly he heard his platoon sergeant bawl from two or three places to his right, 'Grogan! Take your fingers out of your ears, you silly bastard! Listen for the whistle!'

At two minutes to zero, the remaining mines were detonated, including two twenty-four tonners on the La Boisselle road. The earthquake which followed and the gigantic columns of debris gave a foretaste of the force and violence of the coming battle.

There was a shocking silence.

Then Lieutenant Hebden's voice rang out, 'Right, let's be off, chaps.'

The British barrage had stopped and with it Peadar's heart. The sun shone clear and bright. Birdsong started.

Hebden blew a short blast on his whistle. Other whistles were heard further and further along the rows of khaki. Slowly the men rose to their feet, looking to left and right. They dusted themselves off and stepped forward at a slow walking pace over No Man's Land towards the German wire. It looked a long, long way, but Peadar now felt more confident of getting across. He felt somehow lighter without God. All his life he had felt like a passenger, without control. He had taken decisions and chosen the way ahead which appeared to be right for him, or right for Sinead and the boys, yet he had no sensation of ultimate control. He was swept along in the current of life. Dear Sinead, on the other hand, took few decisions, was always happy to be advised by others, yet felt she was being steered, directed, competently and wisely, by her Maker. She was never swept by a current. She nestled in the palm of a benevolent hand. But now Peadar had that ultimate freedom. He alone was taking these measured steps over No Man's Land. If he so wished, there was nothing to stop him from turning on his heel and walking in the opposite direction. He had control.

The British barrage started up again with a thunderous roar, as they began to rain shells and shrapnel upon the next line of German trenches. Clanger Hebden walked ahead, as if on a country ramble, but Targett, Soper and Conlon, spread out on either side of Peadar, looked pale and tense, each with his rifle clasped tight against his chest, bayonet gleaming. Along almost twenty miles the first few khaki waves flowed forward, over the long-untrodden tufts of No Man's Land.

For several paces nothing happened. Peadar fixed his eyes on passing stones and leftover puddles. His guts were full of wind. Thank God no-one could hear him farting all the time. Then the German guns started. Dozens of men fell, unheard in the din, but the wave did not falter. Peadar was scared now. Men fell to his left and to his right. They fell ahead of him and behind him. The Boche wire was less than four hundred yards away now and a lot of it was still intact. Peadar knew that he and his pals were an easy target, upright, slow moving, unwavering, getting closer to the enemy front line with each step. Whose bleeding barmy idea was this? Only someone who was never going to try this caper could possibly have suggested it. There were big gaps in the waves but still the survivors plodded forward. Peadar could even hear the machine guns now. Each step he took was another second of life, precious, vulnerable life. With each footfall he said to himself, 'Live! Live! Live!' Each new step meant his flesh was still intact. No blood was leaking. He was still farting. All was well.

But the Germans were recovering. The seven-day bombardment had clearly not wiped them out. Their artillery opened up on No Man's Land and deadly accurate shell fire burst all around. Peadar was astonished, so astonished that his fear subsided. His own superiors had assured him that this could not happen!

Out of the corner of his eye Peadar realised that Alf was slowing his pace. Turning towards him, he saw he had a severe wound to the side of his face and that most of his right cheek had gone, although he was still staring straight ahead. Peadar reached out to him but Alf pushed his hand aside.

'I'm as right as rain, mate!' he shouted to Peadar. But he spat blood thickly as he spoke and swallowed convulsively to avoid choking on it. Peadar felt tears well in his eyes. He could see Alf's side teeth through the hole in his face, like part of a hideous grin.

'Alf, you're hurt, mate. Let me . . .'

Then there was a loud smack and Alf buckled without a murmur, first to his knees, then flat on his face. Had Peadar been marching a few feet further to the left, that would have been him, a cadaver with half a face and a hole through the forehead. So why did he happen to be just to the right of where the bullets flew at that crucial moment? Why did Alf happen to be in the wrong place at the wrong time? Was it because Alf deserved to die more than Peadar? That was unlikely. Had a conscious decision been made by a God? Any God who had a hand in this was just not worth the name. What would Sinead make of it? Was Alf one of her so-called ants, being crushed underfoot by a greater being who was running to put out a massive fire? Was God trying to stop the war through the very humans who had started it, and, in so doing, having to sacrifice some of them? But his own survival mattered much more to him right now than all these possibilities. Anything he could do to ensure it, he would do. Right and wrong seemed like the luxuries of idle philosophers or of high-ranking commanders sipping vintage port at Querrieux or at Montreuil.

Alf's steel helmet still spouted blood through a neat blow-hole just above its rim. He looked like a baby whale wrapped up in khaki rags and tangled up in a confusion of bags and gear. Through smoke and tears, Peadar then saw his first two German dead by a shell hole. His own wave had been practically wiped out. He had seen Clanger a moment before, urging on his non-existent men, shouting words that no-one was even trying to hear. Soper and Whizzbang were nowhere to be seen. He seemed to have reached the German wire almost alone. Relieved to be free to fall flat now to avoid the raking machine gun fire, Peadar rummaged in his tunic pocket, trying again to find Sinead's letter or crucifix. Instead he withdrew a crumpled cigarette and a stiff handkerchief, the latter given to him by Sophie during his last visit. She had given him the handkerchief to mop up his own semen from his matted belly.

'Who is that? Is it you, Grogan?'

Clanger's voice came from a shallow shell hole to his right, almost underneath the German wire. Peadar looked up to reply and a bullet passed straight through his left eye and lodged in his neck. Slowly he released the handkerchief and the crumpled cigarette. His last words were, 'Sophie, Sophie!'

'Past days I sing in this refrain,
When Vauxhall Road was Pinfold Lane,
And Mary lived at Vauxhall.
Right well she matched the pretty spot,
And enviable was her lot
At Vauxhall in those old days . . .'

'Seamus, love, that was wonderful!' Sinead clapped her hands in the gathering summer dusk. Some of the strollers smiled. Most of the drunks ignored all three of them.

'Old Mrs Kennedy teached us that song, ma!' clamoured Padraig, tugging at his mother's sleeve, desperate to attract some of the attention.

'But Paddy never really tried to learn all the words.'

'I know them words as good as you, soft lad!' Paddy bobbed his tongue.

'Now that's enough, boys! We've enjoyed our airing. It's getting dark now. We don't want to be about much longer. I don't much fancy getting robbed.' This last remark was made more quietly, as much to herself as to the boys.

It was a hot clammy evening, Saturday of August Bank Holiday weekend 1919. Sinead, now thirty-four years old, had been a widow for three years. It was a year since the Armistice and

Padraig and Seamus were nine. They were walking up the Scotland Road on their way back home, approaching Latarche's the jeweller's, where Conal had been run over the previous June. They always stopped when they reached this spot. Sinead usually cried. The twins were never sure why she did that. They all three of them had loved Conal dearly, but their ma was really soft about him.

'Let's stop just for a moment while I pray to Our Lady for poor Conal,' said Sinead, looking down and closing her eyes. Seamus gazed up into his mother's thin, drawn face and closed his own eyes, just like her. Padraig was getting anxious at the rapidly growing crowds of people about. They were getting rowdy and some were shouting. He tugged again at his mother's sleeve.

'Let's go now, ma. I don't like it with no scuffers.'

'"Policemen", son. They're called "policemen". "Scuffers" is a slang word.'

'Well, policemen, then. People can do what they want if there's no police, can't they?'

Sinead patted her thin yellowish hair back round her ears and looked about her. The shopkeepers had put their shutters up early the day before, and doors were all padlocked. Some of the pawnbrokers had boarded up their windows. There had been no 'bobby on the beat' to be seen since the previous afternoon. Her armpits were damp and nightfall was imminent.

'What do you reckon, then, Popey?'

'Whacker, if you please! Folks call me Whacker.'

'Daft name, Whacker.'

'If it was good enough for the lads at the Front, it's good enough for you, O'Hare.'

'You don't outrank me, you know - Whacker. You can't tell me what to do. We're both constables, you and me both.'

'I'm older than you and I could tip you on your head - if I felt like it, which I don't.'

They went on in this way because they were bored. Nothing had happened since the riot at the Stanley Dock that afternoon when the Bank Holiday crowd had gone berserk in the heat and dust and had broken down the dock gates with crowbars. The Flying Column had moved in and beaten the looters off with staves. They had left one man lying in the tobacco warehouse with a fractured skull, attended to by old Nurse McEwan as the ambulance could not get through the city streets. Constables Pope and O'Hare were part of the Flying Column, despite taunts of 'blackleg' from their colleagues on the force, all of whom were on strike.

After demobilisation, Whacker Pope, a single man in his late twenties, had drifted from one casual job to another, gradually ridding his mind of some of the worst horrors of war. Then, in spring 1919 he had joined a demoralised and cynical police force, where many of his new mates were old soldiers who had 'done their bit for King and Country'. He had joined partly on the expectation of an improvement in police pay following the recommendations of the Desborough Committee and partly for the rent allowance, albeit only two shillings a week at that time. An average police constable earned less than an unskilled labourer and was not allowed to supplement his income with outside work. Once in, he could not resign from the force - he could only be dismissed and heavily fined. So why bother to join? O'Hare because his father and his uncle were constables and Pope because he now craved a regular wage, however modest, and some job security. Yet, hardly had they both started, than the government had refused to allow the force to set up their proposed trade union with its declared aim of improving pay and conditions. The *Daily Mail* had run an article stating 'the police are a semi-military body' and rumours rushed through the force like a mighty wind, even up to HQ at Hatton Garden, about a police strike, the closest thing to anarchy on the streets.

Whacker Pope was trained to obey orders and the very idea of striking was unthinkable to him, whatever his muckers said, and he exerted a strong influence upon O'Hare, still less than twenty years old. To O'Hare, Whacker Pope was a hero. He had survived the Western Front and had rained down massive shells on Jerry. If Pope wasn't going on strike, then neither was he, even though the rest of his family were behind it and his own mother had called them both 'bloody blacklegs'.

No-one really believed there would be a police strike until the Friday evening when Pope and O'Hare were on their way to start their shift. Just outside James Mitty Ltd., tripe dressers, of Great Homer Street, the two men found their way barred by by several pickets, their own mates and some from other stations, all in civilian dress. The two constables were told in no uncertain terms to go back home or to join one of the groups of pickets scattered about the city. They told the men they would go home and both went back to Whacker's rooms above Joseph Cummins the pawnbroker's, not far down the street, near the clock tower. There they discussed their next move over a mug of Whacker's excellent tea, which he still brewed in a billy-can, a habit he found quite impossible to break.

Within thirty minutes and three mugs each, the two men had held several shouted conversations from Whacker's first-floor window with uniformed constables coming along the street in groups of four or five.

'Bloody pickets have ordered us off point duty in Scotland Road and Great Nelson Street!' shouted one PC.

'Why didn't you tell them where to bloody get off?' yelled young O'Hare.

'The same reason you're up there, O'Hare, instead of on your beat! We didn't want to get get beaten to death, mate!' O'Hare signalled his appreciation of these sentiments by raising his tea mug in the open window.

He and Whacker resolved to go down to Lime Street Station next morning early to meet the 'paper train' on platform seven and read the *Daily Herald*, fresh in from London.

'Ma, let's be going,' murmured Padraig, as his mother opened her eyes once more.

'I wish me da was here,' said Seamus, placing his arm protectively around his mother's scrawny waist.

'Oh, so do I, love, so do I!' She took his warm little hand and squeezed it hard. 'Maybe,' she went on, 'maybe I should be praying for your da instead of dirty old Conal.'

Seamus squeezed back. He noticed his mother's normally dry, flaky hand was sticky with sweat. The dim air was hot and heavy, heavy with ale breath and dirty bodies. A large, noisy crowd was building up, reeking of the dockland pubs. Men were playing pitch and toss openly on the pavement, calling 'What the law doesn't know about, won't hurt it!'

Sinead looked desperately about her but there were people all around, hemming in the three of them. The language became foul and the pavement was no place for children now. The mob overflowed on to the road and stopped the traffic. The neighing of panicking horses was confused with the screech of brakes as vehicles made vain attempts to turn round in the road.

'Jesus, Mary and Joseph!' Sinead said under her breath, grasping the twins for all she was worth. Then she saw Clodagh.

Standing taller than many of the men, Clodagh strode through the rabble, as if unaware of any atmosphere of menace, her navy blue summer dress sweeping over the dusty kerbstones. Clodagh's self-assurance and the crowd's acceptance of her, even in expensive garb, filled Sinead with hope and relief. She saw the boys first and smiled broadly, tossing her glossy hair aside as she stooped to talk to them, nodding to Sinead, who bobbed her head awkwardly back.

'You look lovely, Clodagh!' said Sinead levelly, seeing several weeks' wages in that outfit.

'John just dropped me off. He couldn't get the automobile any further. The crowds . . .' She threw up her long arms and a thick gold bracelet slid down towards her elbow.

'John?' shouted Sinead above the hubbub.

'John Corkhill, secretary to the Lord Mayor.' She threw her head back and laughed. Sinead was unsure how to react. She was always unsure with Clodagh. The woman was a sinner, sure, but such a lovely person. How could you not like her?

'What's happening, Clodagh?'

'The scuffers are out. There's a police strike. This lot's about to go on the rampage, I shouldn't wonder.'

'Ma!' shouted Padraig, 'Auntie Clodagh said "scuffers" and you told me . . .'

'Shut up, Paddy!' She jerked his arm and he pulled a face.

'There's not a scuffer on the streets of London, so the *Daily Herald* said, or so John said when he'd read the *Daily Herald*, and lots of other unions are offering to support the boys in blue.'

'My God, Clodagh! Are you certain?'

'Am I certain? "London Police Defy the Government", so the *Herald* said.'

'We've got to get away from here,' said Sinead, shaking slightly.

The arrival of the London paper confirmed it all for Whacker Pope and O'Hare. The *Liverpool Daily Post* provided further confirmation, as if any were needed. A few early risers showed mild interest and cracked a number of predictable jokes about policemen with the newspaper vendor. As the two men passed the steam bakery and flour mill and turned left into Richmond Row on their way back to Whacker's rooms, the streets were eerily quiet and almost deserted. The previous evening, Whacker's pawnbroker landlord had boarded up his windows and padlocked the street entrance. He had written boldly in white chalk right across the window boards, 'No Cash Kept on Premises'.

'I reckon that old Jewboy knows something we don't, mate!'

Whacker had said to O'Hare, prompting the latter to nod, wink and spit in the dust.

After a council of war and more mugs of Whacker's tea, they set out towards Police HQ at Hatton Garden.

'Eh, Whacker, don't you feel funny - in civvies, like, when we should be on shift?'

'Life is all about swapping uniforms, mate, swapping one uniform for another.

'How do you mean, like?'

'Well, didn't I swap the old khaki serge for the police uniform?'

'Yeah, you did, but then there was no more foe, eh?'

'No more Hun, boy, just the bleeding Sergeant Major!'

Both men laughed, the old soldier and the young lad, with less than ten years between the pair of them.

'D'you think God was on our side in the war, Whacker?'

'Somebody was.'

'But didn't the Germans think he was on their side too?'

'Reckon they did. But they were wrong, weren't they, soft lad?'

'Perhaps God was on both sides at once - or on nobody's side - to let them both work it out for themselves.'

'God doesn't play dice, son.' And O'Hare sensed that as far as Whacker was concerned, that was that. You didn't argue for too long with a man who had fired a big howitzer.

'I hope God's on Frank Caldwell's side.'

'Who's Frank Caldwell?'

'Your boss, Whacker. My dad's always on about him. He's the Head Constable of Liverpool. I saw him once.'

'What's he like?'

'Tall, looks kind of straight like a soldier. But he's knocking on a bit, must be going on sixty. Do you feel bad about being a blackleg, like?'

'Words, son, just words. I obey orders, I don't follow the mob. I'm just a pebble on the beach, no more than that.'

'What do you mean, a pebble?'

'Life is very big, son. And you and I are very small. A man

should obey orders and keep his head down. That's why I'm still bloody here talking to an eejit like you! Because I obeyed orders and kept my head down. Remember a man is nothing, no more than a small part of a motor engine. As long as he does his bit, the motor runs smoothly but as soon as he gets fancy notions, and goes off on his own, the motor goes wrong. Then he suffers too. Like my Uncle Sean before the War.'

'What happened to him?'

'He was a bachelor gay, loved the ladies, the dogs and the music hall. One night with a full wage packet he was away to the dog track, when he was robbed and beaten to death by a gang of blokes.'

'That wasn't his fault though, was it?'

'Who's to say, son?'

'Was he a copper?'

'No, Sean was a docker.'

Over a hundred policemen in civilian dress were crowded on to the steps of the Police HQ at 'The Garden'. Cheering and chanting and blowing their whistles, they were happy to open up a gangway for Whacker Pope and his young colleague, until they realised that the two men were going inside the building. Cries of 'blackleg bastards' and 'traitors to the working class' were hurled in their faces. Attempts were made to trip them up. Someone thumped O'Hare in the back, but when Pope turned and looked the man full in the face, he backed off and moved to a lower step.

They made their way towards the sound of voices. It was in the parade room that the Lord Mayor of Liverpool, Alderman John Ritchie, was addressing a meeting of constables, a few of whom were still in uniform. The Lord Mayor, an ex-army officer himself, was asking the men to sign up for a small, platoon-sized corps d'elite, called the 'flying column'. Its function would be to protect the City of Liverpool against riot, looting and anarchy, and it would be whisked from one trouble-spot to another by motor lorry.

Within fifteen minutes, Pope and O'Hare had joined, and within a couple of hours they had helped quell the rioting and looting at Stanley Dock. After this baptism of fire, the only remaining question was what would happen in the Scotland Road after dark, the Orange and the Green, the Pope and King Billy.

It was on the tip of Sinead's tongue to tell Clodagh that the good Lord would protect the four of them but she looked at Clodagh's healthy frame, then thought of her own wasted one and wondered just who was protected and who was not. She had hold of Padraig now and Clodagh clasped Seamus to herself and the noise grew louder in the heat and darkness. Unable to move anywhere, they just huddled together at one side of Latarche's boarded up shop front, being sucked this way and washed that way by the human tide. Then an iron bar slammed into the boards by Sinead's head, making her scream with the shock of it. A fierce, dark-haired youth began to prise the planks off the shop window. Clodagh seized hold of the back of his waistcoat and screamed, 'Have a care, there, you daft bastard! Mind the lady!'

The youth half turned, his stubble almost in Clodagh's face, 'Step back then, if you don't want to get hurt!'

But they could not. There was nowhere to step. The first plank came away after much tugging and cursing, and he threw it at his feet, waving to the cheers and whistles without turning, his mind on his task. Then a second, then a third plank was levered away, revealing an unlit but unmistakeable array of silver rings and trinkets. The young man turned to his crowd, blowing kisses to left and right and giving a shallow bow. The ear-splitting applause and the enormity of what was happening terrified Sinead. Seamus had his eyes tightly shut, while Padraig's were wide as dinner plates. Clodagh was simply impatient to move on and tutted and rolled her brown eyes and tapped her foot.

Then, from the midst of the mob, after repeated scuffling and yelling for silence, a man rose up on a box, which placed him head and shoulders above everyone else. The hush spread all around and took hold like fire, until all was quiet. All faces turned towards the raised arms of the rickety, underfed individual who stood, waiting to speak. Like a scarecrow come to life, the sickly young man nodded knowingly at his audience. His bony hands patted the sticky night air placatingly. Had his timing not been so uncannily well judged, he would have started speaking by now. But he waited. He was good.

After a good fifteen seconds of near silence, he slowly raised his upturned palm in a gesture of despair, eyebrows raised.

'And what, ladies and gentlemen, have we here? He indicated the exposed glass front of the jeweller's. 'The imposing jewellery emporium of Mr Latarche.' The sea of caps and hats stood becalmed, holding its breath.

'And what, comrades, does this here emporium remind you of?' Still they waited, hoping he was going to tell them.

'It reminds you of your own empty pockets, does it not?' Murmurs of agreement.

'It reminds you of your own poverty, does it not?' Louder agreement.

'It is a symbol, brothers, of the rich man's buying power. How many of you here in Scotland Road tonight have ever shopped in there?' He jerked his head up to emphasize his question, his eyes bulging, full of irony. Cries of 'Hear! Hear!' and outbreaks of cheering followed. He raised his hand for silence.

'And tonight, comrades, the police, the protectors of the rich and their property, are sadly not with us!' Raucous laughter and more cheering.

'And so, fellow workers, we have been granted a chance here to redress the balance of things, have we not?' Excitement ran like electricity round the crowd, as the realisation dawned of what was being suggested.

Then another voice piped up, 'To redress the balance indeed! You tell 'em, Morrison!'

'Thank you, brother. Another voice to bring moral support to the workers!' He pointed to the unhealthy-looking figure with the gaudy check cap who was wrestling to loosen his collar as if he were about to be suffocated.

'Moral support it is,' he gasped. 'Support to the workers!'

Morrison nodded at his supporter and continued, 'So how, comrades, are we to show our intention to bring about a more just spread of the good things in this life?'

'How indeed? How indeed, Morrison?' The red-faced man in the check cap forced his way through the crowd to the window of the jeweller's and pointed gleefully at the silver inside.

'That's how, Morrison, that's how!' A roar went up and chaos broke out.

Sinead now understood that she and the boys were right in the line of fire. She slid down the wall to a sitting position, dragging Padraig with her. Clodagh stood tall and proud, facing the mob, hands on hips, releasing the quivering Seamus to his mother, who was clawing the air for his hand.

One of the planks was taken up by two men like a battering ram and thrust straight through the window with a satisfying crash and a shower of glass splinters. There still not being room for a man to walk through into the shop, they rammed the remains of the window and barely managed to stagger clear before the mob charged past them, through the gaping hole and into the darkness of the shop.

Sinead and the boys crouched motionless, covered in glass, while the shop was ransacked. Clodagh had thrust her way in with the looters, saying to Sinead, 'In for a penny, in for a pound!'

The next thing Sinead knew was that somewhere a whistle was blowing. Inside Latarche's there was confusion as the heavily laden looters struggled back out through the shattered window. Cries of, 'The scuffers!' and the sound of clogs and boots pounding over broken glass were followed by hesitation and confusion.

'There isn't no scuffers!' came a voice. 'The scuffers is on strike!'

There came a loud revving of engines and a squeal of brakes, then the clumping of lots of men jumping to the ground and coming nearer, running, blowing whistles. The looters inside Latarche's held their breath, as did Sinead, Padraig and Seamus, cowering just outside, still covered with bits of broken window.

About a dozen men in civilian clothes stood in line, facing the gaping hole, all carrying staves. One of them stepped forward, crunching on the remains of the glass. He cupped his hands to his mouth: 'Drop your goods and stand still!'

A defiant voice from the darkness within replied, 'And who the bloody hell might you be?'

'Special police. The Flying Column. Stand still and put the items down.'

'Bugger off! We ain't taking no notice of you!'

Something heavy flew out of the darkness and struck one of the policemen on the side of the head. It was a large silver trophy cup. The man went down without a sound, bleeding. The 'column' charged and the looters, far from trying to flee, came forward to meet them. Scattered all over the floor were shards of glass, silverware of all shapes and sizes, rings and watches. The looters began to fall back under the well-orchestrated deluge of blows which left groaning heaps rocking in the gloom.

Whacker Pope thought the job was more or less over and was thinking about herding the looters on to the trucks when he heard a sound to his right and saw a man with a heavy sack. The noise he had heard was the man's laboured breathing and he was attempting a getaway through a side door, his sack so full of booty that he could scarcely drag it along the floor. Pope took in the weasel features and showy check cap, so oddly mismatched. The man might have looked laughable had he been in a comic paper cartoon or in the music hall. They eyed each other.

'Drop it!'

The weasel did not drop it. More vehicles could be heard drawing up nearby. His black little eyes cast round the shop and up and down, his breath rasping.

'I said drop it!' repeated Pope. He did not drop it.

Heavy footsteps approached.

'It's the army, man! Drop the sack and don't be a fool!' Still he clutched at the sack.

Pope turned to see the squaddies coming in and at that moment the other man lunged at him with a short iron bar. Pope dodged to one side and the blow landed on his arm instead of his head. His arm immediately went numb along its whole length and Whacker guessed it was broken. The weasel came forward again. Whacker was not ready. He had been caught on the hop. He braced himself instinctively, his good arm protecting his head. There was an ear-splitting bang. A pistol shot. Pope opened his eyes slowly, confused. Who had fired and who had been hit? The looter slumped forward into the broken glass, his sack disgorging its contents all over the floor.

Sinead, still crouching outside, had frozen to the spot at the sound of the soldier's gunshot in the enclosed space. She had heard the man fall to the floor and she gazed in astonishment as his bright check cap rolled past her across the kerb and into the gutter. She stared at it as if hypnotised. She could not take her eyes off it and began to tremble uncontrollably. As Whacker Pope and the squaddie carried the body out of the shop, through the broken window and on to the pavement, where they set it down, Sinead began to sob. The corpse lay only feet away.

Pope stooped to her and the two little boys.

'You all right, missis?'

'Yes, thank you.'

'Those little lads all right?'

'Yes, thank you.'

'Did you know him?'

'Not really.' That struck Whacker as a strange answer.

'Never mind,' he said, and then, as an afterthought, 'My Uncle Sean used to wear a cap like that, God rest him.'

But Sinead was not listening.

'"The city was in a state of anarchy," said John Corkhill, secretary to the Lord Mayor.' Sinead let Clodagh's *Echo* slip to the floor. Clodagh! Clodagh! She took money from Mr Corkhill, she then helped to ransack a jeweller's, then bought a newspaper to read what one said of the other! She was a bit like Auntie Dora only more so. Sinead wondered whether she felt a grudging admiration for the pair of them, not for what they represented but for their sheer survival power. They had a philosophy that worked, however ungodly. What on earth must Clodagh's confessions sound like?

That Wednesday morning Sinead had felt more than usually sick, although she had neither been near any TNT nor been in paid employment at all since the Armistice. The night sweats were still robbing her of her sleep and her skin looked seriously jaundiced. Her hair, a faded yellow, resembled a clematis that has died down to dry sticks for the winter. She patted it back, such as it was, and adjusted her framed embroidery half-heartedly.

The boys were unwilling to go to school and they were going to be late. It had been harder to get them off to school since Conal had been run over. Spreading the dripping on their bread had nearly made her sick and she was aware of Seamus's concerned little face, though she avoided looking at him.

'Eat up, both of you. You're going to be late.'

Even her voice was feeble. She turned aside, so as not to see them chomping. Her face was going hot and her mouth started to fill with saliva. God! she thought, I'm going to throw up. But she was wrong. She fell off her chair and crashed sideways to the floor.

Seamus panicked: 'She's dead, Paddy. Ma's dead!'

Padraig knelt to his mother and put his ear to her face, moving her chair aside.

'Sure she is not, soft lad! She's fainted.'

Seamus knelt to join his brother. They looked down at her sunken, yellow face, which looked more dead than alive, much more dead than when she was asleep. Padraig shook her arm. Seamus whispered in her ear, ' Ma, it's Seamus and Paddy. Come back to us, Ma'

Then Padraig sat back on his heels and started sobbing: 'First me da and now her! They're going to leave us on our own, you know.'

Seamus was horrified. 'Don't say that, Paddy! She loves us and she'll wake up in a minute.'

'No! She doesn't care. She'll just die and leave us here. It's not fair!' He poked his mother twice on the shoulder.

'Stop it, Paddy! She's tired because she works all hours for you and me, first in the factory and now at home.'

'Well, she shouldn't if she's going to leave us both alone like orphan boys in the workhouse.'

'You're a pig, you, you're a pig like the Germans in the War. Ma's took bad and you just complain. Think about our ma, will you?'

'She's all we've got left!' wailed Padraig.

'So, let's help her and take care of her.'

'She's lying very still, Seamus.'

'Yes, she is.'

Sinead Grogan's funeral took place at St Anthony's Roman Catholic Church, Scotland Road, at half past two in the afternoon of 4th October 1919 in the rain. She was thirty-four. The cause of death was stated to be 'yellow jaundice'. No-one bothered to delve further.

The poor rough coffin was so light, Jabez said, as he and Mr O'Brien lifted it on to the waiting cart, you could believe it to be empty. Both coffin and cart were provided by Lionel Hunt at Clodagh's suggestion, though Lionel himself was kept away by his 'poor, poor feet'. Nurse McEwan had supervised the laying out, assisted by Mrs Morrison, who still clung stubbornly to life having seen off many stronger than herself. She insisted that the cold and

Larry's beatings made her 'resistant to passing over'.

As was customary, only the menfolk were present at the graveside, but away in a far corner of the cemetery, huddled together under one leaking umbrella, Ethel and Weena from the armament factory wept silently. Clodagh and Mrs O'Brien organised the wake at No. 12 Oswald Street, financed by the secretary to the Lord Mayor, though Mrs O'Brien did not know it. Father Brendan's latin clattered from his mouth, for the man was clearly frozen to the very marrow.

The childless O'Briens of No. 12, still adamant they sometimes saw Conal out of the corner of their eye, welcomed the boys into their home. They knew each other very well, as the boys had lived much of the war years in the O'Briens' place anyway. Mr O'Brien, now working full-time at the Abercromby, was better placed these days than before the Armistice. So, by a circuitous route, some of old Mrs Kennedy's few sticks of furniture found their way back to No. 12, where they had started. Poor Sinead's sea still washed this way and that, nudging people and chattels all round the city.

The O'Briens' place boasted two rooms, which had always impressed Padraig, trotting from one to the other, to check both really existed at once. There was the front parlour, where old Mrs K. had been laid out, and there was the scullery at the back with an enormous sink in which Conal had been scrubbed, when they could catch him.

At first Seamus cried a lot for his mother and kept stepping up to straighten her framed embroidery BE STRONG IN THE LORD which now hung in the O'Briens' parlour. Padraig told all his school friends that he and his brother now lived in a much bigger place, though he thought less and less about No. 8 as the months went by. Seamus, in contrast, often spent the duration of a large sticky bull's-eye gazing at the back entrance and sloping privy roof of his former home. One large family had come and gone at the Grogans' old place - moved in in autumn 1919, to be evicted for non-payment of rent in early spring 1920. For weeks after that, the room remained unoccupied. 'Locked up like a museum,' Mrs Morrison announced to the O'Briens each time they passed No. 8. Mrs O'Brien shook her head sadly at all the dogs' mess and litter spread over the steps there, not like in poor Mrs Grogan's time.

It was in that spring that Seamus went missing. One Saturday morning, Padraig realised that he was stacking the beds in the scullery alone. He folded the bedclothes into an untidy heap in the far corner by the yard door and leaned the two heavy bedsteads together on their sides against the wall. It was hard work for a ten year-old and he cursed Seamus aloud for not being there to help him.

'Auntie O, Seamus has gone!'

'He'll be around,' came Mrs O'Brien's reply from the front parlour, drifting across on a waft of Johnson's wax and Brasso. She was meticulous just as Padraig recalled his mother being meticulous, before she had gone out to work at Maguire Street. Mrs O'Brien sang as she worked too, usually something by Marie Lloyd about 'what a silly girl I am' or her husband's favourite *The Coster Girl in Paris.* Sinead had always insisted that cleanliness was next to godliness, yet, although the O'Briens were not churchgoers - and indeed Mr O'Brien held some quite daring modern views - their two rooms were cleanliness itself and never a rat to be seen. So, decided Padraig, you didn't really need God in order to lead a good life with nice things. He would think of his mother's shrunken body and exhausted face as she dragged herself, him and Seamus to Mass, and wonder whether she was not so much noble as rather misguided and foolish.

At midday, Mr O'Brien knocked off from the Abercromby and came home whistling 'Now give three cheers and one cheer more' from *HMS Pinafore* and reeking of animal fat and oil cake. A spruce, greying forty year-old with a heavy moustache which fascinated Padraig, Matt O'Brien was brought up to date in the parlour about the disappearance of Seamus.

Ní maith liom é, Caitlin,' he muttered.

'English in front of Paddy, please, Matt.'

'I don't like it, Kate.' He brushed his moustache aside with the back of an index. 'Paddy and me shall go and look for him.'

Padraig was delighted. He liked to be seen with Uncle O'Brien, because he noticed how all the ladies nodded to him in the street and smiled a funny sort of smile. Padraig hoped they would do that to him when he was older. He could not be sure what the smile meant but he sensed it meant excitement and some kind of mastery. When women had greeted his da, it was more with respect than any kind of private knowledge. And his da had only one room!

Man and boy hammered on doors as the spring shadows lengthened along Oswald Street. Matt O'Brien's breath came faster with growing panic. Twice Padraig complained that he was squeezing his hand too hard. They went down Dryden Street to the biscuit works. Nothing. Again they knocked on doors. Some folks were sympathetic. Some told them to 'piss off'. They went up to St Anthony's and walked round the church and the school building, shouting Seamus's name. No response in the thickening gloom. Matt was beside himself: 'Ró dhorcha, Padraig, ró dhorcha! It's too dark! We've lost him!'

'Let's try one more place, Uncle.'

Matt just looked down at him, grateful, his own inspiration all drained. Now it was Padraig who led him by the hand, back along the Scotland Road, left into Dryden Street and left again into Oswald Street and another left half way along into the black ginnel that ran between the last few courts on that side of the street. At the back of No. 8 they halted. The stench of the Abercromby hung in the air, although neither man nor boy noticed it.

'Wait here, Uncle O.'

'Where the divil are you going then, Paddy?'

In response the boy took a run at the wall, reached up and hauled himself up on to the top. Then he swung his legs down the other side and unbolted the back yard door. Matt tipped his cap farther back on his head and crept into the yard behind him, as they approached the back door of the house in the pitch dark. Neither said a word. Padraig took the door handle in both hands and, with a practised movement, lifted the whole door and jerked it hard against its hinges. He then pushed it open, the lock still protruding in the engaged position.

They were greeted by a smell of damp and lamp-oil. A sliver of yellow light showed under a door to their left. It was the door of the Grogan's old room. Matt envied Padraig's self-assurance as they moved towards the door. 'Ignorance is bliss,' he said to himself, picturing drunken scallies and homeless cut-throats. While he held back in the darkness, Padraig moved forward and took hold of the door knob.

'Wait, Paddy!' rasped Matt. 'How do you know who's in there?'

'Listen!' Padraig whispered back.

'What?'

'Just listen!'

Very faintly from inside the room came the sound of humming, tuneless but cheerful.

Padraig turned the knob and tip-toed in, followed by Matt, who slipped off his cap and pressed it to his chest as if he were going into church.

Inside, the room was touched by the low shallow glimmer of an oil lamp, placed low and turned right down. The corners were in darkness and huge shadows played on the ceiling. Squatting cross-legged in the middle of the bare floor was a rocking figure. Hands braced on his knees, he rocked to and fro, humming softly, the oil lamp on the floor in front of him. It was an arresting picture. Padraig knew his father would have crossed himself.

'Seamus!' said Matt quietly, wondering why he was not shouting, Seamus, where the divil have you been? We've all been sick with worrying.'

Seamus turned and beamed disarmingly, 'I've been here where I used to live.'

'We saw no light from the street,' struggled Matt.

'I've only just lit it.'

'Seamus, you're soft!' said Padraig. 'Uncle and Auntie O. thought you was dead.'

'Paddy, that dirty square on the wall there is where "Be Strong in the Lord" used to hang.' He sounded as if he were talking in his sleep. Matt, speechless, was searching the floor for inspiration.

'Why did you come creeping in here then, soft lad?'

'I didn't creep, I just came. I came to think and look back. We've hardly thought about Ma and Da since they went over. Anyway Paddy, you showed me how to get over the wall and through the back yard door in the first place.'

Padraig ignored that and instead continued to crow, '"Went over"? You mean "died", don't you?'

'No, I don't mean "died". That's the wrong word for what happens.'

'Well now, Seamus,' offered Matt, now endeavouring to become master of the situation, 'You stay a few more minutes if you want, lad, then come home, because we're all worried.'

'All right, Uncle O.'

It was in the summer of 1922 that the rest of Padraig's life really started. A misty Sunday morning sun chased the shadows along the walls of Oswald Street. It lit the crown of the soft felt hat of the rag and bone man whose cartwheels graunched and ground over the cobble stones by No. 12. Mrs Morrison's scabby little mongrel sat and scratched itself in the warm, dusty gutter, showing only a passing interest in the raucous cries of 'Any old iron and rag bone? Any old iron?' as the laden cart trundled past within a couple of inches of his motionless tail. An old dear with a besom appeared on her steps opposite O'Briens' and set to sweeping furiously, ignoring with stalwart and practised deafness the screams of numerous small urchins coming from inside her place. Little had changed here since the War, though there were more motor cars on Scotland Road for sure. Padraig had got into the habit of sitting on the wall outside his school on a Saturday morning, watching the traffic chuff past, mesmerised, oblivious of the time. It even beat sneaking into the moving picture show at the Homer, because here were sounds, smoke and smells - petrol and hot oil, rubber and, if you could get close enough, leather.

All Padraig wanted was a ride in a motor car. He dreamed of being a motorist and of enjoying the glamorous existence that went with that dream - of racing the Blue Train down to Cannes, whatever that meant - it was something Uncle O. joked about whenever Padraig raised the subject of motoring.

'All you need, Paddy, is as much money as Jack Dempsey or Rudolf Valentino or even the Prince of Wales! Then you can race the Blue Train down to Cannes!'

This would start Padraig sulking until Seamus whispered to him, 'At least we're not in the poorhouse, Paddy.' They always had to be grateful to their guardians for that. Gratitude, however, was too poor a food to satisfy Padraig's hunger.

Even he had to admit, though, that the charabanc trip to Southport was about the most exciting prospect in his whole twelve years, and it was this morning and, as Seamus said, God knew it too, because He had made the sun shine for them. Padraig had been sick in the night with excitement and the fear that something would go wrong in the fragile and untrustworthy universe - he would be taken seriously ill, Seamus would start wheezing, the O'Briens would run out of money, the house would fall down in the night . . . .

Seamus had emptied his sick bowl since he himself would not even look at it and had told Padraig that if it was to be, it would be and nothing could prevent it, but that if it was not to be, then nothing upon this earth could make it happen.

'You talk just like our ma,' was all Padraig could say as his brother rinsed the bowl out and felt his hot forehead like Nurse McEwan.

For Seamus, it was just their first family day out ever, and something to look forward to. He was equally concerned that Uncle and Auntie O. should enjoy themselves, because they were their guardians and they deserved a good time as a reward. For Padraig it meant the opening up of a whole new world, motoring for fifteen whole miles right out of Liverpool to another town. It meant 'travel'! In the charabanc, they would share the main road with rich people in Tin Lizzies, Morrises, Rileys and even Rolls Royces. He wanted desperately to sit next to the driver. It was the driver who had the mysterious knowledge of all the dials, levers and pedals. It was he who had control of the powerful beast and his seat was a most obvious position of authority. Padraig asked Seamus to put in a word for him with the driver but his brother smiled and said, ' Look, Paddy, as long as we get a seat and we can see where we're going, who cares where the seat is?'

'You always seem to know where you're going,' whinged Padraig, disgruntled.

'You always need to be the one in control. Uncle O. said that. You've got no trust. That's what our da used to tell you.'

With a wedge of bread and dripping each they shambled down to Dryden Street to wait for the charabanc, which would avoid Oswald Street, being unable to turn round there. Matt and Caitlin joined them after a few minutes and there the four of them stood with the warm sun on their backs. The dark brooding courts perked up, to become brighter and more cheerful in the light that would brook no shadow later. Sash windows flew up with a bang and net curtains floated out to brush stone window sills. The Abercromby, the Vauxhall and the biscuit factory seemed to be turning dark yellow in the brightness. It was a new feeling; instead of doing up your coat against the cold, you closed your eyes against the sunlight and luxuriated in the redness before them.

When the charabanc turned into Dryden Street, Padraig's heart missed a beat and his stomach cartwheeled with excitement. Seamus just felt relieved that they would soon be setting off at last. It chugged alongside the family group, the passengers already aboard squinting curiously down at them. Padraig noted with satisfaction that they looked windblown, although the morning was perfectly still. It was sheer speed that had ruffled their hair and billowed their coats and scarves. Coats and scarves on such a summer's day! It all seemed to speak to Padraig of a toff's life. He tarried on the kerb, while the others clambered on to the lower of the two running boards, where they clasped the hands reaching down to pull them up on to the next one and in to a seat. Padraig took in the big, heavy-spoked, solid wheels, like the wheels of a cart but smaller and more racy looking, the five rows of seats. each with its own door on either side and the collapsible black hood, all concertinaed together at the very back behind the rear passengers. He was filled with thankfulness that the morning was not wet, so that today he would feel the wind and see everything.

He heard Uncle O. shout to the driver, 'Driver, could one of my lads sit beside you, if you please?'

The driver nodded without turning, and elbowed the youth beside him to move over so there was a space between them.

The driver growled to the youth, 'And you can wipe that scowl off your face as soon as you like or you'll be bloomin' walking to Southport!'

Seamus, Uncle and Auntie O. sat three rows from the front, whilst Padraig squashed in past the driver and sat at the front, beaming at the insect-covered windscreen, over the fuel filler cap and along the sweeping bonnet, down to the radiator cap.

'Keep your eyes on the road for me, son,' said the driver.

Padraig was far too excited to do more than swallow and nod, unable to remove the foolish grin from his face. Seamus was thinking what a shame it was that his ma and da could not be there with them, going out of town on a trip to the seaside. He could not remember either of them ever leaving Liverpool, until his da went over to France to fight in the War.

Matt was muttering greetings through his moustache to his small team of oil-seed press operators, their wives and children, when an abrupt clank signalled that the vehicle was now in gear. Padraig pressed his hands down into the worn leather and arched his back to get the best possible view of the road ahead. The engine's tone fell an octave and Dryden Street began to move by. Having turned round at the junction with Oswald Street, the charabanc was soon cruising north up the Scotland Road. The breeze, the burr of cobblestones and the buzz of adult conversation sent Seamus into a doze, his cropped head lolling against Caitlin's shoulder. Matt shouted right along the vehicle, announcing how much was left in the kitty after the return journey was paid for. Six whole months' savings were there, to include a meal in a cafeteria or tea room. Padraig felt vaguely proud of Uncle O's being a sort of leader but he did not turn round to listen to him. Instead his eyes followed the to-and-fro and side-to-side shifts of the long gear lever. His ears rejoiced in the changing song of the engine, now high and urgent, now low and purring. The driver turned to him and winked. Padraig felt like a member of an exclusive club. He looked at passing motor cars as if to say, 'I'm one of you lot! I do this sort of thing too, you know!'

They passed all sorts of other vehicles from lorries laden with coal sacks or barrels to motor cars whisking elegant couples towards the smoky city behind them. The air became clearer than Padraig had ever known it. The houses and shops thinned out and the green countryside began to assert itself. It was a scene from his own fancy!

Just ahead of them was a smart couple spooning in a Model T. Padraig was curious. The man sported a cap and gauntlets, while his partner's soft hat had a broad, drooping brim garlanded with flowers, and her her black coat had fur-covered lapels and cuffs. The car looked small, shiny and black. It was sleek and hard, like a projectile in Padraig's mind. It represented determination and aggressiveness. Down low at the front were two large gaping headlamps. The shiny little grille, Padraig knew, had 'Ford' written along the top in wavy script. The two sidelights squinted farther back on either side of the tiny, wafer-like windscreen. The hood lay casually folded back at the rear. The running board was the minimum possible and the steering wheel looked like a child's model. So careless and yet so chic - the whole picture!

People like them always looked good, whatever they were doing.

Again and again the lady kissed the driver on the cheek and nestled her face against his coat. The man, unmoved, leaned his arm along the top of the door as he drove, a man who had everything - a motor car and a pretty companion! Padraig could only guess at his self-assured conversation, the throwaway comments, the lack of anxiety or preoccupation, the cavalier disdain of financial constraints. Could an orphan kid from Oswald Street ever be like that? The alternative - a job in the Abercromby, saving six months for a day out in a charabanc, was too awful to contemplate.

School days came to an end a few months after that.
Easter 1923 found Seamus bagging sawdust at the saw-mill in Ashfield Street near the corner with the Vauxhall Road. It made him wheeze and hawk, though young Mairead Ryan. Still at Saint Anthony's Girls' School, brought him juvenile solace with her Saturday afternoon visits at the mill - a cheese sandwich like a manhole cover and a warm, damp kiss. Padraig, whom nowadays everybody seemed to know as Paddy, worked at Harding's Garage and Cycle Repair Shop under Love Lane railway viaduct, opposite Britannia Warehouses.

The next generation of Grogans waded into the sea of life, Seamus regular as clockwork at Confession, often dragging Auntie O along with him, and Paddy, his head turning this way and that at the material things of this world. Father Brendan would sigh and ask of Seamus, 'Now where is that twin brother of yours?'

'Underneath a motor car, Father!' would be the reply.

'Dear Lord above! I hope he's not hurt?'

'He is not, Father. He's repairing the steering on a Morris.'

'I wish he'd steer himself back to God. I fear we shall lose him, Seamus.'

'We never had him in the first place, Father.'

1924 - 1939

God and Mammon

For what is the hope of the hypocrite, though he hath gained, when God taketh away his soul?

Job Chapter 27 Verse 8

Stan Gardner still made the occasional detour in his Rolls Royce to see his old factory in Maguire Street. What a money spinner that had been! During the war years and through 1919 his artillery shells had lined his pockets with gold. He had retired in 1920, a fortnight before his forty-second birthday. While shaving every morning he would reflect that each time one of his shells exploded at Ypres, on the Somme or in the mud of Paschendaele, more coins cascaded into his coffers. Even if some failed to explode at all, still Stan stood to gain. And gain he did - with an eight bedroom mansion in Speke, an assortment of mistresses and all the trappings of sudden wealth. When a reporter from the Echo asked him whether he felt he traded in death, he had snorted, 'No more than your family butcher does!'

Starting out at twenty-one with a modest inheritance, Stan had 'done all right'. He had anticipated the need for ordnance early in 1914 before Britain had joined the war. He had acquired the Maguire Street factory for a song and borrowed massively to refurbish and equip it. He broke even within six months with a loss of only four girls - two in a small explosion and two from 'yellow poisoning', a condition he insisted was 'in folks' own imagination'. Since that time of course there had followed many more deaths. But Stan had had the stomach to take the sort of risk that lesser men would pale at.

'You can't make a good meal without breaking a few eggs and whipping the bloody cream!'

He had just come from Maguire Street to see the levelled site of the old factory, cleared for houses, and was driving south down Love Lane for the second time, when he plucked up courage and pulled into Harding's for petrol.

'Harding's Motor Engineers and Cycle Repairs' announced the sign over an arch of the railway viaduct. On the rubble- and puddle-strewn yard stood a single petrol pump. Taller than a man, it was open at the front, displaying its mechanical innards to passers by on Love Lane. Upon its round head were tattooed the letters 'BP'. It had a long white hose and brass nozzle, like a thin, pale arm, stuck in its ear. In place of a heart it had a round gauge, showing how much petrol had been transfused into the gasping motor car.

Stan stopped at the pump, his heart pounding with anticipation. He tried not to look towards the lock-up but gazed casually at the Silver Lady in frozen gracefulness atop his radiator grille.

Hilda Harding had married a younger man who had fallen at Mons, leaving her, a pretty young widow, with a rather grimy but quite profitable garage business, and a daughter Greta, just fifteen years old. Stan was especially excited by Hilda's dark blue hat, like a blue bell, with its ribboned rim which shaded her eyes and made her look at once mysterious yet modest, that modesty which seems to hint at the potential for unbridled passion.

'Like an inverted piss-pot,' thought Stan, but on her head it became a thing of beauty. Then she would wear a dark-coloured blouse and calf-length pleated skirt or, if she were actually serving at the pump, blue dungarees. Hilda's dungarees were Stan's most vivid erotic fantasy. When she bent and stretched to pump the petrol, Stan's chest became quite uncomfortably constricted.

His day now took a turn for the worse when, instead of Hilda, a thin, hungry-looking youth with cropped brown hair and an expression of intense alertness, loped towards his vehicle. Carrying the cranking handle to work the pump, the youth might have appeared threatening, had he not had a lost look about him, like a poor swimmer treading water.

'How now, young Paddy?' Stan forced a smile at the youth.

'Mr Gardner,' mumbled the youth, touching his forehead in an awkward salute.

'Fill her up, if you please.' His eyes scanned the lock-up as Paddy unscrewed the filler cap.

'Yes, Mr Gardner.'

He fitted the handle on to the winding capstan, unlooped the hose and poked the nozzle into the Rolls Royce's echoing tank. Stan slid out of his seat and stepped outside. He stretched his arms and closed his eyes into slits, looking for a moment as if he were being crucified, the hem of his fur coat lifting several inches.

'And how is Mrs Harding?' He avoided Paddy's eyes and held his breath.

'All right, Mr Gardner.'

Stan swallowed his irritation. 'Well, is the lady on the premises today?' There, he had said it!

'Yes, Mr Gardner. She's inside at the back, doing the books.

'I'll just go and pay my respects. Clean the windscreen, Paddy, and you can sit inside and turn the wheel.'

'Yes, Mr Gardner!' Padraig's face lit up at once. This man and his Rolls Royce were a direct link in the golden chain which could pull him in to the world of money, if only he could think of a way of attaching himself to it. This gnawing need gave him no peace, from the moment his eyes opened in the morning till the moment when at last he found fitful sleep at night. Sometimes even in his dreams he smelled thick, blue cigar smoke, leather motor car seats and perfume like Mrs Harding's.

'Do you want a mug of tea, Paddy Grogan?' Greta stood watching him turn the pump handle, cool in her long, dark blue dress with its little white buttons all the way down and her crisply permed brown hair and wide hazel eyes.

'Yes please.' He felt hot and dirty.

'Yes please who, Paddy Grogan?' One hand was on her hip, the other toying with her ear-lobe.

'Yes please, Greta.' It was no skin off his nose if that was the way she wanted to play it.

'What happened to "Miss Harding" or "Miss Greta"?'

'You said we could drop all that mullarkey.' His posture was sheepish but there was no mistaking the growing cocksure look in his eyes. 'Tell your ma that her pump attendant and dog's-body has jacked it in and she can look for another eight months for the next one.'

'Don't be so cheeky. Do you want one or not?'

'If Bob's having one, I'll have one.'

'Bob's a mechanic, not an unskilled labourer.' She pouted and smiled triumphantly.

'So will I be soon, Greta Harding.'

'We'll see, slum boy!' Spinning on her heel, she flounced off in the direction of the lock-up. Paddy watched her go before he started pumping again. He carried on watching until she had disappeared inside. Then he pumped with desperate vigour, as if exorcising some demon.

'Do you mind if I smoke, Mrs Harding - or may I call you Hilda?' Stan reached inside his fur coat and carefully withdrew a long thick Havana.

'We have a business relationship, Mr Gardner. I certainly would not dream of calling you Stanley. You buy my petroleum, I service your motor car. What more is there to it?'

Hilda nodded assent to his box of matches and raised eyebrow. Blue smoke rose in the small office.

'I like to think there might be more - Hilda.' She rolled her eyes and clasped her hands together upon the well-organised little desk which separated them.

'I trust you are not being improper - Mr Gardner!' Her smile was relaxed.

'Not in the very least - Hilda!' His was even more relaxed. 'I'm merely thinking business, that's all.' He exhaled smoke noisily and squinted at Hilda against the grey light from the window behind her. Her hair was translucent, like a chestnut halo.

'What business have we to discuss? Surely you are not going to ask for credit arrangements for your petrol?' She leaned forward slightly, her eyebrows perfect arches, her mouth a perfect cupid's bow, in fact she was perfection itself! Stan thought about kissing those lips - very, very softly. He squirmed slowly in his chair, but not slowly enough for Hilda to miss it. He drew hard on his cigar.

'As you are aware, Hilda, for I shall call you Hilda, I am a wealthy man.' He waited for her agreement. Instead she rose and reached up to take an ashtray from a shelf stuffed with ledgers. She placed it in front of Stan, who was starting to look warm and flushed. He nodded and tapped off a long grey inch of ash. Inside the ashtray was a motif of a bent and bearded St Christopher carrying a man on his back, above the legend 'Christopher, be my Guide'. Stan observed in passing that his ash had fallen full in St Christopher's face, obscuring it.

Undeterred, he went on, 'And I am also a bored man, a man with time on his hands.' He examined the nails of his left hand and threw a sideways glance to see whether Hilda might be looking at him. She was looking at the clock on the wall behind Stan, just above the door.

'Money does not impress me, Mr Gardner. This business, though small in your estimation, I am sure, keeps me and my daughter very well, thank you. My late husband also left me provided for with savings and a modest war pension. . . .'

'Quite the contrary, I do assure you. I am your most ardent admirer - as a businesswoman of course!' How confounded hot the little office was!

'Very kind of you, I'm sure.' A large part of Hilda now wanted this man with his big cigar and fancy notions to leave and let her get on with running her business, but a small part was intrigued and ready to allow this cat and mouse conversation to continue. She knew Stan had seen her glance at the clock. He appeared uncomfortable and possibly had other fish to fry. So she ventured, 'You see, the business runs itself. Bob is the mechanic, Paddy is the apprentice and Greta helps me with the clerical work.'

Stan sat back in his chair and blew smoke down his nose: 'Bob is old and tired and lives for the day when he can graze on his allotment up by the Liverpool Locks. Paddy is only a young lad but he's keen and hungry and he's very good. If you don't keep his fires stoked up, you'll lose him to a bigger garage.' And as for Greta, thought Stan, all she wants is to spend all day spooning with Paddy, though she probably doesn't even know it herself!

'Greta is very good at selling the cycles,' offered Hilda weakly, watching another gobbet of ash fall on the saint's face.

'Forget about cycles, Hilda! The future lies with the motor car. Soon, almost every family will own a motor car and they will buy vast quantities of petrol and they will need skilled mechanics like Paddy.'

He saw Hilda grimace with disbelief at the idea of the motor car ceasing to be the plaything of the better off. 'Hilda, I've stood outside your workshop out there,' he jerked a thumb behind him towards the door, 'and heard people ask for Paddy Grogan by name. He's keen and he's thorough.'

'What is your point - Stanley?'

'That's better! That's much better!' he beamed. 'My point, Hilda, is that you might consider purchasing another garage in addition to this one, keep old Bob here and get another mechanic to supervise Paddy in the new place. Then buy a third garage and put Paddy in charge of it in three or four years' time.'

'Just a moment, Stanley! How on earth am I supposed to finance all that?'

She already knew the answer, so it came as no surprise when Stan replied quietly, Not you, my dear - me!'

Now who is that plump young thing mincing down Ashfield Street with her battered straw hat, her white blouse, her black skirt and her black, laced boots going click, clack over the cobblestones? She is only just in the teens of her years if she's a day! Thirteen years old and no more. She draws the shawl closer about her shoulders for the damp coming in off the docks. Her raven-black hair is cut so short, it all but hides inside her hat. She is not pretty, but she is trim and those are good child-bearing hips, unless I am much mistaken! And what might she be carrying in that greaseproof paper? It looks like sandwiches to me. Why now she comes closer, I can see it's the young Ryan girl - now what in Heaven is her name - Mary? Marie? No, I seem to recall she has a good Irish name. Mairead! That's it, Mairead, Mairead Ryan.

'Good day to you, Mairead!'

'Good day, Nurse McEwan!'

Aye, thirteen years ago I delivered her, around 1911 I suppose it would be, twelve months after the Grogans came over from the Old Country.

'And where would you be off to then, young lady?'

'I'm away to Dayntree's just along the street.'

'Dayntree's, is it? Now what would you be wanting there, pray?'

'I'm seeing my young man, to take him his snap.'

'Works at the sawmill then, does he?'

'He does so. He bags the sawdust. It's a responsible job, bagging the sawdust,'

'To be sure it is, child, to be sure it is. And who might this young beau be?'

'Seamus Grogan, Nurse McEwan. He's very God-fearing. He goes to Confession regular as clockwork and he goes to the Mass more than once a week.'

'Well well, Seamus Grogan is it? To think I brought the pair of you into this sad world and now here you both are billing and cooing, so to speak.'

'Seamus isn't too eager for the billing and cooing, Nurse, though he gives me a nice kiss when he gets his cheese sandwiches. He's fourteen and his voice is changing. He'll be a real man soon.'

'And what does all that sawdust do to his poor chest, Mairead Ryan?'

'It's a torture, Nurse, so it is! But he's a brave soul.'

'I know, child. It's a special young bucko you have there at Dayntree's. You take good care of him.'

'I'll do better than that. I'm going to keep him for ever!'

'He's down the back, love, teaching that no-good wastrel Cassidy the reading and the writing.'

She click-clacked past the foreman who touched his cloth cap with a smile. Clutching the cheese sandwiches tight to her chest, she sidled by the big circular saw, with its vicious, whirling, sabre-toothed blade and terrible high-pitched rasping scream. Her round young face all screwed up tight with fear, she was deaf to all the cries of, 'Hey, are those for me, darlin'?' and, 'Wait just outside, my pretty, and I'll be out directly to see you!'

Eventually, at the far back, she came upon her Seamus and Ciaran Cassidy sitting on a sack of sawdust, craned over a tattered envelope which rested on Ciaran's knee. Seamus was pointing to the letters of the alphabet, which he had drawn in capitals, and poor Ciaran was stammering out each one in turn.

'If you'd paid attention in school instead of getting the birch every five minutes, you'd be able to do that by now and Seamus could have his snap in peace!'

Seamus looked up at her with a beatific smile which melted her instantly. He put his arm round his student's dirty neck: 'Don't shout at him, Mair! He's really having a go.'

'It's your break, boys. I'm the one who'll have a go as you call it!'

'Listen to him say his letters, Mair.'

'Seamus, I came traipsing all this way to see you, not to be back at school!'

'Just this once, please, Mair!'

'Hurry up then. I want to see you start your sandwiches and I want a kiss.'

Ciaran gave Seamus a nudge and smirked down at the floor, stirring his boot in the shavings.

'Come on then, Ciaran!' said Mairead, tapping her foot and gazing up into the rafters.

Ciaran stumbled obediently through the alphabet, encouraged all the way by Seamus, who looked him in the face, nodding and smiling.

'There! What do you reckon to that now?' Seamus jumped to his feet and took Mairead by the shoulders.

'Very good, I'm sure.' She tried not to smile. She felt more sure of her ground behind a rather severe front. 'Now eat.'

She held out his sandwiches, which she made for him every Saturday, there being no school. If ever she was late, which was rare, the men would pipe up, 'She's left you, mate! She's run off with a sailor!' But they all knew she would come in her own good

193

time.

After Seamus had chewed and swallowed his first bite, she would embrace him hard without embarrassment and press her lips on his.

'Does he taste of cheese, gorgeous?' The men would wink and snigger, but for Mairead, now that she had set her seal upon him, the business was done and she could click-clack back home.

Today she asked Seamus, 'Why do you give up what little break they allow you, to improve Ciaran? He wouldn't do it for you, would you, Ciaran?'

Seamus cut in to save his friend's discomfort: 'I do it whether he would do it for me or not, Mair. My reward is in Heaven.'

'And when he's a charge-hand and you're still bagging sawdust, what then?'

'I hope he does become a charge-hand, if it's what he wants.' Seamus began coughing and took a piece of rag from his waistcoat pocket to spit into.

Mairead took her own handkerchief from her sleeve and pressed it into his hand. Still coughing, he shook his head and tried to give it back to her but she insisted.

'While you're worrying about other people, no-good, layabout people,' she looked at Ciaran who quickly lowered his eyes, 'you yourself will be dying and ready for a wooden overcoat!'

'When it pleases God, Mair,' he gasped between bouts of hacking and wheezing.

After she had gone back home, a couple of new operators came to squat on the sacks with Seamus and Ciaran to savour brown, corrosive tea in chipped enamel mugs. One of them jabbed Seamus matily in the ribs: 'You and your lady friend, do you do it together?'

Seamus looked at him, unperturbed.

The man smiled and winked, 'You know, do you do it, together, like?'

There was a pause while they listened to a pigeon cooing somewhere up among the roof beams.

'We don't spoon, if that's what you're meaning,' smiled Seamus good-naturedly.

'But do you ever - you know?' He laughed aloud and his friend, eager to clarify the situation, said, 'He means, have you ever put your John Willy inside the lady?'

Both men roared. Ciaran smirked at the floor. The pigeon flapped once or twice as it shifted its position above them.

'No. Not until she's my wife. That would be a sin. You both know that.'

The laughter died down and the discussion took on a more serious tone. 'Don't you ever feel you want to do it with her, her being your girl and all?'

'Yes, sometimes I really want to.'

Instead of being the butt of this conversation, Seamus was beginning to direct it. All three were listening to him, attentive, ready to learn, as he searched for his words.

'Just because you want to do something, that doesn't mean you should just go and do it, like it might be spooning or it might be murder or something.'

'But spooning with the young lady friend isn't murder, mate - unless she's got long finger nails, like!' No-one laughed at this afterthought.

'No, but it is sinful. We're both too young and we aren't man and wife, so we have to hold back. We have to control the animal part of us. Doing it with your wife is for making children, not for having fun - that's fornication.'

The two older men sat back, looked at each other and shoved their caps back on their heads to let the air get to their pates, with a mixture of amazement and new respect. The talk had changed from a goading session to a more polite enquiry. Seamus leaned forward to cough and spit into the sawdust between his boots.

'A bloke's John Willy is given him by God to make more men and women in His own image, not to fulfil his lust.'

'That sounds a bit like Father Brendan, my young mate!'

'I believe the same things he does, so it might just as well be.'

195

Shaken by another fit of coughing, Seamus took off his cloth cap and fanned his face with it.

'Well, my John Willy,' answered the saw operator, placing his charred churchwarden pipe between his teeth with a click that instantly reminded Seamus of his father, 'has always brought me good luck and quenched the fires of lust!' He rocked back and forth with hearty laughter until, with an audible plop, a generous gobbet of grey and white pigeon dropping landed in his lap. His mate convulsed at the irony of this event: 'Well now, Jacko, mate, that lot's landed in just the right place to quench your fires a bit more now, hasn't it, son?'

IN LOVING MEMORY
OF
SINEAD GROGAN
Born 1885
Died 1919
BE STRONG IN THE LORD

It was a Sunday morning in March 1925 and it had snowed during the night. The sky was overcast and there was no wind. The slow thaw made the air damp and chilly. Apart from the well-wrapped figures of Mairead and Seamus, nothing stirred in St Anthony's churchyard. The two youngsters stood hand in hand before the simple headstone. Seamus stooped to brush away its little snowy cap. He looked about him, as Mairead squeezed his hand. Where was the raucous bickering of the sombre rooks high up in the dripping branches? Where was the rumble of traffic on the Scotland Road? Where were the stray dogs that sniffed around the graves? The whole city was waiting to be thawed out.

Just beneath the headstone, as white as the snow itself, lay a bunch of lilies.

'There they are again, Seamus, the mysterious lilies.'

'I wonder who comes, Mair, every single week.'

'Somebody who knew your ma. Somebody who wants to keep themselves to themselves.'

Footsteps in the slush along the path: 'Hello, both of you! I've brought a few daffs just to cheer the grave up a bit.'

Clodagh strode towards them, tossing her long hair aside with a jaunty movement of her head. She was splendid in a beige knee-length coat, open at the front to reveal a matching dress with dropped waistline and pleated skirt. She carried a bunch of daffodils in one hand and a clutch handbag in the other. Mairead thought even the daffodils looked like a fashion accessory. She squelched nonchalantly through the wet snow in her high-heeled bar shoes.

'What gorgeous lilies!' she drawled with less of a Liverpool accent than ever.

'We don't know who brings them, Auntie Clodagh.'

'Seamus Grogan!' she neighed. 'My name's Clodagh to you now you're practically a man. Do you want to make a lady feel old, now do you?' They all laughed and Seamus felt his hand squeezed again.

She leaned forward and placed the daffodils on the grave - a splash of yellow in the snow. And all at once the dogs started barking and the rooks cleared their throats.

'You have beautiful hair, Clodagh,' ventured Mairead.

'I won't have it cut short to my scalp just to be in fashion, my darling. And I won't wear a ruddy cloche hat either! I'll never make a Lady Duff Cooper, now will I?'

Mairead smiled, feeling small and young, and wondered who on earth Lady Duff Cooper was. They all stood looking at the lilies and the daffodils as the rooks wheeled round and Seamus's memories wandered round 8 Oswald Street. He blinked several times as his eyes filled and he had to use his free hand to brush away the tears. Clodagh turned towards him and murmured, 'You're a good lad, Seamus. I'm sorry I'll never bear one like you.'

'You're very good to come, Clodagh,' said Mairead, sensing that Seamus could not speak.

'I come here to remember a much better woman than I'll ever be.' She made the sign of the cross and slipped away without another word.

A long silence followed after which Mairead turned to Seamus and said, 'I don't see Paddy putting himself out to come to his ma's graveside too often.'

'Don't be hard on him, Mair. He loved her too, in his way.'

'Whatever way that was! I don't believe he's been up here since the three of us came together.' She fidgeted her feet around in the snow. 'And even then all he could find to say was that when he was a rich man he would buy a better headstone.'

'It's just his way. He means well.'

'Anyway, it's thanks to the O'Briens mainly that your ma's got a stone at all. They're good folks, the O'Briens.'

Seamus nodded and sighed, then he had a fit of coughing. Mairead put an arm round his quaking shoulders and led him away.

Together they meandered off towards the Scotland Road, looking for all the world like an old married couple.

How many times had Padraig checked and re-checked his hair, tie and shoes in the oval scullery mirror on that spring morning in 1925? How many times had he begged Auntie O. to brush his brand new suit?

'That suit's worth two whole weeks' wages for your Uncle O'Brien, Paddy! Mrs Harding must think very highly of you or else she's got money to burn!' Caitlin appeared to scold him but she hid her smile behind his well-tailored back as she brushed his jacket and trousers vigorously for the umpteenth time.

'You'd have to ask her which it is, Auntie O!'

'Don't be getting cheeky with me, young man!' She took the

handle of the brush to his backside so that he yelped, and they both laughed. 'Now do, for goodness' sakes, remember your manners, Paddy, if you're going to start mixing with posh folk.'

'The Hardings aren't really posh, Auntie.'

'They're business people and they're employers. That makes them a better class of people than the likes of us in Oswald Street. I do believe your ma and da would be quite proud of you. Tea with the boss! And her a lady and all!'

Paddy had wondered whether he ought to have felt guilty about coming into the O'Briens' house the evening before with such an expensive suit. He knew Seamus would have. But he was not Seamus. The thrill of beginning to get his fingers round the end of the golden chain swamped all other considerations. Even beautiful, snooty Greta would have to make some sort of polite chat with him.

'I'm not going to bow and scrape, Auntie. I'll soon be as good as them.'

She stood back and looked at him, but not at his clothes: 'You're getting a cocky side to you, Paddy. You must either change it or learn how to hide it.'

'He looked at her for a moment, then smiled, 'Yes, Auntie, no, Auntie, run you into town, Auntie!'

She tapped him with the brush again but this time with less of a smile.

'Remember, Paddy, lad, the Hardings don't need you. They could sack you tomorrow and get another young man to do your job. So try to be a bit gracious, won't you?'

'There's still a shortage of young men, Auntie. They advertised for ages for a trainee mechanic. I'm good at it and I've got two years' experience with the same employer. I'm the only person who touches the Silver Ghost now, you know.'

'The what? What's a Silver Ghost when it's at home?'

It was just over a mile's walk from Oswald Street to Westbourne Street, but those neat terraces facing Whitley Gardens might as well have been on another planet. The further he walked down Shaw Street towards the Gardens, the more conspicuous and clumsy he felt, with his contrived working-class spit and polish, the docker's kid from the slums off the Scotland Road! His arrogance sank into his shiny new shoes as he passed some houses with motor cars standing in front of them, just like the Hardings. Yet still he was angry at his own craven spinelessness. This youth was about to become the man who was destined to join in the party, was he not, like the smug-faced rake in the Model T with his elegant lady-friend, like Stanley Gardner in his Rolls Royce? He had to believe in himself, but who was he? Unlike his twin brother he was sure of nothing, except that life might slap you down without warning or reason at a moment's notice. So, to be secure, you needed money, lots of money, and with it, power and influence, what his da used to call 'clout'. Stanley Gardner had plenty of it. Even the Hardings had it. It was reflected in the place you lived. He had none at all, yet.

He rehearsed in his mind his arrival at the Hardings' door. The way he behaved at that door would set the tone for the afternoon. If he made a mess of it, the gold chain would slip from his fingers and he would lose ground, and probably Greta would sneer at him at work and start calling him 'slum boy' again.

When he had confided in Seamus about these anxieties, his twin had said to him, 'I stood trembling at the door for fear of what lay behind it. I let Faith open the door for me and I found the room inside was empty.' All Padraig could reply was, 'Where the bleedin' hell do you get these sayings from?'

'If folk treat you badly because of where you come from and not what you are, the fault lies with them, Paddy, not with you.'

'That depends on where you want to be going, brother. Where I want to be going is more important to me than where I come from.'

'Then you're like a ship with no anchor, Paddy, a tree with no roots.'

'Clever talk, Seamus, but it won't pay today's prices!'

'Your talk is all about prices but never about values.'

47 Westbourne Street had a small garden with a low wall at the front. Paddy looked up and found it intriguing that the Hardings owned the upstairs and the downstairs too, and, what was more, their shiny Bullnose Morris stood in the street, waiting to take them wherever they wanted to go. They also owned the freehold of the Love Lane premises, as Greta frequently reminded him with a sneer and a nod of her infuriatingly pretty head.

He stood at the door patting his hair at the sides and adjusting his tie, vowing that once he had done both, he would forget about them and not fiddle any more.

As the door swung smoothly open, a smell of pot-pourri met him and there stood Greta, hand on hip, looking him up and down. Did that delicate smell come from inside the house or from inside Greta's clothing? Perhaps her very body exuded this tantalising scent. He very much doubted that her body required some of the baser attentions that his did.

 Her big hazel eyes narrowed as she studied him. Her short brown hair was cut shorter than ever and shaped to her head in flat, neat waves with shiny pendant ear-rings on either side.

'Well, hello, slum boy! You look almost presentable.'

Paddy was uncertain whether this was a grudging compliment or simply another piece of Greta sarcasm. He took in the loose, chemise-shaped bodice with the waistband at hip level and the knee-length skirt.

'Good afternoon, Miss Greta.'

He whipped off his cap and stood tugging it, wanting to fling it into the stunted rose bushes.

'Miss Greta! My, My! We are on our best behaviour, aren't we?'

She pivoted on the slender heels of her court shoes and called, 'Mother, the Grogan boy is here. Should I risk letting him in the house?'

Hilda Harding appeared in the doorway behind her daughter.

'Greta, don't be so confounded rude! Paddy, I do apologise for my daughter. In spite of all my efforts she has turned out to be very rude. Go inside, you horrid girl!'

Greta pulled a face at Paddy and waltzed into the house. He would have liked to watch her go but her mother stood in the way.

In the drawing room he did not fail to notice the wireless set sitting on its own little table, nor that it had valves and a loudspeaker instead of a cat's whisker and headset. The Hardings belonged firmly in the new age of the British Broadcasting Corporation, and no doubt when pictures became available with the sound - as at the Homer picture house only smaller - they would have that too. Nor did Padraig miss the bowl of fruit on the front window sill, though nobody was ill.

Greta swayed and hummed to *Love is the sweetest Thing*, as it crooned out of the gramophone. When her mother asked her to turn it off, she just closed her eyes.

Padraig found it hard at first to understand why the front room had a faint odour of cigars. There must have been a male visitor to the house apart from himself. Of course! Mr Gardner! Padraig was treading the same square of carpet as Stanley, and on a social footing too! Wireless, gramophone and Havanas - was Paddy Grogan of Oswald Street really here? Still the real test would be the tea and sandwiches. He guessed Greta expected him to drop food and look gauche with his cutlery, as if he had too many fingers. His previous attempt to get coaching from Greta had been met with, 'Five minutes' training from me can hardly make up for fifteen years of slum living! Now put this accumulator on charge, will you, or the Bednalls will have no wireless.'

The table almost filled the small dining-room at the back of the house, in which the air was rich with cucumber and tomato, sherry trifle and cake. When Hilda showed Padraig to one of the high-backed chairs, they found Greta already seated, her hand hovering over the segmented coffee cake.

'Don't you dare, Greta!'

'Just exercising my hand, Mother.'

'I'll exercise my hand on you!'

Padraig avoided Greta's eyes and concentrated on what Auntie O. had drummed into him. He drew out a chair for Hilda at the head of the table. It was surprisingly heavy. As she thanked him, he felt the colour rise in his cheeks. He waited for Grace to be said, but none came, so, instead of showing surprise, he said, 'May I pass you anything, Mrs Harding?'

He was aware of Greta's eyes but she offered no caustic comments. Perhaps he was winning. He handled his cutlery without faltering and made polite and general conversation. He paused to speak and did not use his knife, fork or spoon to emphasise what he was saying.

When Greta said, ' I don't suppose you've ever had this sort of meal before, Padraig?' he smiled at her and replied, 'It was very kind of you both to invite me, Miss Greta.'

Hilda smiled in turn at her daughter as if to say, 'There! That's told you!'

Yes, he was winning! Soon he would be eating in places beyond poor Auntie O.'s wildest dreams.

'I should never have agreed to this, Stanley!'

'Relax, Hilda! The Worth Tea Room is a very respectable place for a lady and gentleman to be seen.'

'I feel - somehow - furtive.'

'Nonsense! You've never been to Chester before - you told me so - and now here we both are. It's a day out! There's no Greta to spy on us and pass comments we can well do without, and it's not as if we were planning on staying the night here, for goodness' sake!'

'Stanley, will you keep your voice down or I shall walk straight out of here!'

'Most ladies would be pleased to be whisked down to Chester in a Rolls Royce and to be wined and dined for the day.'

'It is nice of you, Stanley - but I'm not "most ladies", as you put it.'

'Don't I know it!'

'Is that some kind of implied criticism?'

'No. I think you're wonderful. That's why I wanted to bring you here, because you're not " most ladies", as I put it.'

'Stop it!'

He thought she smiled for a brief moment but could not swear to it.

Trade was brisk in the Worth Tea Room in one of the Rows in Chester, which was not typical of trade in general in that spring of 1926. Stanley looked across the cups, plates and serviettes at her in her felt cloche hat and casual three-piece jumper suit. He guessed it was not Coco Chanel, although it was her style. Hilda had fashionable taste but not quite enough pounds, shillings and pence to indulge it to the full. But he had!

She toyed with her pearls: 'This seems the most idiotic time to expand, Stanley. There's a recession. Bob says there's going to be a strike with every worker coming out - a general strike, the papers are calling it.'

'A capital time to buy another garage, my dear! You'll get one at rock bottom price. I would like to invest in you, as you know, so I'll buy a proportion of it. I need no income from the venture, so I'll just look for capital growth. All the income is yours. I can have an agreement drawn up by my solici . . .'

'Not so fast, Stanley! I need time to think and I need another cup of Earl Grey.'

She reached for her purse but Stanley's large hairy hand closed gently over her own small, well-manicured one.

He shook his head and smiled confidently: 'These high class Nippies are just like trams in the 'Pool, never there when you need one, then suddenly you get three at once!' He raised his arm to one of the waitresses.

Hilda withdrew her hand slowly from his: 'These girls aren't Nippies, Stanley, and when did you last ride on a tram?'

He grinned and reached again for her hand but it was in her lap under the table, out of reach - for the time being.

He ordered another pot of Earl Grey in a firm and sonorous voice, beaming at Hilda all the time. The waitress scribbled, bobbed and scurried away with the dirty cups and saucers in the direction of the hectic kitchen.

'Paddy Grogan,' began Stanley, 'keeps my car on the road all by himself. The boy is gifted, Hilda. You know I recommended him to my old friend Sir Bert Akers, so he could service the brakes on Bert's Rolls? Well Bert was cock-a-hoop about the work done, both the speed and the quality of it. He's going to be a regular customer now.'

Hilda again moved her hand from the table as Stanley reached for it.

'I know. Paddy is a very ambitious young man, Stanley, and he is proving good for business. Greta says that bicycle sales are down but our income from motor repairs and servicing has increased by a third since Paddy worked for us.'

'Why can't I hold your hand, Hilda. Just for a moment?'

He was leaning forward, staring at her, while she looked away towards the window.

Hilda ignored his question and went on about the business: 'Paddy would be quite capable of working under supervision at new premises.'

'That's more like it! Then, when he's old enough, he can manage a garage of his own, with his own apprentice. Expansion, Hilda, expansion!'

This time he grasped her hand across the table and squeezed it. This time Hilda did not resist.

Shapeless in a cloth cap, striped muffler, loose-fitting second-hand jacket and waistcoat, in spite of the sunshine over St Anthony's, Seamus emerged into the light with Mairead. The muffler disguised the fact that he wore no tie, and he wore no tie because of what he now called his 'Dayntree cough'. The sunlight splattered over Mairead's battered wool-embroidered straw hat, which almost hid her short dark hair. Her long, heavily-creased, belted jacket made her hips look big and her old-fashioned, full, long skirt, falling right down to her buckled shoes served only to intensify the impression of a young girl grown old before her time.

Seamus felt full of warmth and light inside his body after the words and music of the Mass. The sunlight was only an outward manifestation of his own state of mind. God had passed his lips and entered him. It was the ultimate intimacy, paradoxical, because it was both humbling and exalting. He felt at one with everything he saw. Mairead felt rather a sense of duty done. Going to Mass was the right and proper thing to do.

They both smiled straight into the sunlight, two unkempt innocents, as they strolled out towards the wide world.

'More fresh lilies on your ma's grave then Seamus.'

'Perhaps we should keep watch on the sly and see who it is!'

'Sure we should do no such wicked thing, Seamus Grogan! Just be thankful that somebody cares enough.'

'I am thankful, Mair, you know I am.'

'Then leave it, and God bless whoever it is.'

Padraig and Greta emerged blinking into the sunlight from the Homer picture house. In the secure darkness, Padraig always found a respite from the anxieties of day to day living. Holding Greta's hand had awakened his body and shot new sensations through it.

He had always reckoned she would come and step out with him in the end, because he wasn't a bad catch - no money yet, it was true, but plenty of prospects!

They had seen two Buster Keaton films, *Coney Island*, released during the War and now several years old, and *Cops*, with its famous chase scene, during which he had felt for Greta's hand and wondered at how soft and moist it was. He sat there in the blackness, afraid to move in case she guessed at the sticky discomfort in his trousers. He had never had such a ramrod on him before and it affected his breathing and made him sweat. He bet Uncle O. would know just how to handle all that kind of thing, though certainly not with a girl from Greta Harding's background. Greta had left her hand in his and at times his own hand rested partly on her leg. He tried to work out how many inches it was from her private parts now! Not that many, although that was as close as he was likely to get for the time being.

They both paused, dazzled, on the steps of the Homer, to show passers-by what an elegant young couple should look like. Padraig wore his new suit and Greta a severe brimless cloche in the latest style, with a cream dress, unbelted, to just below her knees, and matching shoes with two buckled straps over the instep. For a few seconds they were blinded and could go no further, then Greta put her arm lightly through his and they made their way self-consciously down the steps and into the street.

Seamus always said that the material things of this world only really matter if you invest all your concern and desires in them. Then death really is the end and to be feared; but if you sometimes raise your eyes above these trivia, then death comes more as a junction than as a dead end. Nurse McEwan would call it putting your spiritual eggs in more than one basket, another of her personal insurances.

Yet be all that as it may, Paddy still felt a thrill of excitement as his toast popped up with a click from the toaster. This was the thrill of the here and now, not some chancy guesswork about what might or might not await us in the hereafter.

However much Seamus might smile knowingly at the Grogans' electric toaster, at least Paddy and Greta could pick it up and feel it and polish it! Seamus and Mairead's values were based on abstract ideas - faith, grace and the Trinity. Seamus had never wanted much, which was fortunate, as he never had much. Yet his tranquillity still irritated Paddy at times, even though they were both now married and in their early twenties.

Paddy had become successful and was making respectable money as a director of Harding and Gardner Ltd., with their six petrol stations and motor repair shops, not to mention the car sales and auction business, which he ran more or less on his own. Seamus, however, always gave the impression of being more content than Paddy. Seamus did not strive.

'I neither sow nor reap,' he would say to Paddy and Greta.

'That's just a way off covering up a lack of drive and ambition,' would be Paddy's response.

'My reward will be in Heaven.'

'Mine will be at the end of the financial year!'

For Seamus, in this autumn of 1933, the clicking of his twin brother's toaster was surpassed by the smiles and laughter of his own three children, Peter, named after the boy's grandfather, but spelt the English way, aged four, Sinead, aged two, and baby Matthew, in honour of Uncle O., just eight months. He had married Mairead in the Christmas of 1928 at St Anthony's.

'I've got to marry him, Mrs O'Brien, before the Lord takes him back to His own, that rattling chest and all!'

Once again that dingy old room at 8 Oswald Street rang to Grogan voices, for Seamus had moved his brood into his parents' former place, which had once more lain derelict for months, a refuge for vagabonds and boozers, next door but one to Uncle and Auntie O'Brien, but a whole world away before the new Mrs Grogan got to work on it. While Seamus struggled on, bagging the shavings at Dayntree's, Mairead, trussed up like some gipsy peasheller in a market, had cleaned and redecorated their new place, so that it breathed bleach and distemper. Seamus nonetheless swore he could still smell his da's pipe of Ogden's on a balmy evening and he could still hear his ma whispering, 'Mind the babes, my love!' as she and their da came to bed, thinking he and Paddy were both asleep at the foot, half buried beneath the folds of his old greatcoat that reeked of the docks.

Now in his twenty-fourth year and pale and consumptive, he loved nothing more than to be tugged this way and that by his shrieking children, who would stampede gaily over the bed first thing in the morning, in the stricken slum dawn. Mairead would not call a halt to these happy riots until Seamus's coughing forced him to sit bolt upright and smile quietly at the ceiling, while the sweat rolled down his face. Then the children would go silent and gaze into their da's face and pick at his stubble. Then Mairead, hands on hips, looked on, wishing they had just a wee bit more room, perhaps a few bob to their name, not Paddy and Greta's sort of money, just some of what it could provide for them at No. 8. Seamus insisted God would provide and that what He did not provide must be unnecessary. Having handed over his money to her on a Friday night, he thought no more about it, and certainly never suspected the earthly miracles she worked with those meagre resources week in, week out.

Their love for each other was a close and simple love, a closeness forced upon them in that one room where they ate, washed, slept and made love gently in the stuffy darkness, the children breathing in the cot nearby. Mairead welcomed his poor body into her arms and made him a hero time and again. She never left his side to go and wash afterwards but held him to her breast until he was quiet. Seamus wanted no more than this and thanked God every day for His blessings.

My name is Clodagh Kerrigan, though everybody calls me just Clodagh, not Mrs Kerrigan or anything grand - I'm not really the type to encourage the use of handles. I'm forty - forty-something! I'm in my forties, shall we say? I'm a very tall lady, too tall for some fellas. I think I scare them a bit. They'd love to find out how far up my legs join together but they're too windy to try it on! Still, that's their loss, isn't it? I'm a brunette and I wear my hair long, although I've got more than a few streaks of grey in it now. Yes, I know what you're thinking: doesn't she know it's not fashionable to wear your hair long, especially when you're knocking on a bit, but I don't care. And do you know why I don't care? Because it's making no difference to the jingle in my pocket, if you catch my meaning? Yes, I see you do!

Mick Kerrigan was my husband. The silly bleeder joined up pretty well at the first beat of Kitchener's drum and was blown to bits by a Jerry shell before most of the BEF had crossed the Channel. So now I'm a widow and have been so for nearly twenty years. My two little girls passed over from the typhoid almost a year to the day after I got the telegram about poor Mick; first Louisa - she was four - and forty-eight hours later, Eileen, just two years old, poor skinny little scrap! The doctor ran up and down the stairs like a scalded cat, trying this potion and that, but still they both died, God rest the pair of them! And as for me, well, I stayed as fit as a fiddle the whole time, never so much as sneezed nor coughed while my babes lay dying. Now where's the justice, I ask you? What's God's purpose for me, do you suppose?

Men, you ask? Sure, I've had men, loads of them. Even when Mick was alive. His money was no good. He was only ever a casual worker, never held a regular job down. I've always been good at using my charms. God gave me this body and I use it as a scientist uses his brains to make a living. I don't invent guns, poison gas and tanks, do I? I give pleasure and contentment. So who is the guilty one? All right, I don't invent medicines that cure the sick either but I have cured a few sick men in my time - in my own way - and they've gone home to their wife and children the better for my treatment. I don't say I'm a good woman, either. I suppose I'm not really that good or that bad - just a tiny part of the workings of the city. That Lionel Hunt the grocer was worse than me, so he was. He made himself out to be a good man, a pillar of the business community, but he was a perverted bleeder if ever there was one, I can tell you. I'd waddle away from his shop feeling as though his middle finger was still half way up my arse! Oh, I do beg your pardon. That wasn't very lady-like, was it?

Well, anyway, the city is the city when all's said and done. There's plenty like me in it and there's plenty of priests and all. We all do our bit in our own way. The priest gets his money and I get mine. Not that I'm saying I'm like a priest, because that's a bit of a blasphemy, but we're all grist in the mill of life, as Mick used to say . . . daft bugger!

John Corkhill, secretary to the Lord Mayor, was another memorable one. That was the time of the police strike. I recall I bumped into Sinead Grogan and her twins caught right in the middle of it one really hot evening not long after the Armistice. I could swear she knew that man they shot in the jeweller's shop, nasty little piece of work. I remember how she stared at his corpse when they brought it out. He'd been a rent man for a while. He used to jingle his money pouch at me in the street and stick his tongue out and waggle it at me. I told him I'd cut his cock off for him one fine day. John Corkhill used to drive me out in his motor car, right out of the town. He paid for my clothes, he paid my rent weeks in advance and he was a good lover, bless him!

Even Matt O'Brien, who looked after the Grogan boys, came to my bed once or twice. He used to shout out in Irish when he shot his bolt. You'd think he was dying, the way he carried on! His wife is a good woman, very kind, but I think she was like a sack of murphies between the sheets, if Matt was to be believed.

Any road up, the biggest surprise of all was young Paddy, aye Paddy Grogan, son of Peadar the docker and Sinead, both gone before now, twin brother of Seamus - you know - Seamus, who ought to be a priest but bags wood shavings at Dayntree's by the canal. Well, Paddy's a different kettle of fish, if you please! He's a director of Harding and Gardner, the motor car people. They seem to be all over Liverpool now. He married into the firm with that stuck up Greta Harding, Greta Grogan now. It has a bit of a ring to it, doesn't it, 'Greta Grogan'? Three years' wedded bliss and no babies! Now how could that be? They both look hale and well-nourished and God knows they want for nothing! And I know for sure young Paddy has everything in the right place, as I shall tell you. Auntie Dora whispered to me that they're preventing it deliberate. She would know, I suppose!

Yes! She's stopping herself conceiving, the sinful mare! Now how do you like that? Perhaps because I can have no more, I should keep my mouth shut. The good Lord in His wisdom is doing this woman a favour maybe. Auntie Dora thinks if a lady prevents herself from catching, it's because she wants to put herself about a bit. Now young Greta doesn't go in for that, I'm sure, it's just that she's too taken with the good life to be mithered with babes. You know, I can well understand that but I bet you can't, can you? No, I thought not! But that's today's bright young things for you!

Where was I now? Oh yes! I'm seeing a fit old gentleman who wanted to sell his motor car at auction and bid for a better one, he being in easy circumstances, like. No, it's not fair to say they're all rich! While he was laid up with gout, he gave me the taxi fare and asked me to go over and see Paddy Grogan to find out whether he could put a bargain our way. I turned up a bit late at Love Lane, where he's got a beautiful new office and showroom and a gorgeous flat over the top, all done out in the latest styles by Greta with no expense spared. She's got taste, that woman, I've got to give her that! Still, I'm running ahead of myself again.

When I turned up, I found that I was too late and they were shut. I could see Paddy inside in his smart suit and there was an old dear sweeping up round the motor cars. I was going to go away again when Paddy saw me and tapped on the great big window, beckoning me to come in. He gave the old woman a key and she

212

opened up for me and I went inside the showroom.

The change in Paddy since he tied the knot! He stands taller and straighter and he has a little pencil-line moustache. The Scouse accent has all but gone - unless he gets worked up, and then it's pure Scotland Road!

He was wearing a dark three-piece suit, a dark-coloured tie and a shirt as white as an altar cloth, except for a star-shaped spot of blood on the collar, from a shaving cut, I suppose, but the only thing that marred his Mr Perfection appearance. His face looked relaxed and confident apart from his eyes - they've never lost that anxious, hungry gleam, like an animal waiting to be thrown a lump of meat. He's a very handsome man now, and no mistake, but he has a look about him - a waiting look. His brother's eyes give out light but his seem to draw it all in. He craves limelight so much that there's darkness all about him. But his body is lean and hard like a greyhound's, with muscles lying just underneath the skin, all tense, ready to pounce. You feel you want to touch, just as you'd want to run your fingers and your palm over a statue of one of those young Greek men - you know, like the ones in the foyer of the Homer picture house - exciting but so very, very cold. And his smile was as narrow and thin as his moustache.

'Auntie Clodagh!' It was meant to be cheeky. I was intended to rise to it.

'Little Padraig as ever was! You've left school now, have you?'

The old dear finished her cleaning and put her mop and bucket in a small cupboard. Paddy bade her goodnight and told her he would let me out himself and see to the locking up. I then explained the dilemma of my poor gouty Horace and his automobile plans and Paddy listened and inspected his finger nails one by one in minute detail. He also had a habit of brushing imaginary dandruff off his shoulder. I mean there was no dandruff to be seen, just that little star-shaped blob of blood on his collar.

'I'll do a special deal for yourself and Horace,' says he, staring into the palm of his hand.

'Is it you who puts the flowers on your mother's grave every week, Paddy?'

'I do not. Maybe I should.'

'It's not your brother, it's not you and it's not me. I wonder who the mystery florist can be then.'

The mystery of his mother's grave was of no interest to Paddy, who went on about trade-in values and reserve prices.

'I mustn't keep you from your wife, Paddy. She'll be wondering where you've got to.'

'She's gone to Paris with her mother to do some shopping,' says he, clearly mightily impressed himself and hoping I'd be so too.'

'Paris! Some shopping trip! She'll be away for days then?'

'Only forty-eight hours. They went by aeroplane from Croydon on the Golden Clipper - an hour and a half to Paris! The longest part is the train journey from Lime Street, changing in London.'

'How the other half do live!' That seemed to please him no end. 'So, you're all on your own upstairs?'

'Yes, and Stanley's at Brooklands for the motor racing, so I've been running the whole show myself today.'

'Quite the big businessman, Paddy Grogan!'

He looked at me properly for the first time. I'm taller than he is but he looked me full in the face and ran his eye over me just as if I was a bloody second-hand car! It was dead quiet in the showroom and everything was washed with crimson in the setting sun. I smiled at him as he looked me over, the cheeky young puppy! His eyes were slits in the sunlight but they missed nothing.

'Is the sun in your eyes, Paddy?'

'I'm dazzled by you, Clodagh.'

'Is this the bare-arsed whippet from Oswald Street?'

'No. This is the company director who runs half a dozen businesses.'

'So I should be down on my knees then, should I?'

'Depends what you have in mind.'

'Great Heavens above, listen to him! Is that a respectful way to speak to your Auntie Clodagh?'

'You can't have it both ways, Clodagh, the respect and the thrills as well. You know as well as I do that you must choose one or the other.'

Padraig Grogan, I thought, I'll not stand here to be cheeked and then given a lecture on the ways of the world by the likes of a young, jumped up, arrogant little . . .

'Tea or coffee, Clodagh, or maybe something with a bit more bite?'

'To hell with you, Paddy! We'll find our own car and make our own mistakes!' Seething I was, seething with rage at that puffed up little shit!

Can you wonder? His ma and his da would be turning in their graves. He's done all right for himself, sure, but he has an arrogant side that he cannot always conceal, like another person trying to get out from inside him. But you'd know that as well as I do.

He explained in great detail how he'd give Horace the best part-exchange money for his old car and would then get him a much newer one out of the auction compound and sell it to him for the reserve price, all of which meant that Horace could save four or five guineas.

I knew Horace would hardly believe it and he'd be proud of me for managing to arrange it all without him. Men usually think I'm only good for spooning with, you know, so this was something special for me now and I really wanted to show Horace.

I could sense that young Paddy wanted to show me his easy way with the ladies so I realised I'd have to put up with a bit of his lip, if that's what it took to do business with him.

He turned to me, still squinting and still casting his eye over me: 'The tea and coffee stuff is locked away for the night.'

'That's all right. I'll do without.'

'I can make you a cup in the flat.' I could tell he was holding his breath.

'Now that wouldn't be altogether proper, would it?'

'Altogether, no, I suppose it wouldn't. But who's to know?'

'You're a married man and that's your wife's place too.'

'I am allowed to discuss business, you know, Clodagh. If you were a man, nobody would bat an eyelid.'

'No, but I'm not a man, am I?'

Now it was my turn to look him square in the eye and I've had more practice at it as well, a lot more than Paddy has! He reddened and made as if to smirk, but his poor nervous face couldn't quite manage it. He will be very good later and very dangerous, if he keeps on trying, but at the moment he's just a beginner, I'm afraid. Still, be all that as it may, upstairs we both went, Paddy leading the way.

Though I'd strolled past that new Love Lane showroom building many times, I simply wasn't prepared for the Grogans' flat over the top. The building is a big white, square thing, very white, as if it was coated with icing sugar. There was the showroom at ground level with its big windows and there was the flat above it with a balcony and more big, square windows, all very modern looking. The position isn't very nice, just underneath the railway viaduct with the Bolton and Bury line racing past the kitchen and bathroom at the back and the Love Lane motor traffic going by below the drawing room and the dining room. Opposite, you can see the Britannia Warehouse over the road. But talk about luxurious! It's the sort of place you and I can only dream about. Paddy said it was inspired by the pavilion at Bexhill on Sea. Well, I should just think it was! Some would say it's vulgar but, as Paddy himself says, they're all folk who couldn't afford such things anyway, and when they find they can, then they can build their place how they like, can't they?

I followed him into his kitchen. Well! Everything was electric - electric clock above the electric cooker, electric kettle, electric toaster. He made us a pot of tea, moving over the shiny lino floor like a skater, very graceful but very self-conscious too. Though he didn't actually point out each individual gadget to me, he clearly wanted me to notice the general effect, which I did.

We sipped our tea, facing each other across the kitchen table. A goods train rumbled by, puffing heavily. A goods train sounds quite different from a passenger train, doesn't it? Passenger trains go diddly-dum, diddly-dum and goods trains go dum dum dum dum. Anyhow, there we sat without a word, just sipping. From time to time he looked at me but I kept my eyes on the tea in my cup.

'Greta wants to move away from the railway, get somewhere quieter.'

It was like a cock-eyed apology for the noise, as if he felt it spoilt the impression.

'Are you happy with the deal, Clodagh?'

'It's most kind of you, Padraig.'

'Oh, Padraig is it now?'

'Well, business is business, as you would probably say to your other customers.'

'You're a very handsome woman, Clodagh. I've always - admired you, your style.'

Dear me, thought I inside my head, here we go, Clodagh!

'I was a friend of your mother's, Paddy. She would be forty-eight if she was alive today and I'm not far off that age myself.'

'So what? What's twenty-five years?'

'A quarter of a century!'

He put his cup down slowly in the saucer and looked up at me, searching for his words. His face looked as if there was real torment inside. I thought, this is not a happy young man.

'Clodagh, I think you're a very attractive woman - lady. I think I could learn a lot from you.'

It was my turn to look across at him. His poor young face, it was a picture!

'Do you now? And what do you think you would learn from me, Paddy Grogan, director of six companies, owner of an all-electric kitchen?'

That floored him and he just sat there, staring down at the table.

I felt guilty then and decided I had to help him. 'What do you want me to teach you? You make a decent cup of tea.'

'It's Greta. I believe she's - disappointed with me - you know, with my - sort of - performance.' His face looked like a beetroot!

'You mean she thinks you're no good between the sheets, is that it? You tell your Auntie Clodagh!'

'Don't make fun of me, Clodagh! I need advice while Greta's away.'

He got up and began to pace about the kitchen, touching things as he went round, like somebody in a shop, as if the things didn't really belong to him.

'Clodagh, supposing I gave you and Horace that car for nothing?'

'Hold hard, Paddy. Nothing's for nothing in this cruel world! What's the price of this so-called "free" motor car?'

Of course I was beginning to guess at the the answer to that one! He turned his back on me, a straight and manly back, I should add!

'Teach me, Clodagh. Teach me how to be a man in bed. Show me how to please my wife. I've made out I've had experience, but she's obviously had men before me.'

He turned to face me and bless me if there weren't tears in his eyes, nice brown eyes like his old fella's before him.

'Well now, Paddy lad, there's a surprise for sure!'

'Will you do it? Will you show me?'

'For a free motor car? That's the best offer I've had for a long time - and me over forty!'

'But will you?' He was really pleading now, surrounded by his luxury flat.

'How could I explain it all to gouty Horace?'

'How jealous is he?'

'Probably not at all. A free motor car would certainly go a long way towards containing his virile fury!'

Paddy seemed so relieved, it warmed my heart. I asked him to top up my cup, which I noticed was bone china, and escort me to the scene of the crime, an expression which did not please him at all. But, you know, I could tell he didn't so much feel guilty as afraid of being found out, and he was intrigued, as I confess I was, about the idea of him and me - you know - he being the son of one of my old friends, me remembering him crawling about the floor in that room in Oswald Street with a bit of wet rag dangling from his mouth. I thought of Sinead, though the memory didn't trouble me as I wasn't seducing the man. He'd invited me, and, old acquaintance aside, how many offers does a lady get when she's past forty, from a handsome and wealthy young blade in his twenties? Anyhow, most of my men friends are married. That's the way of the world. I didn't create it, I just try and survive in it.

In the bedroom was a gas fire with a beige tiled hearth and surround and a shiny parquet floor with a big Chinese rug - all greens and orange - I could almost taste the colours, they made my mouth water. The walls were beige distemper with no pictures or hangings, rather sterile, a bit symbolic, eh? The bed was a whopper! The pillows looked full fit to burst their down all over the room. Paddy sat on the edge of the bed, knees squeezed together, hands in his lap, like a maid waiting to be asked to dance!

I stood in front of him, pulled out my kirby grips and took off my pill-box hat, laying it on the bedside table, without taking my eyes off him. You mustn't lose the man's attention during this bit. This is when he starts getting aroused. Then I slipped my fox fur stole from around my shoulders and let it slide to the floor at my feet. Next my shoes - and you try taking your court shoes off gracefully, standing on one leg and looking into a man's eyes! I threw my brown suit jacket to the foot of the bed, wondering if it would get kicked off there later, unbuttoned my blouse, untucked it all round my skirt and drew it up over my head, shaking my hair free. I tossed the blouse at Paddy. He managed a smile at that. Well, some men like to sniff your clothes as they come off you, armpits and all . . . pigs, aren't they? I unclasped my brassiere and let my bouncers free. They're still in good shape, though breast-feeding my poor babes did more damage than the passing of the years. I have a few little stretch marks on my belly, as you know, but I'm still fairly flat in that area, especially when I suck it in and push my tits right out!

I made a four course meal out of the stockings and suspenders, as you may imagine, and knew that Paddy was past the point of no return. I have a way of pivoting forward at the waist to take my knickers down, keeping my legs straight and letting my tits sway from side to side while I'm bent over. Then I stood up straight and proud, hands on hips, and smiled at him. He looked very serious and a bit flustered. He tried to speak but I knelt and put my finger to his lips. I laid him back and undressed him, though he made a mess on his belly before I'd finished. I told him different ways of saving his ammunition and then coached him for an hour, showing him where to touch, how firmly or how gently and how to know when it was working and how to know when it was time to change to something else. How many men get that from their wives, even if the ladies know about it themselves? It takes a real dyed-in-the-wool whore to do that!

He was fit and strong, but in such a bleeding hurry to begin with. Then I made him say it all back to me, all he'd just learnt, like in the schoolroom! He was so grateful that I felt quite prepared to accept the car for Horace! Then we lay quiet in each other's arms and shared one of his awful Turkish cigarettes, while his willy shrivelled to a slippery little button and I lay feeling his lukewarm juice oozing out of my Mary Jane. Oh, I know I'm earthy in that way, I'm sorry. I see you disapprove. Still, it's all part of the love-making process. It tells you more about a man than all the clever conversation in the world.

What did it tell me about Paddy, you ask? Well, let me explain over this last milk stout, since it was you who brought him into the world. Your continuing good health, Nurse McEwan!

Paddy is a young man who will never find contentment. He thinks it's just round the next corner or the next or the next. Whatever he owns, he believes that he will get happiness with the next thing he buys, always the next thing, always in the future, never here and now. Everything he does is a rehearsal for a better time of life ahead. Learning to satisfy Greta will be his first ever effort at making someone else's 'now' a happy one, setting his own plans aside. I told him that grace, or whatever you might like to call it, comes from everyday little things, like washing the pots, blacking the grate, struggling to satisfy the wife. You have to slog for it. He thinks you just screw up your eyes and wait for it to be handed to you on a plate, because he's Paddy Grogan, and somehow deserves it. I tried to show him how his cock is a thing for his lady's pleasure and not just for his own. I don't think he'd ever seen it that way. I told him that if he could lose his own selfish self inside Greta, he might be on his way. He seemed to understand but I don't think he can really do it.

I ought to go into business, shouldn't I, Nurse? Well, yes, I know I am in a sort of way, but I tend to neglect the spiritual for the joys of the flesh. I usually only do half the job with these men . . . .

In the small front parlour of 12 Oswald Street, Matt and Caitlin O'Brien sat having high tea. Matt was quite hot in his collarless white shirt and dungarees. His hair was sparse now and his moustache greying. His rolled-up sleeves revealed bony but still well-sinewed forearms. His eyes still twinkled but from a sunken distance. And Caitlin? She looked severe at first glance, her grey hair parted in the middle and her round blackrimmed spectacles sweeping round the room. Her black, spotted dress seemed to be gathered, rook-like, about her, buttoned up to within an inch of her chin. Yet anyone who knew her would pick out the lattice-work of laugh lines round her eyes and the prim but generous mouth, ready at a moment's notice to erupt into gales of mirth.

Matt sat in silent satisfaction at the fact that he could cause her to do this at will. The small, low table, resplendent in its starched and ironed cloth like some kind of secular tabernacle, was crowded with cold ham, eggs, kippers and tea-things, all white and shiny in the dim surroundings.

Matt and Caitlin sat quietly together as if posing for a photographer, complete in each other's company. On the far wall, above the enormous wireless, BE STRONG IN THE LORD hung on a tack against the flowery wallpaper. The stuffy little room was rich with the smell of food and tea. Trinkets cluttered the mantelpiece above Matt's head, tiny vases, photographs, a pipe-rack in tarnished brass and not a crucifix or rosary in sight.

Now and then, sleepy Caitlin would close her eyes into slits and see old Conal curled up before the red hot grate, whingeing softly in his dreams of the chase, his matted fur steaming. Even now she sometimes swore she had plucked a dog hair from the scullery plug-hole.

'You're daft, woman! It's from my moustache.'

'You've got a funny moustache, then, with Alsatian hairs in it!'

Matt was redundant from the Abercromby now, with a small pension. They both missed the boys, though neither mentioned it in so many words. Seamus, Mairead and the children came round a lot, but Paddy was never seen in Oswald Street.

Matt and Caitlin sat in the parlour, listening to the clock ticking, ticking away their hours and days at No. 12. Caitlin was afraid Matt was bored but he would never own to it She set before him the best she could with the money they had but she suspected that, though his stomach might be filled, his other manly needs were always left unserved. When he had been earning good money, she guessed he took his business elsewhere and she felt relieved because he was relieved. But what could he do now? She had never really liked what she called 'that side'. She loved Matt right enough but could not abide his weight upon her and all the shoving and grunting and the mess. To think that a beautiful baby could come from all that!

Caitlin visited Sinead's grave at St Anthony's every week or so and admired the fresh white lilies each time. Seamus couldn't afford them so it had to be Paddy. She knew it wasn't the tall tarty Irish woman, because she'd asked her outright when they met one afternoon at the graveside.

'And how is Mr O'Brien these days?' she'd asked down her nose. Hussy!

'He is well enough.'

'Has poor Seamus still got his Dayntree cough, Mrs O'Brien, you being near neighbours?'

'He has.'

'Padraig seems to keep very well.'

'Does he? We don't see him in Oswald Street.'

'I saw him recently. He sorted out a car for a friend of mine.'

'Did he now?'

'Beautiful flowers they are, Mrs O'Brien, but it's not Padraig who provides them.'

Caitlin wondered indignantly how she would know but chose to hold her peace on the matter.

When Matt was really low, he whistled, *Buddy, can you spare a dime?* the recent Bing Crosby song, and then Caitlin would rush to the range and put the kettle on to boil for a cup of tea. That did the trick for a while at least. It was a song of the Depression and it was the Depression that had robbed him of his job at the factory. Then Matt would look up as if waking from a dream and look at the tea table.

'How can we afford all this food, Kate?'

'It's thanks to the Grogans again.'

'You mean the rich Grogans?'

'You know who I mean. It comes from Seamus and Mairead, who can barely get by for themselves.'

July 1939, and that same southwester that used to blow smoke from the Vauxhall chimney all those years ago, was driving the smell of smoke through the darkness into Oswald Street once again. This time, however, the fire smelled much closer. The smoke slipped into the hallway of No. 8 and under the door of the sleeping Grogans. It slithered across the lino and up the legs of the bed. Peter, now ten years old and in his own camp bed, did not stir. Matthew and Sinead at the tail-end of their parents' bed, lay open-mouthed in each other's arms, like dead lovers.

Mairead's eyes slid half open. She sniffed: 'Seamus!'

He coughed. Matthew and Sinead turned over in opposite directions.

'Seamus, I can smell smoke.'

Now he was awake and propped himself up on one elbow.

'Seamus, go outside and look down the street. There's a fire burning somewhere near.'

Both crossed themselves. Seamus shambled, coughing and sneezing, out of bed.

In the street it was warm and mothy. The acrid smell of fire was unmistakeable and a group of men and women had formed in the pool of light beneath a street lamp.

'There's a whole row of terraces alight in the Scotland Road,' said one man, clad in his dressing gown, pyjamas and slippers. 'My eldest just got back home and told me.'

'I didn't know the pubs stayed open till three of a morning,' muttered a fat woman in a nightdress and an old grey jumper.

'You bugger off, Mrs Elwell!'

She was not deterred: 'Did he tell you about it or did he slur it to you?'

'I told you to bug . . . .'

'Where is the fire exactly?' Seamus was starting to wheeze.

'Just before the Medical Mission Hall and Bevington Hill, Mr Grogan, so my boy said, who was stone cold sober!' The last part of the message was fired defiantly at Mrs Elwell who sneered, gathered her ample nightdress and flounced off.

'Auntie Dora!' gasped Seamus to himself.

'Aye, that's right, Mr Grogan. The old besom who cooks the scouse for the down and out folk Must be bloody ninety if she's a day.'

Seamus turned on his heel and flew up the court steps: 'Up! Everybody get up! Auntie Dora needs our help!'

Peter groaned and sat up as his father switched the light on. Fire engines were heard ringing along Scotland Road, as Mairead, now grossly over-weight, waddled over to fill the badly deformed kettle.'

'Who needs us, Dad?' piped Matthew, standing up in bed, pulling all the bedclothes off his sister.

'Auntie Dora, son. The very old lady that we see in church.'

'The old lady with the beard?' Seamus and Mairead exchanged a fleeting smile.

'That's it, son, and the big hat. My dad, your grandad, used to laugh at her big hats.'

Mairead rested the heavy kettle in the crook of her arm and frowned at Seamus: 'It's the middle of the night and you've woken the whole family! What can we do of any use?'

Seamus gently took the kettle from her and using the voice that he reserved for reasoning with the children, said, 'She has been a good Christian soul all her life and was one of my parents' original friends when they came to this country, and she gives to those worse off than herself, though she has less money than even we have, God bless and keep her!'

Mairead knew she had to capitulate after this stirring speech and set to getting the children dressed while Seamus made the tea.

The little ones' excitement grew as the smell of burning intensified. Peter pretended to be a fire engine and broke a saucer, which earned him a slap on the leg from his mother.

'I think I should stay at home with the children, Seamus. It's not a family outing, it's a big fire. It's not safe for them.'

Predictably the children sent up a chorus of indignation. Now that their sleep had been interrupted, they were ready and eager to go outside and begin the day's adventures.

'Have you no faith these days, my love? God will protect us if we are doing His will. Now, are we all ready to leave?'

Seamus found his own personal vision of Hell belching forth in reality just beyond the bobbing hats in Scotland Road. Three terraced houses were ablaze from all their windows, casting a white glare into the surrounding dark. In front of the crowd, three fire engines and their crews blocked the worst of the heat out. One fireman was hosing the roofs from the top of his mobile ladder, while the others fought the flames pouring from the windows, showering sparks into the night with their cascades of water. The fire roared like an express train, as it sucked and surged through the gaping window holes. Mairead clutched at Seamus's hand and gathered the children to her bosom, speechless in the terrifying din. The crowd, men and women who knew in their hearts that they had never really mastered fire since their forefathers first caused it to spark into life, looked on in awe. It was a monster, it was a god and it was more powerful than all of them. Their fear, their respect were instinctive, going back centuries, like respect for the sea and for destructive winds, a part of their collective instinct, the folk memory. Like a macabre firework display, each deluge of sparks sent up an 'Oooh, Aaah' from the among the watchers, as it eddied up then faded into the night. The heat bellowed forth among them like blasts of hot breath, forcing them to stagger back, gasping, fortified in the relief that this was someone else's property burning, not their own, so that it was intriguing rather than devastating.

'Seamus, what are we doing here?' screamed Mairead, her eyes screwed up against the smoke.

'I'm going to help,' he shouted back, the dribble visible on his chin from his coughing.

'Don't be so daft!' she cried in disbelief. 'This is just what you of all people should keep well away from! This smoke will do for you if you stay here.' She tried to drag him away. The children were frightened now and Sinead was sobbing into her mother's coat.

Seamus was trying to shout above the noise: 'Auntie Dora's place hasn't caught properly yet. I'm certain she's still in there!'

'How could she sleep through all this, love? Be reasonable.'

'She'll be blind drunk, that's how.' And with that, he tugged his sleeve free and was gone away into the crowd. The screams of

Mairead and the children were borne away by the gusts of heat and the tumult of fire and people. She made a step as if to follow him but a woman close by them suddenly found that her hair was alight and there was pandemonium. The woman was knocked to the ground as well-meaning helpers fell upon her, yelling confused instructions at nobody in particular. Then an old man fainted. Mairead felt a growing sense of panic.

The position was clear: on the one hand there was the fire and on the other, herself and her children. Seamus was now fending for himself. But what of God? Where was He? Was He in the fire? Was He with her family now? Of course! How foolish she was! God was in neither place yet in both. That would be Father Brendan's answer. But was God working with the fire or with the Grogans? Or was his overall purpose so broad that the Grogans were dispensible? How was she to act? Faith: that was the only solution to all the doubts. Do as you would do and yet accept God's will. It was futile to agonise about what God was doing. One just had to act and trust. That was it! Act and trust.

The fire was almost under control now in the three houses, though they were all gutted. The stench of saturated charcoal and steaming brickwork was overwhelming. The fire teams' attention turned to the fourth house, which was burning fiercely at the front.

'There's people in here too! They must be deaf and dumb or something!' came a fireman's shout, as he emerged from where Auntie Dora's street door had been axed in.

Mairead's stomach churned as the crowd surged forward. More bells were ringing. The police were here. But where was Seamus? She looked wildly about her, seeing only faces lit up by flames and excitement, children being hoisted up by their fathers to get a better view of the destruction.

Then, across the far side of the road, she noticed a lonely huddle of a dozen or so people of various ages, draped in overcoats and blankets, their pyjamas and nightdresses visible underneath. Silent, their saucer eyes gaped at the spectacle, unseeing. They said nothing to each other, each person alone in private torment -

no home, no furniture, no food, no clothes, no toys - nothing left but the future.

'My God!' said Mairead to herself. 'Those are the victims. They ought to parade themselves in front of these beasts here and see how charitable these folk are and whether they'd be ready to pay for their night's entertainment.'

Then, turning to the children: 'Peter! Matthew! Sinead! Hold on tight to each other and Peter hold on to me. We've got to squeeze to the front. I've got to talk to one of the policemen.'

'Is daddy dead, Ma?' came Sinead's little voice from somewhere near the ground.

'Of course not, love. He's very brave. He's helping.'

His wheezes temporarily forgotten, Seamus lunged through the smoke, down Auntie Dora's side passage and into her back yard. There he was doubled up with coughing for a moment. Still hacking, he struggled out of his overcoat, bunched it up and held it tight against his mouth. Breathing through it gave a little relief. His coughing eased, allowing him to cast about in the smoke for the back door. There it was! Unlocked as always. As he opened it, he felt the fire breathe out hot on his face. He stumbled inside, his eyes streaming, his breathing noisy. Feeling his way along the wall, as if reading braille, he found a doorway and kicked around desperately for the bottom of the stairs. Got it!

'Auntie Dora!'

The only response was the rush of hot air past his ears.

'Auntie Dora! Is anybody there?'

His heart was pounding now. This was very dangerous. He had no training of any sort to cope with this situation. He could die here. He had a wife and three children. Padraig would manage so much better! Yet he had the certain feeling that Padraig was somehow near, he could sense his nearness. If only he were with him right now!

He knew it was Paddy and not God. God was with him but with a different kind of certainty. Seamus never felt alone, because he believed he never was. Aloud he cried, 'God, help me!'

Then he knew he would either be successful or slip easily and fearlessly into death, whichever God willed. It was a choice he found acceptable. It was not a dilemma but another solution handed to him, a solution of which he believed he was unworthy. Thus, at peace, he slogged up the steep, narrow stairs.

He lowered his coat from his face to call out but no answer came. For the first time he faced the possibility of coming upon a corpse in one of the two upstairs bedrooms. Perhaps he should have knocked up Ciaran Cassidy and dragged him along, although Ciaran was his boss now - senior charge hand. The door of the first room stood open. He could hear the fire inside, a low, rushing noise, as if he were approaching some big machinery. He forced his eyes open in the smoke, dabbing at them with his coat and imagining Mairead scolding him: 'Don't put that thing near your eyes! It's filthy and you don't know where it's been!' Dear Mair! What a strange thought to have here and now. Was he dying? He did not believe so. Where were the firemen? He could hear nothing but the fire. Maybe they had had to give up and he was trapped here. Then he stumbled against something. It moved. He knelt down, his wheezing now louder in his ears than the fire.

In fact all he could hear at all now was his own wheezing. His hollow chest heaved and fell with the supreme effort of each precious breath. He fought for each one, guessing that each one was killing him a little more surely than the one before.

He reached out and his fingers felt a man's trouser leg upon a threadbare piece of carpet. Both the leg and the carpet were almost too hot to touch. A hand reached for his and grasped it feebly. More tears pricked Seamus's eyes but not this time from the smoke. He fell upon the man and shouted, 'Where is Auntie Dora? Is anyone else here?' The man whispered, 'Three more,' and sank to the floor again.

Seamus crawled on all fours around the man to the far side of the room, the side where the fire was fiercest. There, amidst the stink of burning timber, he was able to locate and touch three other men. Two of them responded. One did not.

There was smouldering bedding on the floor, probably makeshift sleeping arrangements. Who were these men? Why would a ninety year old woman, who had remained a spinster all her life, entertain four men? And where was Auntie Dora? He rose shakily to half his height and staggered into the other room. His head was light and his back ran cold with sweat, though his face burned. He felt rather sick now. He had had enough. But the job was not finished. His thoughts became confused. Once or twice he thought he was back in Oswald Street and this was his own house. He called out for Mair and the children. Then he heard a crash in the room he had just left and realised that part of the ceiling had come down. He must act, not daydream!

It took him no time to find the little cast-iron bed facing the window, which had now lost its glass and was billowing black smoke from within. Dragging Auntie Dora's heavy, shapeless body out of bed and on to the floor almost finished him. The foot of her bed was on fire and her vast, flabby arms and shoulders offered nowhere to grasp or lift. She offered no resistance, there was no sweat in her armpits when Seamus put his hands under there, and her eyes remained closed. Somewhere inside his head, Seamus noted wryly how he tugged the old dear's heavy flannel nightdress down to cover her dimpled legs for the sake of propriety, so she should not be exposed to the onlookers when she emerged outside.

He remembered little about how he brought her down into the yard. He remembered his surprise at the length of her white hair, normally shoved up inside one of her huge hats. He remembered her bare feet going bump, bump, bump from stair to stair. He remembered how she had landed on top of him at the foot and he had lain wheezing into her expressionless face, her stubble chafing against his own. Then there were firemen all round him. He was lying on his back in the open air.

Of the five people in that house, only one survived - a man of thirty-seven, a man who had drunk less than all the others and the only man among them who was able-bodied. Auntie Dora was dead. Seamus had risked his own life to drag a corpse out of the inferno.

He lay gasping for air on the far pavement, a rough blanket up to his chin, sympathetic faces smiling down at him. A woman's voice said to him, 'They're bringing the bodies out now. Pity about the old lady but you were quite the local hero. The Echo's got the story.'

'And one man was alive, thanks to you. The fireman said he knew exactly where to find him and get him out quickly, because of your instructions,' said the kneeling doctor, withdrawing his stethoscope and getting to his feet.

'Very well, Mrs Grogan, he's all yours now but he must go to hospital for observation.'

Mairead's tears fell upon him and he could hear the children crying too. The sound was like music.

The crowd parted at the arrival of the Rolls Royce. They thought it was the Lord Mayor and flash bulbs popped in the darkness, lighting up tired but expectant faces for a split second. The dying fire, now assigned to second place, hissed and spat, bare windows and doorways pouring out sooty black smoke. The flash bulbs, the spitting of the fire and the clouds of smoke created a strange, unreal world, into which the impossibly lustrous and immaculate limousine slipped without a sound.

The vehicle came to a halt. The driver's door opened and a spotless hand-made brogue slid to the wet cobblestones, followed slowly by the other, as if testing the temperature of the puddles. The tall, slim man stood up, adjusted his camel coat and threw his cigar down, leaving it to hiss and die. He signalled to his lady passenger to stay in her seat and beckoned to a police constable.

'Where is my brother, constable?'

'Your brother, sir?' He saluted.

'Yes, constable, my brother, Seamus Grogan. I received a

telephone call from his wife.'

The policeman stood staring at the man in disbelief.

'Well? Will you take me to him, please? I have to start work in a couple of hours.'

'So, you - you are the other Mr Grogan then, sir?'

'I am Mr Padraig Grogan, yes. Now can we please get on?'

'Certainly, Mr Grogan, sir.'

Padraig allowed the striped cuff to guide him through the crowd and over the slick snakes of fat water hose. People stepped back and murmured as they passed. Paddy drew a snow-white handkerchief from his trouser pocket and pressed it to his nose, keeping his eyes on the ground. At length they came upon a knot of craning people beneath the glow of a street-lamp. Without his escort he ventured towards the central figure, lying in a blanket, haloed by light from above. People were leaning over him as if in worship. Seamus lay brightly lit, surrounded by faces in penumbra and, beyond them, blackness. He lay, smiling reassurance, the light seeming to emanate from within as much as from above. He gave the impression of receiving these people in an ambassadorial capacity! The wood shavings man! Paddy was mildly irritated. Mairead had implied that Seamus's life was in danger.

As Padraig broke through to his brother's side, Seamus's sooty, black face spread into a broad grin.

'Paddy, Paddy! I knew you'd come!'

He took his brother's hand and tried to tug him down into a kneeling position beside him. Padraig rapidly scanned the cleanliness of the pavement and sank shakily into an awkward squatting position, gathering the skirts of his coat cautiously about him, like a fussy old hen settling upon her eggs.

Seamus struggled to speak into his brother's ear: 'Paddy, Auntie Dora is dead. I couldn't save her.'

Paddy noticed the foulness of his brother's breath and kept his handkerchief in position.

'Paddy, only one man survived,' Seamus croaked.

Now Mairead was right beside them, kneeling in the water. 'He's a hero, Padraig! My man's a hero.'

Paddy observed how fat she was becoming and how she smelled of perspiration. Greta never smelled of perspiration, neither would she kneel in water. But he did get the uncomfortable feeling that some kind of fraternal gesture was expected of him by these folk - a hug or some such. His very attire made him an object of curiosity, so that any failure to display what might be considered everyday behaviour would single him out even more.

But these were his people as much as they were Seamus's. He did not need to make efforts to blend in surely? Yet when he had used to blend in, all he had desired in the whole world had been to stand out. So where did he stand? In or out? His problem was not where God was, but where he himself was! He could not stand outside himself because he was all he had! He compromised by putting his handkerchief away and tousling his brother's hair. The act felt rather unnatural but it sent a ripple of sympathy through the crowd. Still he remained aware of his need not to start the next working day tired and dirty. Greta tended to shun him when he was tired and dirty.

'I bet you want to know why Auntie Dora had all those men in her house, eh?' Seamus was smiling up at him. Paddy realised he should want to know, so he nodded and looked interested. If the press could close in now, it would be useful free publicity for the business, one of its directors showing family concern and solidarity.

'Third anniversary of the start of the war in Spain.'

Paddy looked at him blankly.

'The civil war in Spain, Paddy! Two thousand British volunteers went out to join the International Brigade, including those four at poor old Auntie Dora's!'

'What were they doing at her place?'

Mairead looked at him now with a mixture of wonder and disgust: 'They were here for their reunion, the big one at the

Volunteer Drill Hall by the Servicemen's Club in St Anne Street.

'A lot of them were disabled from the Spanish war,' Seamus went on, while Mairead stroked his blackened forehead, 'and Auntie Dora offered to put them up after the "do".'

'They were all the worse for wear, including Auntie Dora,' said Mairead, 'That's why all but one died. He says he didn't drink much and he was able-bodied. Still, he was for the cemetery too if it hadn't been for my Seamus.'

Paddy reflected. Auntie Dora's passing was the end of an era. A door into his childhood had closed for ever. He was more of an orphan than before. He longed for the warmth and comfort of his car and the relief of recounting everything to Greta, without the mess or weariness of actually having been involved in it. Anyway, the Grogan name was going to be in the Echo. That was something.

What Paddy had never understood was why any family of five, living in one room, would consciously seek to compound its chaos by adding a large Alsatian dog. However matey the communal fug of cooking, breathing and farting might be, a huge, hairy dog must seriously increase the demands on space and patience, not to mention the question of hygiene.

'It must eat as much as a small man,' drawled Greta from the dressing room of their new luxury home in Speke. 'God alone knows how they can afford to put food in its enormous mouth! The children aren't actually overweight, are they?'

'It wouldn't suit us, that's for sure.' Paddy was searching the drawer of his bedside table for the keys to the Rolls Royce. He hung about, having found them, waiting for Greta's inevitable, 'Check my face, will you, darling? It feels like a bloody bombsite!'

He knew, as she knew, that her face, like the rest of her, would be perfection. She was as desirable to every man as she was unattainable to Padraig. They still made love occasionally but

Greta deplored the mess. She would come to bed with a fistful of old handkerchieves and an expression of brave perseverance. Even as he thrust desperately into her, he saw how she turned her head to one side. Then she would suddenly say something like: 'When you've finished, I'll 'phone about that tap in the kitchen.' She had a knack of making it all sound like going to the lavatory, not very nice, but it had to be done. He did not know for certain whether Greta had a lover but he supposed she had. Perhaps her lover's mess was more acceptable than his.

Stanley would sometimes take him on one side and ask whether everything was 'hunky dory'. His concern was genuine enough but, at bottom, Stanley believed that a woman was like a horse - to be broken to its master's will. He would understand no other approach. Hilda had certainly not been broken to his will but Stanley was a man who could easily overlook his own inconsistencies and even persuade himself that they were a figment of his own limited imagination.

Mairead now trundled to the shops astride an ancient bicycle of uncertain colour and origin. Wobbling about like a circus act, she would stop at the Love Lane premises of Harding and Gardner Ltd. whenever fate took her that way. Sometimes the Alsatian would trot along the pavement beside her. If Stanley's heart sank at her arrival, he never showed it, nor did Hilda, both now in semi-retirement. Padraig and Greta however did their best to make good their escape to the washroom adjoining their office, hissing to their manager, 'We're not here!'

Mairead would park her bicycle noisily against the showroom window and shout, 'Stay!' to the dog. As she waddled inside, her bicycle would often, with a grace it never possessed when she rode upon it, slide gently sideways and crash to the ground, whereupon the dog would lunge, barking at the window to advise his mistress of the disaster.

'I know you don't do bikes,' she would begin apologetically and then go on to mention the loose saddle or defective brake, and one of the mechanics would be dispatched unwillingly outside to solve the problem. They never accepted payment, just Mairead's cheerful assurance that their reward would await them in Heaven.

'So long as she doesn't await me there as well!' the mechanic would confide to his grinning workmates.

On this summer's afternoon, Padraig was too slow. Mairead came bowling on to the the forecourt with the Alsatian loping in her wake. The big doors of the service bay were wide open and inside in the shadow stood Paddy and his manager at the Love Lane site, John Eccles, sturdy, bald and dressed in a dark suit, like a bullet with arms and legs. In the service bay, parked half over the inspection pit and half in the doorway was Paddy's Rolls Royce.

' Look who's here, boss,' growled Eccles, running his hand over his glistening pate. Paddy squinted out into the sunlight but was dazzled and saw nothing.

'Who is it, John?'

'Your sister-in-law, boss.'

'Christ! Have I got time to disappear?'

'No, boss. She's seen you.'

'Bugger!'

Dismounting like an avalanche, Mairead barked 'Stay!' at the dog and smiled helplessly as the dog ignored her and trotted purposefully into the service bay.

'Mairead, how lovely to see you!' managed Padraig through compressed lips, glancing at Eccles to see whether he was grinning.

'Mrs Grogan.' Eccles tapped the place on his forehead where his forelock would have been, then straightened the lapels of his suit and jerked his blue chin out.

Mairead took this as a signal to advance. While the dog went on a sniffing tour of the service bay, Paddy, Eccles and a young mechanic stood in line before Mairead, as if waiting for her to take a photograph of them. Grasping the handlebars to her bosom, she ventured, 'It's the chain, Paddy.'

There was a silence. Everyone stood waiting in the heat.

'Mr Grogan's got an oil leak . . .' the young mechanic's words died on the warm air. Without looking at him Paddy motioned him to be silent.

'Shall I come back another time? I can tell you're all busy.'

Eccles opened his mouth, but it was Paddy who spoke: 'No, no, certainly not! We won't hear of such a thing, will we, Mr Eccles?'

'Definitely not, Mr Grogan, sir. The very idea!' He jutted his chin out again, like a boxer sizing up his opponent.

'I don't want to be any trouble.'

'No trouble at all, Mairead.'

Paddy's eyes darted about the shadows to locate the dog. He had never felt at ease with dogs. Not like Seamus. Seamus was like St Francis of Assisi with the animals! Paddy had to know where the dog was at all times. He could not relax. Turning uneasily to his mechanic, he said, 'Here's a little job for you, young McArdle. This lady's bike.'

He pointed to Mairead and her machine.

'Yes, Missis.'

McArdle put his wheelbrace reverently down on the concrete floor beside the pit and took Mairead's bicycle, wheeling it round the Rolls to the far side of the pit, Mairead cataloguing its mechanical faults like a rosary, as she brought up the rear.

To Paddy's growing alarm and irritation, she appeared to have forgotten the existence of her dog, which was snuffling all around the edge of the pit, occasionally craning its neck into the abyss below. Paddy really wanted the animal right outside. Its soft, wet muzzle, its teeth and its smell appalled him, together with the knowledge that dogs sometimes devoured their own excrement.

He took the rash step of calling to it and beckoning with his hand. Eccles looked at his boss in amazement, fully aware that he could not abide animals, especially dogs.

To Paddy's consternation, the dog's eyes lit up at the prospect of some attention which might even culminate in some food. It turned towards him, ears pricked up, head slightly askew, attentive. It gave a little yelp of anticipation, then launched itself towards this newly declared playmate. Filled with alarm now at the forces he had unleashed, Paddy took a step backwards towards the pit. Keeping his eyes riveted on the dog, he caught his foot in the wheelbrace. He tripped and fell without a sound, striking the side of his head against the rear bumper of his Rolls Royce, down into the inspection pit. For a second, nobody moved. The only sound upon the heavy air was the panting of the dog, as it stood on the edge of the pit, staring down into the darkness, impatient for the fun to continue.

Eccles ran to throw a switch on the wall, which lit up an inspection lamp clamped somewhere under the chassis of the Rolls, thereby illuminating the bottom of the pit.

There lay Padraig, looking completely at peace, gazing up towards the light, the wheelbrace on his chest like a huge dull crucifix. Eccles, Mairead and McArdle moved towards the edge, slowly and gingerly, like a child turning a page in a book to a picture which it fears to look upon. Mairead muttered and crossed herself. Eccles swore.

'Get down that ladder and see to Mr Grogan, McArdle!'

The youth descended the ladder as if lowering himself into freezing water. He shook Paddy gently, calling, 'Mr Grogan! Are you all right, boss?'

But they all knew he was quite dead.

The dog scampered round to Mairead, its tail wagging frantically, looking for new distraction.

A gaggle of tousled schoolchildren chirruped past the warm wall of St Anthony's cemetery, swinging pumpbags bursting with belongings and a gasmask each - another rehearsal for full-scale evacuation. Seamus stood in the church porch with Father Brendan, their bodies in shadow but their faces lit by a slant of afternoon sunlight.

Neither man said a word for a while, just looked out into the light. It was a week since Paddy's funeral and now he lay beside his mother in the shade of a wise old oak.

Seamus thought about all the people dead and gone recently - Auntie Dora and now Paddy, half his own flesh and blood, and a few years before - old Mrs Kennedy and his own ma and da. He heard Father Brendan stifle a belch, pat his belly then place his hand on his shoulder, saying, 'Aye, Seamus, lad, the world is changing.'

'You can read my thoughts, Father.' He coughed into his hand. The Dayntree cough.

'The worthwhile ones, yes,' he smiled, his cheeks inflating like cherry balloons with the gas from another belch.

'Did you see Clodagh during the funeral, Father? How upset she was? I had to take her outside, you know.'

'There was an attachment there of some sort, I dare say.'

'With my brother? What sort of attachment?'

'Not for me to know. Nor for you now. That's all for his Maker now, Seamus, lad.'

Seamus nodded. 'But Greta was furious. I suppose because here was a woman who was more upset than she was!'

'Maybe so. Maybe so.'

As they basked just inside the porch, a Rolls Royce slid to a halt at the kerbside just round the corner to their left in Chapel Gardens. A portly middle-aged man got out and looked about him, stepping on his cigar butt. He was wearing a long camel coat in spite of the warmth of the afternoon and appeared to be concealing something in it, something bulky. Seamus thought of the gangster films he had taken the children to see at the Homer. As the man drew nearer, Seamus realised he knew him. He stepped back into the shadow and drew the priest back too, as the man went past, still looking round suspiciously.

'Mr Gardner.'

'Who's that, Seamus?'

'Mr Stanley Gardner of Harding and Gardner.' The man walked towards the graves.

'Poor Paddy's father-in-law?'

'The same, Father. The man I would not speak to at Paddy's wedding.'

'The man who used to employ your dear mother, is it, down at Maguire Street during the War?'

'It is. The man I hold responsible for poor Ma's death so early. She helped to buy his Rolls Royce for him and she paid with her life.'

Both men followed the visitor with their eyes as he descended the gently grassy slope towards the more recent headstones.

'Sure, such bitter thoughts are not the sort of stuff that normally fills your head, Seamus.'

'No Father, but that man over there in the coat then went on to draw my brother into business with him.'

'He didn't draw him in, as you put it. Paddy went in willingly.'

'You mean he didn't care that Mr Gardner helped to kill our ma?'

'I mean he didn't see it that way. Business is business. Gardner provided employment for your mother, God rest her soul, and she could have left the factory at any time she wanted.'

'That was the one thing I could never talk to him about.'

As they stood and watched, the man stopped at the graves of Sinead and Padraig. He bowed his head at Padraig's grave, then knelt beside Sinead's. As Seamus watched, time seemed to hold its breath and many days and many years telescoped together. The man opened his coat and reached inside, still kneeling. Into the dancing sunlight he drew a bunch of purest white lilies and laid them on Sinead's grave, as if laying out a small child.

All at once, the 'unmentionable odour of death' was dispelled and Seamus's happiness was complete.

Bibliography

First Day on the Somme - Middlebrook - Penguin
Women Workers in the First World War - Braybon - Routledge
Conchie - Spring - Cooper
Liverpool, a City at War - Perrett - Hale
Old Ordnance Survey Maps: Liverpool North 1906 Godfrey
The Home Front - Pankhurst - Cresset
Victorian and Edwardian Sailing Ships - Greenhill and Giffard - Batsford
The Cunard Story - Johnson - Whitlet
Beyond Orange and Green - Probert - Zed
Britain since 1700 - Cootes - Longman
The Somme - Farrar-Hockley - Pan
Where we used to Work - Hudson - Baker
Britain at War 1914 -1918 - Mair - Murray
Police Strike 1919 - Sellwood - W.H.Allen
Veteran and Vintage Cars - Roberts - Octopus
The Dawn of Motoring - Merecdes-Benz (UK) Ltd
Visual History of Costume of the 20th Century - Byrd - Batsford
History of Twentieth Century Fashion - Ewing - Batsford
Dressed for the Job - Williams-Mitchell - Blandford
Rolls-Royce, the Complete Works - Fox and Smith - Faber
Between the Wars - Symons - Batsford

Acknowledgements

For their advice and interest:

Jenifer Cummings   Dominic O'Rourke
Tony Moore   Daniel Hudson
Mike Nestor   Jane Hartley

For their facilities:

The Picton Library, Liverpool
Lichfield Public Library
Birmingham City Public Library